The Economics of Futures Markets

Jerome L. Stein

Basil Blackwell

To Sam, Sherry, Emily and Benjamin

Copyright © Jerome L. Stein 1986

First published 1986
First published in USA 1987
Reprinted 1989
First published in paperback 1990

Basil Blackwell Ltd
108 Cowley Road, Oxford OX4 1JF, UK

Basil Blackwell, Inc.
3 Cambridge Center
Cambridge, Massachusetts 02142, USA

British Library Cataloguing in Publication Data

A CIP catalogue record for this book is available from the British Library.

Library of Congress Cataloging in Publication Data

Stein, Jerome L.
  The economics of futures markets.

  Bibliography: p.
  Includes index.
  1. Commodity exchanges. 2. Financial futures.
  I. Title.
  HG6046.S674 1987   332.64′4 86-12924
ISBN 0-631-15139-7
ISBN 0-631-16884-2 (pbk.)

Typeset by Unicus Graphics Ltd, Horsham
Printed in Great Britain by
Billing & Sons Ltd, Worcester

Contents

Preface

The spectacular growth of the new futures markets in interest rates and stock market indexes has generated a demand for an economic theory of the effects of futures markets upon the economy. For example, the United States Congress, the Federal Reserve System and the Commodity Futures Trading Commission demanded an analysis of the effects of these new futures markets upon the rate of capital formation. This book provides a unified theory of the effects of futures markets – in commodities, financial instruments, stock market indexes and foreign exchange – upon the intertemporal allocation of resources.

Futures markets have two opposite and undeserved reputations. Some groups regard them as pure gambling markets. Others regard them as markets for insurance against risk. Unquestionably, there are amateurs who use futures markets to gamble. They consistently lose money. Futures markets, in fact, are dominated by large commercial firms who interact with professional risk bearers. Those who want insurance against price risk should either buy options or engage in forward transactions. Futures markets are used by commercial firms to manage, but not to eliminate, the price risks inherent in their ordinary business. For example, major users of futures markets are dealers and financial intermediaries who are professional risk bearers. If they did not use the futures markets, the risk premiums that they would have to charge their customers would significantly decrease the demand for their services.

The excellent surveys of the literature and description of the development of futures markets by Goss and Yamey (1976), Kamara (1982) and Peck (1985) supplement the material covered here.

The first and last chapters of this book can be read as a unit, and should be of interest to government regulators and industry participants. Chapter One describes the empirical phenomena that a good theory of futures markets must explain, and demonstrates why the traditional finance approach is deficient. The last chapter (Seven) applies the abstract theory, developed in Chapters Two to Six, to the 'real world'. It explains the effects of interest rate and stock index futures upon the rate of capital formation, and thereby answers the question posed by the Congress, cited earlier. This chapter is based upon my monograph 'Futures markets and capital formation' (1985). The American Enterprise Institute has granted me permission to use this material here.

Chapters Two to Six are for economists interested in the theory of how futures markets affect the intertemporal allocation of resources under conditions of risk and uncertainty. The ideas developed here are certain to be controversial. The two foci of my theory are: (a) what are the real effects of futures markets and (b) how should they be evaluated in terms of economic welfare. With respect to the first question, I show how futures markets fundamentally change the supply equation, and accelerate the convergence to a Muth rational expectations (MRE) equilibrium. In the absence of these markets, an MRE equilibrium is most unlikely to occur in a changing environment. Chapter Six, which is the second focus, develops a quantitative measure of the welfare benefits of different futures markets.

This book has benefited from the criticisms and suggestions by Akio Yasuhara, Anne Peck, Rama Ramachandran, Harl Ryder, Mark Rzepczynski, Christian von Weizsäcker, Jürg Niehans, Peter Abken, Haim Levy, Yoram Peles, Fred Arditti, George Borts, Geoffrey Heal, Graciela Chichilinski, Franklin Edwards, Ronald Anderson, Avraham Kamara, Bernard Dumas, Martin Beckmann and Robert Selvaggio. Marion Wathey typed the manuscript with her usual skill and sense of responsibility. My wife Hadassah has been a continual source of good advice and encouragement. I thank each one very much.

Providence, Rhode Island, USA
February 1986

1

Futures Markets: The Phenomena to Be Explained

This book on the economic theory of futures markets focuses upon the following interrelated questions. (1) How do the futures markets affect the intertemporal allocation of resources? (2) To what extent do these markets pool relevant information concerning supply and demand at a later date? (3) How do these markets affect the risk premiums that producers charge, when the prices of output or of input are uncertain? These questions can be combined into the following. How do futures markets affect the supply functions of output, when there is price uncertainty? (4) What are the welfare effects of the futures markets? How can we evaluate the extent to which a particular futures market has changed economic welfare?

These questions are of great interest to the policy makers as well as to the academic economists. The simultaneous occurrence of extensive trading in financial futures and increased volatility in security prices and interest rates since 1976 caused concern for the Congress and Federal Reserve System. The government had experience with the economic role of traditional commodity futures and learned to understand it. The new and rapidly growing financial futures seemed to be different. Traditional commodity futures markets had been studied by academic economists for many years. Financial and stock index futures had not been analysed theoretically by economists, so that there was no model by which their effects upon the economy could be analysed. This lacuna induced the Congress in 1983 to request the Board of Governors of the Federal Reserve System, the Commodity Futures Trading Commission (CFTC) and the Securities and Exchange Commissions to study 'the effects, if any, that trading in ... [futures] has on the formation of real capital in the economy (particularly that of a long-term nature) and the structure of liquidity in the credit market; . . . the economic purposes if any, served by the trading in such instruments.' The economic theory developed in Chapters Two to Six is used in Chapter Seven to answer the specific questions posed by the Congress.

The quality of positive economic theory must be judged by its ability to explain with precision, clarity and simplicity the key elements of a complex economic phenomenon. Section 1.1 describes the basic characteristics of futures markets. Theories which ignore or cannot explain these characteristics cannot qualify as relevant or good theories of futures markets. One set of theories of futures markets, based upon the capital asset pricing model (CAPM) or the intertemporal CAPM has been extensively discussed in the literature. Section 1.2 draws upon Section 1.1 to explain why the CAPM type of models are incapable of explaining the essential features of futures markets. For this reason, an alternative research strategy is used in this book. Section 1.3 contains an outline and summary of Chapters Two to Seven.

A commodity is a vector of characteristics of interest to buyers and sellers, such as physical characteristics, quantity, time and place of delivery, financial and liability provisions. Trading occurs in three types of markets: cash (spot), forward and futures. *Forward* markets are simply cash (merchandizing) markets for deferred delivery. There are as many forward contracts as there are commodities for deferred delivery. Each forward contract is custom-made to the specifications of the buyer and seller. A contract to purchase a new automobile from the dealer in his showroom is an example of a forward contract.

Futures markets are quite different from forward markets. Futures markets are characterized by a small number of actively traded commodities. These markets deal in standard homogeneous contracts for the delivery of a specific quantity of specified grades of a commodity at designated delivery points within a stated interval of time. There are very few elements to the vector which defines the commodity traded in the futures market, so there are few commodities traded in futures markets. Futures contracts are perfectly fungible and are traded by open outcry on organized exchanges.

Trades are cleared by a central clearing-house which becomes the opposite party to each side of private transactions. Several noteworthy aspects of this arrangement must be stressed. First, the clearing arrangement permits any party to reverse a previous transaction without contacting the original second party, whenever it is advantageous to do so. The party simply reverses the transaction and settles the difference between the purchase and sales price by certified check. This flexibility does not exist in a forward market which deals in a particular narrowly defined vector of characteristics. Physical delivery against futures contracts is infrequent (Paul, 1985, Table 5-5, p. 324). The risks of default are low because the clearing house is the opposite party to the futures transaction. The integrity of the clearing house in a futures transaction replaces the integrity of a particular buyer or seller in a forward transaction. The clearing house protects itself by a marking to market settlement of accounts on a daily basis and by requiring maintenance margins.

Secondly, futures markets reflect the buying and selling activities of many buyers and sellers of the homogeneous contract. Firms often have the power to affect the market price in cash and forward markets because these are merchandizing contracts custommade to the two parties. However, a single party is less able to affect the price in the broad futures market than in the cash or forward market. This liquidity of the futures market, i.e. the ability of firms to trade large quantities without affecting the price is one of the main reasons why the new futures markets in financial instruments have flourished. This is discussed in Chapter Seven.

Thirdly, futures markets disseminate information quickly, effectively and inexpensively, and thereby reduce monopoly power. In the cash and forward markets, a large firm has a substantial advantage over a smaller firm. The larger firm has more extensive and reliable information concerning current and impending developments. A small onion grower, cotton farmer, cattle feeder or heating oil distributor meets a local dealer, who may represent a national firm, concerning the sale of a particular product at a later date. It is difficult for the producer to gauge the reasonableness of the dealer's offer because the costs of search are high. When there is a futures market, potential buyers and sellers have a means of gauging what a broad group of buyers or sellers expect will be the subsequent price of the commodity specified in the futures contract and there is a historic relation between the price of the specific commodity in question and the commodity specified in the futures contract. The parties evaluate the reasonableness of the dealer's offer in terms of its relation to the futures price.

1.1   Characteristics of Futures Markets

The main characteristics of futures markets, to be explained by a good economic theory, are described in this part and are summarized by 1–10.

1   There is only a small number of actively traded commodities with futures markets. The trading unit is large and indivisible.
2   Almost all of the open interest is concentrated in the nearby contract, which has a maturity of no more than three months.
3   The success ratio on new contracts is about 25 per cent. Some new contracts succeed and others, which seem to have similar useful features, fail.
4   Futures are seldom used by farmers. Instead, they use forward contracts. The main users of agricultural futures are intermediaries (dealers) in the marketing process.
5   There are both commercial and noncommercial users of futures contracts in interest rates and foreign exchange. The commercial users are to a large extent dealers: intermediaries in the marketing process.
6   The positions of the commercials and dealers in interest rate futures are almost evenly divided between long and short positions.
7   The main use of futures by the commercials is to hedge corresponding cash and forward positions.
8   The positions of the noncommercials are almost entirely speculative positions.
9   In foreign exchange futures, the positions of the commercials are unbalanced. In some currencies they are net short and in others they are net long. However, their positions are primarily hedging against corresponding cash and forward positions. The noncommercial positions are overwhelmingly speculative positions.
10   Futures are used in the underwriting of fixed income securities but not in equity underwriting.

What economic theory of futures markets can explain these phenomena? In Section 1.2 it is shown that the variants of the CAPM cannot explain these characteristics and hence cannot be considered to be a relevant theory of futures markets.

1.1.1 There Is a Small Number of Successful Contracts

On 18 October 1985 there were only 56 commodities with futures prices listed in the *Wall Street Journal*: 15 grains, 4 livestock and meat, 7 food, fibre and wood, 12 metals and 18 financial. The visual contrast between the small number of traded futures contracts and the large number of traded securities listed over several pages of the newspaper makes the point that there are very few successful futures contracts relative to financial assets traded. Table 1.1 contains the open interest (i.e. number of outstanding contracts) of a representative sample of different types of futures contracts: Treasury bonds and bills, the Standard and Poor (S&P) 500 futures contract, wheat and heating oil.

Table 1.1 Open interest (number of contracts) in a sample of actively traded contracts 18 October 1985

Commodity (unit traded)	December 1985	March 1986	June 1986	September 1986
Treasury bonds ($100 000)	182 961	55 167	17 942	9 477
Treasury bills ($1 million)	27 555	5 071	2 275	603
S&P 500 futures ($500 × index)	57 352	3 762	176	
Wheat (5000 bushels)	18 561	8 363	3 134[a] 4 846[b]	263
Heating oil (42 000 gallons)	13 045	7 244[c]	4 125[d]	1 330[e]

Notes: (a) May 1986; (b) July 1986; (c) January 1986; (d) February 1986; (e) March 1986.
Source: Wall Street Journal, 21 October 1985.

The unit traded is a large indivisible quantity: $1 million of Treasury bills; $100 000 of Treasury bonds; 5000 bushels of wheat and 42 000 gallons of number 2 heating oil. In the case of the S&P 500 futures contract, the unit traded is $500 times the index. The price of the December contract is $500 times the index 186.85, which equals $93 425 per contract.

There are few contracts per commodity, and the open interest is concentrated in the nearby contract which has a maturity of no more than three months. The open interest is the number of contracts outstanding, where one party is long and the other party is short. In the case of Treasury securities and stock market index, practically all of the open interest is concentrated in the nearby contract which, in October 1985, is the December 1985 contract.

Futures markets are broader and more liquid than the corresponding cash or forward markets. On a given day, the value of the S&P 500 futures traded is substantially larger than the value of securities traded on the New York Stock Exchange (NYSE). The Treasury bond futures contract is generally the most active futures contract in the world. On 24 January 1986, 160 000 contracts were traded representing $16 billion.

Futures exchanges are producers of futures contracts and attempt to maximize the collective interest of their members. The common interest of the members, who range from retail brokerage firms to large floor traders, is the maximization of trading revenues. The supply of contracts generated by the exchanges can be viewed as the desired output of the industry. Contract innovation will be successful if the exchanges can correctly anticipate the demand for futures contracts by customers in the market.

It is not easy to predict the demand for a new futures contract. Foreign exchange, both spot and forward, is traded on the interbank market. Futures contracts in foreign exchange were first traded in 1972 on the International Monetary Market of the Chicago Mercantile Exchange. There seemed to be a demand for foreign currency futures as the foreign exchange markets were free and there was exchange rate volatility. The Canadian dollar, Deutsche Mark, Swiss franc and Japanese yen were successful contracts, but the Dutch guilder, French franc and Mexican peso contracts were unsuccessful. Table 1.2 describes some successes and failures of futures contracts in foreign exchange.

Table 1.2   Annual volume of futures contracts by foreign currency 1972–80

Year	Canadian dollar	Deutsche Mark	Dutch guilder	French franc	Swiss franc	Japanese yen	Mexican peso
1972	38 804	19 318	–	–	17 721	43 989	9 717
1973	29 161	77 264	11 327	–	22 013	125 653	120 337
1974	3 699	49 447	1 527	11 359	42 505	7 239	90 941
1975	2 677	54 793	927	6 238	69 933	1 790	48 547
1976	17 068	44 887	392	5 968	37 246	1 449	51 439
1977	161 139	134 368	2 812	3 150	106 968	82 261	17 029
1978	207 654	400 569	3 585	4 449	321 451	361 731	17 844
1979	399 885	450 856	22	406	493 944	329 645	29 982
1980	601 925	922 608	4	144	827 884	575 073	10 301

Source: International Monetary Market 1979–80 Yearbook, Section 2

Following the work of Sandor (1973), Silber (1981) examined the success and failure of new futures contracts. Table 1.3 presents the basic data on innovations between 1960 and 1977. Two criteria of success were used: (a) what percentage of these contracts traded in 1980 and (b) what percentage of these innovations traded 10 000 or more contracts in 1980. Inspection of Tables 1.2 and 1.3 reveals that futures contract innovation is risky. The success ratio for all exchanges ranges from 25 to 32 per cent, depending upon the criterion used. The five largest exchanges had higher success ratios than did the smaller exchanges. There is only a demand for a small number of futures contracts and the public prefers that they be traded on the largest exchanges.

Table 1.3   Success rate of contracts introduced between 1960–77

Innovating group	Percentage trading in 1980	Percentage trading more than 10 000 contracts in 1980
All exchanges	32.3	24.6
Five largest	43	30.2
Excluding five largest	11.4	13.6

Source: Silber, 1981, Table 2

The above description of futures markets shows immediately that the theory of state contingent claims (Arrow-Debreu securities) does not correspond to observed futures markets. In the Arrow-Debreu model a set S of contingent claims are traded, where each security S_i in the set is characterized by commodity, date, place of delivery and state of the world that will obtain. This is an infinite dimensional space because of the infinite dimension to the possible states of nature. There is a market determined price for each state contingent claim S_i. Consumers have utility functions and producers have production functions, defined on set S. Consumers and producers select their respective optimum consumption and production on the set, given the budget constraint. The prices of the state contingent claims adjust to equate desired consumption to desired production. Since there is a separate market for each contingency, there will be a competitive equilibrium allocation of state contingent claims which is Pareto optimal.

There must be an infinite number of state contingent claims to correspond with the infinite states of nature. But the number of futures contracts is small, their success rate is low, they are concentrated in the nearby maturities and they come in large indivisible units. In no way do futures contracts that are traded correspond to the infinite set of state contingent claims that appear in the Arrow-Debreu model.

1.1.2 Forward and Futures in Agriculture and Livestock Industries

The CFTC under the direction of John Helmuth conducted a survey of grain and livestock farmers in the autumn of 1976 concerning their uses of forward and futures markets (Helmuth, 1977). The main results shown below are that farmers sell their output forward to dealers and hardly use futures markets directly. Dealers are much more important users of futures than are producers. However, a large fraction of the producers do take the futures price into account when they make forward contracts with the dealers. The following conclusions emerge from the survey.

1 During the entire period 1972–76, approximately 10 per cent of US farmers traded futures at one time or another. Among those with annual sales of $100 000 or more approximately 20 per cent traded futures some time during the period. This is summarized in Table 1.4.

2 In 1976, approximately 6 per cent of the farmers bought or sold futures. Of this group, 33.4 per cent traded in commodities they used or produced. Thus only 2.2 per cent (6.6 × 0.334) of the grain farmers traded futures in commodities they used or produced. The remaining 4.4 per cent (6.6 × 0.67) of the grain farmers used futures for pure speculation in other commodities (Helmuth, 1977, Table 6 and p. 24).

3 Forward contracts, unlike futures, are tailored to the needs of the parties to the transaction in terms of quality, quantity, time and place of delivery and financial arrangements. A grain or livestock farmer can get a local buyer to give him a firm bid on his current or prospective output on any business day; and this is a forward contract. Farmers use forward markets to a considerably greater extent than they use futures markets. The extent of their use of forward markets varies from year to year. In 1976, 17.2 per cent of the grain farmers used forward contracts but only 6.6 per cent of them used futures contracts.

Table 1.4   Percentage of farmers trading futures in 1976 and at some time during 1972–76

Value of annual gross commodity sales	1976 (%)	At some time during 1972-76 (%)
$10 000–19 999	1.0	3.8
$20 000–39 999	7.0	9.2
$40 000–59 999	6.0	10.4
$60 000–79 999	4.6	7.7
$80 000–99 999	3.7	19.1
Over $100 000	*13.1*	*20.9*
US total	*5.6*	*9.8*
Type of Farm		
Grain	6.6	11.9
Livestock	3.4	7.0
Other	11.1	12.9

Source: Helmuth, 1977, Tables 6 and 8

Table 1.5   Frequency of hedging in the futures market by types of grain marketing agencies

Type of business	Never (%)	Occasionally (%)	Routinely (%)
Single owner or partnership	71.2	20.8	8
Cooperative	60.3	25.1	14.6
Corporation	50.7	27.0	22.3

Source: Helmuth, 1977, Table 10

In 1974, 63 per cent of the corn, 51 per cent of the wheat and 60 per cent of the soybeans purchased from farmers by grain marketing entities was done through forward contracts.

4   Farmers sell their current or prospective output forward to intermediaries. The latter tend to use futures markets for hedging to a much greater extent than do producers. Table 1.5 presents data from the US Department of Agriculture Grain Industry Survey indicating the frequency of hedging by various grain marketing entities by various types of business ownership.

5   Although only a small percentage of farmers use the futures market, approximately half of the farmers who signed forward

contracts in 1976 took the futures price into account to some extent. Some merely looked at the futures prices in the newspapers before they entered into a forward contract with the intermediary. Others signed some form of forward contract that was priced off the futures market (Helmuth, 1977, Table 17).

1.1.3 Financial and Foreign Currency Futures

The significant innovation in futures contracts was the development of the Government National Mortgage Association (GNMA) financial futures contract. It was conceived by Richard Sandor in 1972 and first traded on the Chicago Board of Trade in 1975. Sandor's innovation of financial futures created a new industry which quickly overshadowed traditional commodity futures and the foreign exchange futures which were trading since 1972. New products in this industry were Euro-dollar futures; Treasury bond, bill and note futures; certificate of deposit futures; municipal bond index futures; S&P 500 index futures; and New York Stock Exchange composite index futures.

The magnitude of these financial futures markets can be seen by looking at the volume of just three financial futures: Treasury bonds, Treasury bills and the S&P 500 index. On 18 October 1985 the estimated volume was greater than $31 billion which was almost ten times that of the volume of the New York Stock Exchange.

Treasury bonds:
$$180\,000 \text{ contracts} \times \$100\,000 \qquad = \$18 \quad \text{billion}$$
Treasury bills:
$$7\,425 \text{ contracts} \times \$1 \text{ million} \qquad = \quad 7.43 \text{ billion}$$
S&P 500 index:
$$62\,881 \text{ contracts} \times (\$500 \times 187.04) = \quad \underline{5.89 \text{ billion}}$$
$$\$31.32 \text{ billion}$$

The CFTC under the direction of Ronald Hobson conducted a survey of open positions as of the close of trading on 30 November 1977 in each of the interest rate futures trading at that time and five of the more active foreign currency futures. The survey obtained information on the occupation or business of all traders holding open contracts in these markets, and the size of each trader's position and type of position (hedging or speculation).

This information was obtained from clearing members of the Chicago Board of Trade and the Chicago Mercantile Exchange and from nonclearing futures commission merchants. The aim was to learn who are using these futures markets and the composition of these markets.

The open interest in a particular futures contract is held both by 'commercial traders' and by 'other traders'. Commercial traders use futures trading as an input into their merchandising operations in the cash or forward market. The price of the futures contract traded is highly correlated with the price of the underlying commodity that they buy or sell in the spot or forward market. The category 'other traders' represents the complement to this set. Their futures trading is not related to their main business.

For example, the distribution of the traders in GNMA mortgage futures by occupational groups was as follows (Hobson, 1978, Table Vd). *Commercial traders* include mortgage banks, commercial banks, securities dealers, savings and loan associations, investment companies, institutional investors, other financial institutions, real estate developers and builders. *Other traders* include employees of financial institutions and the futures industry, investment and commodity advisers, private investors and investment clubs, retail proprietors and employees, other managers, proprietors and officials, clerical and kindred workers, sales workers and purchasing agents, craftsmen, foremen and kindred workers, labourers and other primary workers, insurance and real estate workers, accountants and auditors, engineers and others in physical sciences, school and college personnel, lawyers and judges, physicians and medical personnel, other professional occupations, farmers and farm managers, housewives, retired persons, students, military and civilian government workers.

The three major interest rate futures (Tables 1.6–1.8) can be characterized as follows.

1 Commercial firms constitute three quarters of the Treasury bond futures market, are almost half of the GNMA futures market, and a little more than a third of the Treasury bill futures market.
2 In each case, long positions of commercial firms are approximately equal to their short positions.
3 Most of the long and the short commercial positions are hedging positions against underlying cash instruments.
4 Practically all of the long or short positions of noncommercial firms are speculative.

5   Dealer positions account for a large part of the commercial positions, and tend to be net long.

6   Most of the dealers' long and short positions are hedging positions against underlying cash instruments.

Table 1.6 describes the Treasury bond futures contract. Line 1: commercials are approximately balanced between long and short positions. Commercials account for 74 per cent of the long and 76 per cent of the short open interest. Line 2: dealers constitute 71 per cent of the long and 65 per cent of the short commercial position. Lines 3 and 4: the average position of the commercial

Table 1.6   Characteristics of the open interest in US Treasury bonds futures

		Long	Short
1	Commercial position as fraction of open interest	0.74	0.76
2	Dealer position as fraction of commercial position	0.71	0.65
3	Average number contracts per commercial	66	67
4	Average number contracts per noncommercial	6	5
5	Commercial hedging as fraction of commercial position	0.75	0.74
6	Other trader hedging as fraction of other trader position	0.05	0.21
7	Dealer hedging as fraction of dealer position	0.65	0.64
8	Hedging to open interest	0.57	0.62

Source: Hobson, 1978, Table Va

Table 1.7   Characteristics of the open interest in US 90-day Treasury bill futures

		Long	Short
1	Commercial position as fraction of open interest	0.37	0.35
2	Dealer position as fraction of commercial position	0.54	0.47
3	Average number contracts per commercial	33	30
4	Average number contracts per noncommercial	7	7
5	Commercial hedging as fraction of commercial position	0.68	0.64
6	Other trader hedging as fraction of other trader position	0.03	0.06
7	Dealer hedging as fraction of dealer position	0.83	0.77
8	Hedging to open interest	0.27	0.26

Source: Hobson, 1978, Table Vc

Table 1.8 Characteristics of the open interest in GNMA futures

		Long	Short
1	Commercial position as fraction of open interest	0.48	0.47
2	Dealer position as fraction of commercial position	0.42	0.30
3	Average number of contracts per commercial	50	49
4	Average number of contracts per noncommercial	13	13
5	Commercial hedging as fraction of commercial position	0.89	0.88
6	Other trader hedging as fraction of other trader position	0.03	0.03
7	Dealer hedging as fraction of dealer position	0.80	0.70
8	Hedging to open interest	0.44	0.43

Source: Hobson, 1978, Table Vd

trader is more than 12 times that of the average noncommercial trader, on either side of the market. Line 5: 75 per cent of the commercial position, either long or short, is a hedging position. Line 6: the position of the noncommercials, either long or short, is overwhelmingly a speculative position; Line 7: 65 per cent of the dealers' long positions and 64 per cent of the dealers' short positions are hedging positions; Line 8: hedging accounts for 57 per cent of the long and 62 per cent of the short open interest.

Table 1.7 describes the open interest in Treasury bill futures and Table 1.8 describes it for GNMA futures, using the same format as Table 1.6.

The foreign exchange futures can be characterized as follows.

1   Commercial firms have unbalanced positions. The direction of the imbalance varies with the currency.
2   Commercial firms only dominate one side of the market.
3   As a rule, most of the commercial long and short positions are hedging positions.
4   Practically all of the noncommercial positions on either side of the market are speculative positions.
5   As a rule, the dealer position accounts for a large part of the unbalanced position.
6   Dealer positions are primarily hedging positions.
7   Hedging is a large part of the open interest only on one side of the market.

Tables 1.9 and 1.10 illustrate these points with the Canadian dollar and the Swiss franc respectively.

Table 1.9   Open interest in Canadian dollar futures

		Long	Short
1	Commercial position as fraction of open interest	0.55	0.25
2	Commercial hedging as fraction of commercial position	0.79	0.56
3	Dealer position as fraction of commercial position	0.59	0.28
4	Dealer hedging as fraction of dealer position	0.94	0.87
5	Other trader hedging as fraction of other trader position	0.07	0
6	Hedging as fraction of open interest	0.47	0.14

Source: Hobson, 1978, Table Ve

Table 1.10   Open interest in Swiss franc futures

		Long	Short
1	Commercial position as fraction of open interest	0.26	0.57
2	Commercial hedging as fraction of commercial position	0.70	0.90
3	Dealer position as fraction of commercial position	0.38	0.86
4	Dealer hedging as fraction of dealer position	0.96	1.00
5	Other traders hedging as fraction of other trader position	0.09	0.24
6	Hedging as fraction of open interest	0.25	0.62

Source: Hobson, 1978, Table Vf

1.2 Capital Asset Pricing Models (CAPM) are Unable to Explain Futures Markets

Harry Markowitz (1959) and James Tobin (1958) developed the theory of optimal portfolio selection in a world of uncertainty. This normative theory was extended by William Sharpe (1964) and John Lintner (1965) to a general equilibrium model of asset prices. The main results of this class of general equilibrium models are as follows.

1 Market equilibrium prices or expected returns on assets can be derived solely as functions of measurable parameters.
2 The equilibrium expected return on any asset is the sum of the riskless rate of interest plus a risk premium.

3 The appropriate risk premium on any individual asset is proportional to the covariance of its own rate of return with that of the market portfolio, and it does not depend upon its own variance.

The Sharpe–Lintner CAPM is a general equilibrium theory which is elegant, simple and follows logically from the basic structure of the assumptions. Its theoretical predictions are capable of being tested empirically.

As is indicated below, Lintner and many other subsequent researchers found that the general equilibrium CAPM theory is inconsistent with the evidence. The Sharpe–Lintner model was later utilized by Katherine Dusak (1973) to explain pricing or rates of return in futures markets. Her article stimulated other studies of futures markets which treated futures contracts as just another asset in a general equilibrium CAPM.

The approach taken in this book is quite different from the general equilibrium CAPM because the latter is not only inconsistent with the evidence concerning stock returns but also is *qualitatively* incapable of explaining the empirical phenomena of futures markets presented in Section 1.1 and summarized by the ten characteristics mentioned. In this section, I first briefly summarize the evidence which rejects the general equilibrium CAPM model. Then, I specifically explain why CAPM reasoning is both qualitatively and quantitatively incapable of explaining futures markets.

1.2.1 Theory of CAPM and Empirical Evidence

The general equilibrium model is based upon assumptions (A1) to (A7). The first four are crucial in obtaining the basic qualitative results. The last three simplify the analysis and lead to precise quantitative results.

(A1) All investors select portfolios based upon the mean and variance of return over a single period.

(A2) All investors are price takers and there are no transactions costs.

(A3) The quantities of all assets are predetermined.

(A4) All investors know the means and variance–covariance matrix of rates of return.

(A5) All investors can borrow or lend an unlimited amount at an exogenously given risk-free rate of return.

(A6) There are no taxes.

(A7) All assets are divisible.

The basic implications of the CAPM are as follows.

(CAPM-1)   All investors hold in their portfolios all the risky assets in the same proportions as these assets are available in the market, independent of the investor's preferences. Define the excess expected return as the expected return on an asset $E(R_i)$ in excess of the risk-free rate, r. Then, the next implication is:

(CAPM-2)   The expected excess return on a given asset $E(R_i) - r$ is proportional to the expected return on the market portfolio $E(R_m) - r$.

(CAPM-3)   The above factor of proportionality β_i is the covariance of the return on asset i with the return on the market portfolio, divided by the variance of the return on the market portfolio. This is summarized by

$$E(R_i) = r + \beta_i[E(R_m) - r] \tag{1.1}$$

and

$$\beta_i = \text{cov}(R_i, R_m)/\text{var} R_m \tag{1.2}$$

where $E(R_i)$ is the expected return on ith asset, r is the risk-free rate and $E(R_m)$ is the expected return on market portfolio. Combining the above two implications, the fourth implication is:

(CAPM-4)   The appropriate measure of risk on an asset is not its own variance, but the covariance between its rate of return and that of the market portfolio.

Factor of proportionality β_i is also the percentage increase in the risk on the market portfolio resulting from a marginal increase in the weight that asset i has in the market portfolio:

$$\beta_i = \frac{1}{\sigma_m} \frac{\partial \sigma_m}{\partial w_i} \tag{1.3}$$

where σ_m is the standard deviation of return on market portfolio and w_i is the weight that asset i has in market portfolio. Equations (1.2) and (1.3) are equivalent ways of viewing the risk premium on an asset. If β_i is zero, then the asset will not command a risk premium over the risk-free rate r, regardless of the magnitude of its own variance.

The empirical results of the tests of the CAPM are inconsistent with the theory (see Jensen, 1972; Levy, 1978). The research design of the tests is to use time-series data on securities to estimate β_i in equation (1.1). Using the β_i derived from time series, cross-section regressions as described by equations (1.4) or (1.5) were estimated:

$$\bar{R}_i = \gamma_0 + \gamma_1 \hat{\beta}_i + e_i \qquad (1.4)$$

$$\bar{R}_i = \gamma_0 + \gamma_1 \hat{\beta}_i + \gamma_2 \sigma_i^2 + e_i \qquad (1.5)$$

where $\bar{R}_i$ is the average return on ith risky asset during the period, σ_i^2 is the variance of return on ith risky asset, $\hat{\beta}_i$ is the systematic risk estimated from time-series regression and e_i is the residual.

If the CAPM model is valid, then equation (1.4) should correspond to equation (1.1). Specifically, the following hypothesis should be true.

(H1)   Coefficient γ_0 corresponds to the risk-free rate $\bar{r}$.

(H2)   Coefficient γ_1 corresponds to the average return on the market less the average risk-free rate $(\bar{R}_m - \bar{r})$.

(H3)   Coefficient γ_2 in equation (1.5) should be zero because of (CAPM-4): the only relevant risk is systematic risk β_i not the security's own variance.

Douglas published one of the first direct tests of the CAPM. He examined seven separate five-year periods from 1926 to 1960. The main result was that the average realized return was significantly positively related to σ_i^2, the variance of the security's return over time, but not to β_i the covariance with the index of returns. Lintner (1965), Miller and Scholes (1972), and Black, Jensen and Scholes (1972) did further tests of the general equilibrium CAPM model over a sample period 1931–65 for returns on ten portfolios which contain all securities on the NYSE. The conclusion was that the CAPM model described in equation (1.1) is not an adequate description of the structure of security returns.

Haim Levy (1978) examined rates of return on a sample of 101 stocks traded on the NYSE during the period 1946–68. He calculated monthly, semi-annual and annual returns. First, he used time series to estimate systematic risk β_i of each security. Secondly, he used the estimated β_i and variance σ_i^2, from the time series, in deriving cross-section regression equation (1.5). His main results are summarized in Table 1.11.

The results summarized in Table 1.11 are devastating for the CAPM. The estimate of systematic risk $\hat{\beta}_i$ adds nothing to the explanation of price behaviour. For annual returns, $t = 0.9$. By contrast, the own risk σ_i^2 is a significant explanation of asset returns. For annual data, $t = 5.2$. Thus (H2) and H3) are rejected

Table 1.11 Tests of the CAPM model $\bar{R}_i = \gamma_0 + \gamma_1 \hat{\beta}_i + \gamma_2 \sigma_i^2$

	γ_0	γ_1	γ_2	R^2
Semi-annual returns				
Coefficient	0.0528	0.0099	0.1771	0.23
Standard error	(0.0050)	(0.0072)	(0.0808)	
t	10.6	1.4	2.2	
Annual returns				
Coefficient	0.117	0.008	0.197	0.38
Standard error	(0.008)	(0.009)	(0.038)	
t	14.2	0.9	5.2	

Source: Levy, 1978, Tables 2 and 3

by the data. There are variants of the CAPM which attempt to rectify the deficiencies of the classical CAPM model described but these variants do not have the clarity, objectivity and simplicity of the classical model. Those which allow expectations to be heterogeneous no longer permit the theory to be tested empirically. The empirical performance of the consumption beta model is distinctly inferior to that of the classical model (Mankiw and Shapiro, 1985).

1.2.2 CAPM Reasoning Applied to Futures Markets

Keynes viewed the futures market as one where commercial firms hold inventories of commodities and sell futures to transfer the risk of price fluctuations. 'Speculators' are on the other side of the market and purchase these futures at a discount below the expected price. The magnitude of this discount is the risk premium demanded by the speculators. His theory of 'normal backwardation' has been the subject of controversy. Brennan (1958), Cootner (1967) and Telser (1958) debated the issue of whether 'normal backwardation' exists. This debate was continued by Dusak (1973) and by Carter, Rausser and Schmitz (1983).

Dusak (1973) applied CAPM reasoning to the issue of what is the risk premium that speculators must receive to accommodate the commercial interests on the other side of the market. Her frame of reference was implication (CAPM-4) above. The appropriate measure of risk on an asset is not its own variance, but the covariance between its rate of return with that of the market portfolio.

As a measure of the risk premium, which is the expected rate of return on a futures contract in excess of the risk-free rate, she used the discount of the futures price $P_f(0)$ below the subsequently expected price $EP_i(1)$ as a percentage of the current cash price $P_i(0)$, This is the left-hand side of equation (1.6). According to (CAPM-2) and (CAPM-3) above, it should be proportional at rate β_i to the expected excess return on the market portfolio (the right-hand side of equation 1.6):

$$\frac{EP_i(1) - P_f(0)}{P_i(0)} = \beta_i[E(R_m) - r] \tag{1.6}$$

The appropriate market risk premium demanded by the 'speculators' is dependent upon β_i, the systematic risk. Is it positive, as claimed by Keynes? Dusak estimated regression equation (1.7) for futures in wheat, corn and soybeans during the period 1952–67:

$$R_i = \alpha_i + \beta_i R_m + \epsilon \tag{1.7}$$

where R_m was the return on the value weighted S&P 500 index of common stocks and R_i is the return on the futures stated on the left-hand side of equation (1.6).

Her conclusions (Dusak, 1973, Table 3) are that both the mean return and relative risk β_i for wheat, corn and soybeans are very close to zero. Consequently, there is no systematic risk to adding futures contracts to the market portfolio. The futures price should not be at a discount to its expected price and 'normal backwardation' does not exist.

Subsequent researchers, particularly Carter, Rausser and Schmitz (1983), arrived at opposite conclusions. For example, Bodie and Rosansky (1980) examined the distributions of annual rates of return on 23 commodity futures contracts during the period 1950–76. Their conclusions were as follows.

1 The data are inconsistent with CAPM reasoning. A regression of cross-section rates of return on the $\hat{\beta}_i$ derived from time series (the form of equation (1.4) above) yielded a significantly *negative* value of γ_1. Theoretically, γ_1 should be an estimate of the expected excess return on the market portfolio $(\bar{R}_m - \bar{r})$ which *must* be positive.

2 The mean excess returns on commodity futures contracts are positive, which supports Keynes's view.

3 The mean rates of return on futures and stocks were about the same.

4   An investor could have reduced his risk without lowering his mean rate of return, by diversifying his portfolio through mixing stocks with futures. By switching from an all stock portfolio to one with 60 per cent in stocks and 40 per cent in commodity futures, an investor could have reduced his standard deviation of return by one third without sacrificing any of his mean return.

1.2.3   Inapplicability of CAPM Reasoning to Futures Markets

Many studies continue to view the pricing of futures contracts within the framework of the CAPM general equilibrium model or of modifications to that class of model. The unifying characteristic of these studies is a search for the appropriate β_i systematic or nondiversifiable risk. Such a quest is inconsistent with the basic empirical phenomena of futures markets, for the following reasons.

1   An important implication of the general equilibrium model is (CAPM-1): investors hold risky assets in their portfolios in the same proportions as they are available in the market. This implication makes no sense for futures contracts because the open interest is equally divided between the long and short open interest. There is a zero net position in the market because the sales of the shorts equal the purchases of the longs. How then can both the longs and the shorts be holding the market portfolio in the same proportions?

2   Assumption (A3) of the CAPM model, that the quantities of all assets are predetermined is inapplicable to futures markets. The open interest (i.e. the quantity of outstanding contracts) is an endogenous variable determined by economic conditions and the open interest varies considerably during the course of a month. Table 1.12 describes the open interest in the two nearby contracts of Treasury bond futures during December 1983 and wheat during January 1983. The range during the month in each case is huge. In the December Treasury bond contract, the open interest ranged from 47 408 contracts to 2672 contracts at the expiration date. In the March contract, the open interest varied from 81 760 to 113 076 contracts. A similar situation existed in January 1983 for the March and May wheat contracts.

Therefore assumption (A3) above, that there is a fixed vector of risky futures contracts whose prices adjust according to the CAPM model, is grossly at variance with the phenomena

Table 1.12 Intra-monthly variation in the open interest in two nearby contracts: Treasury bonds and wheat 1983

US Treasury bonds			Wheat		
Date (December 1983)	December contract	March contract	Date (January 1983)	March contract	May contract
1	47 408	81 760	3	116 919	32 495
2	41 971	85 388	4	112 520	32 555
5	37 827	93 483	5	112 680	33 760
6	34 490	89 764	6	114 365	34 195
7	27 324	92 736	7	111 935	37 430
8	23 610	97 917	10	108 780	38 210
9	21 956	99 409	11	108 560	38 795
12	16 575	103 685	12	103 905	37 820
13	14 487	106 976	13	99 000	39 665
14	13 508	111 877	14	98 080	40 920
15	10 988	113 076	17	98 895	40 790
16	10 716	109 197	18	103 270	43 260
19	7 167	108 760	19	97 970	41 695
20	2 751	109 029	20	96 685	40 820
21	2 685	109 606	21	96 740	42 135
22	2 672	108 604	24	96 255	42 650
23	2 672	106 851	25	96 935	45 875
27	2 672	107 436	26	97 965	46 360
28	2 672	108 888	27	96 520	45 045
			28	94 565	45 275
			31	98 490	45 385

Source: Chicago Board of Trade 1983 Statistical Annual, Interest Rates and Metal Futures, p. 74; *1983 Statistical Annual Cash and Futures Data: Grains, Forest Products and Energy*, p. 9

to be explained. *Both the quantity and price of futures contracts are to be determined simultaneously.*

3 Almost the entire open interest (i.e. outstanding contracts) is concentrated in the nearby contract with a maturity of no more than three months. This is shown in Table 1.1. *The futures contracts are short-lived securities, whose quantities are determined by the volume of transactions in the cash and forward markets.* Instead of the CAPM type of model where prices adjust to clear the market for fixed quantities of securities, an economic model must be adduced to explain the demand for and supply of futures contracts.

4 Line 1 of Tables 1.6–1.8 for interest rate futures shows that commercials are on both the long and the short sides of the market, and that their positions are close to balance. Line 2 of these tables shows that dealers are on both sides of the market but, on balance, tend to be long. How can CAPM reasoning account for this extremely important characteristic of the futures market?

5 Bodie and Rosansky (cited above) claimed that all investors could reduce the risk on their portfolios without sacrificing mean return, by switching from an all stock portfolio to one with 60 per cent in stocks and 40 per cent in commodity futures. This is logically impossible. The rate of return R_i to a long is minus the rate of return to the short. How can both the long and the short achieve the same risk reduction without sacrificing expected return? What the group that is long adds to its assets in futures, the opposite group to the transaction (which must be short) is adding to its liabilities. CAPM reasoning founders on the arithmetic fact that the long open interest in futures is exactly equal to the short open interest. The Bodie–Rosansky result is simply a simulation of a situation which cannot exist in the market for all individuals.

6 The main users of futures are intermediaries in the marketing process. Table 1.4 shows that between 5 and 10 per cent of the farmers used futures. Instead, they use the forward market in their transactions with dealers. Table 1.5 shows that co-operatives and corporate grain marketing agencies are frequent users of futures. CAPM type of reasoning is incapable of explaining these phenomena.

The inescapable conclusion is that a very different approach is necessary to explain the empirical phenomena of futures markets.

1.3 Outline and Summary

As a unit, Chapters Two to Four are addressed to the following questions. What are the optimization equations of and the interactions among the agents which ultimately determine the market-clearing futures price and total quantity of output produced? What determines the futures price? What is its information content? What is its role in the production process? What determines the variability of the futures price? What is the magnitude of the market-clearing volume of hedging and its ratio to total planned input or output? The determinants of the uses of futures markets by commercial firms are precisely the determinants of the success or failure of futures contracts. Under what conditions will they succeed or fail?

In Chapter Two, the subjective price expectation of the subsequent period's price by the ith class of agents is treated as a predetermined variable. In Chapter Three, the analysis is carried further by deriving the endogenous subjective price expectations of the different classes of agents. The speed of convergence to a Muth rational expectations (MRE) equilibrium is analysed. For theoretical reasons, there should be a diversity in the forecasting ability of large and small commercial firms, professional and amateur speculators. This leads to the next question. To what extent does the diversity in the forecasting ability of the futures speculators simply result in transfers of wealth among themselves and to what extent does it affect the output produced, the price paid by the consumer and the variance of that price? How does the existence of futures markets affect the level of expected production and the variance of the price paid by consumers, relative to the situation that would prevail if there were no futures markets?

The commercial firms are transactions oriented: they are concerned with the income statement, not with the balance sheet, in their use of futures. Contracts in futures are used to manage risk in connection with input price or output price uncertainty involved in near-term transactions. They are not used to eliminate risk but to manage it.

The reason why futures markets are simultaneously useful to both the commercials who are long and to those who are short is implied by the analysis of Chapter Two. The volume of both short and long hedging depends upon first, the quality of the hedging instrument which enables the commercial firms to diversify away the absolute price risk of the product of the broadly defined industry and secondly, the magnitude of the absolute price risk compared to the risk of changes in the relative price of the firm's output or input. A quantitative measure of the usefulness of the futures contract to the commercial firm is the maximal percentage risk reduction possible, even though the agent will generally not select this point. The maximal percentage risk reduction is the square of the correlation coefficient between the price relevant to the firm and the futures price. Several examples of declines in the use of a futures market illustrate the point that its usefulness to commercial firms is positively related to the maximal percentage risk reduction.

Another implication of the analysis is that dealers (i.e. inter-mediaries between producers and consumers) are the main users of futures. Moreover, dealers in fixed income securities in both the primary and secondary market will actively use futures but equity underwriters will not. On the other hand, stock block traders in the secondary market will use futures.

The market-clearing futures price $q_T(t)$ at time t of a contract which matures at subsequent time T is the sum of the subjectively expected price by the market $E_m p(T; t)$ plus or minus a risk premium h/w:

$$q_T(t) = E_m p(T; t) - h/w \qquad (1.8)$$

The numerator h of the risk premium is the net hedging pressure: the excess supply of futures by the short and long commercials that would occur if the futures price were equal to the expected price. There is no reason why h should be positive, because futures markets are used by commercial firms which hedge prospective input purchases as well as by those which hedge prospective output sales. Tables 1.6–1.8 show how balanced commercial hedging is in interest rate futures. Tables 1.9 and 1.10 show that, in foreign exchange futures, h can be positive or negative. Denominator w of the risk premium reflects the risk sharing by commercials and non-commercials.

Chapter Three is addressed to the following questions. What determines the subjectively expected prices $E_i p(T; t)$ of the ith group of agents, when purchase or sales decisions are made at time t but the price will only be known at date T? What determines the variance of price var p which is the source of risk? Only when these questions are answered can one compare the price and output with and without futures markets. The questions are answered in Chapter Three which considers a nonstorable good.

Emphasis is placed upon the theoretical determinants of the diversity of price expectations among agents. The forecast error ϵ_i of the ith agent between the subjectively expected price $E_i p(T; t)$ and the subsequently realized price $p(T)$ can be written as the sum of two elements

$$\epsilon_i(T) = E_i p(T; t) - p(T) = [E_i p(T; t) - Ep(T)] + [Ep(T) - p(T)]$$

$$= \quad y_i(t) \quad + \quad \eta$$

forecast error $\quad = \quad$ Bayesian error $\quad + \quad$ unavoidable error

$$(1.9)$$

The first element $y_i(t)$ is a *Bayesian error*, which reflects the inability of the ith agent to locate the objective (true) mean of the distribution of prices $Ep(T)$. The second element η is the deviation of the actual realization $p(T)$ from the objective mean. This is an *unavoidable error*, which reflects the fact that demand is not always at its mean value.

The MRE hypothesis assumes that the Bayesian error in the market is zero: the subjective estimate by the market of the mean price $E_m p(T; t)$ is indeed the objective mean $Ep(T)$. I prove that the variance of the Bayesian error is positively related to the variance of the objective distribution of prices and inversely related to the total number of samples that an agent has taken from the information set. Agents who have taken larger samples have smaller variances of the Bayesian error than do agents who operate on a small scale. As time continues and repeated samples are taken by each agent, the variance of the Bayesian error declines. However, the variance of the Bayesian error for those who operate on a large scale converges at a faster rate to MRE than for those who operate on a smaller scale. I call this process asymptotically rational expectations (ARE) whose limit is MRE.

The conclusions of Chapter Three are as follows.

1 Futures markets change the structure of the model by changing the supply of output equation. This changes both the expected price and the price variance.
2 There is an optimum ratio of professional to amateur speculators to minimize the variance of the market forecast error. The optimal ratio of the position of professional to amateurs is equal to the ratio of the variance of the forecast error of amateurs to that of professionals.
3 Even though the observed composition of speculation is not optimal, given the parameter estimates, as long as the variance of the market forecast error of amateurs is less than six times that of producers, the entry of amateur speculators will not increase the variance of the market forecast error.
4 A large total volume of speculation can be expected to lower the expected price, primarily through risk sharing.

Chapter Four is concerned with storable commodities where inventories are always carried and production and consumption are continuous. The cash price equates production with the sum of consumption and the desired rate of change of inventories. The desired level of inventories depends upon the cash price. A dynamic process inevitably results.

I derive a rational expectations dynamic solution for the evolution of the cash price and level of inventories over time, when there are developed futures markets. The expectation of the cash price converges asymptotically to the flow equilibrium price, which is defined as the price where current production is equal to current consumption. The main conclusions are as follows.

1   The speed of convergence depends positively upon three elements: (a) the average price elasticity, a, of current production and current consumption; (b) the slope, c, of the marginal carrying cost function; and (c) the risk premium, R, which depends negatively upon the degree of speculation by non-commercials. A rise in the risk premium lowers the current cash price but increases its rate of change to the flow equilibrium price.

2   A change in the flow equilibrium price produces an immediate corresponding change in the cash price.

3   The variance of the change in the cash price is equal to $[(c + R)/a]$ var u, where var u is the variance of the sum of the intercepts of supply of current production and demand for current consumption.

4   The variance of the change in the futures price relative to the change in the cash price is negatively related to the distance to maturity of the futures contract. The longer the distance to maturity, the relatively smaller the variance of the change in the futures price.

Chapter Five evaluates empirical evidence concerning several issues discussed in the previous chapters. First, to what extent do producers pay a risk premium to futures speculators for the transfer of the risk of price changes? Secondly, are the subjective expectations of the subsequent price held by the market participants equal to the objective expectations? If the MRE hypothesis were correct, then the two expectations would always be equal. There would be no Bayesian errors. Then futures markets would not affect the relation between the subjective and objective expectations. An alternative view is that the futures markets speed the convergence of the market's subjective expectation to the objective expectation. Unless the underlying distribution of prices has been stationary for a long time, without futures markets the MRE hypothesis is unlikely to be correct. Lastly, to what extent does the existence of futures markets change the structural equations which determine the quantity produced and price paid by the consumer?

An analysis of empirical studies shows that the 'backwardation MRE' hypothesis is inconsistent with the evidence. Instead, there are significant differences in forecasting ability between professional and amateur speculators, and between larger and smaller agents. The profits of the agents generally derive from their superior forecasting abilities and not from 'backwardation'.

Moreover, the existence of futures markets accelerates the convergence to MRE and changes the structure of the supply equations. In the absence of futures markets, each producer must act exclusively upon his own information. With futures markets, the information of the various agents is pooled in the determination of the futures price. I show that with the advent of a futures market in potatoes the cobweb cycle was eliminated. Basic changes also occurred in the supply equations of continuous inventory products when futures markets developed, in the manner implied by the theory in Chapter Four.

Chapter Six derives, on the basis of the theory in Chapters Two to Four, quantitative measures of how well futures markets are conducive to the optimal intertemporal allocation of resources. The ex-post social loss is shown to be a multiple of the square of the price deviation between the subsequently realized cash price and the futures price. The analysis applies to both storable and nonstorable commodities. There are three components to the price deviation and hence to the social loss: An unavoidable error (η), Bayesian error (y) and a risk premium R. The expected social loss is a multiple of the variance of the sum of the three components, var $(\eta + y + R)$.

In an ideal market, the unavoidable error resulting from unpredictable stochastic variations is the only component of the price deviation. Then the variance of the unavoidable error var η is the minimum expected social loss. My measure of social loss is the ratio of var $(\eta + y + R)$/var η. The closer this ratio is to unity, the better is the performance of the particular market. Several empirical studies are examined to determine the measures of social loss: Which markets perform better than others and what are the sources of the welfare loss?

Chapter Seven is addressed to the questions posed by the Congress: what are the effects of the new futures markets upon the rate of capital formation? It draws upon the theory developed in the earlier chapters to evaluate the effects of new institutional arrangements upon the supply of and demand for loanable funds (Table 1.13) which determine the rate of capital formation. The level of security prices or rate of interest adjusts to equate the two

Table 1.13   Supply of and demand for risky securities during a time interval

Supply	
(1)	Planned investment by firms (FNMA, GNMA)
(2)	Government budget deficit

Demand	
(3)	Savings less change in the demand for money (institutional investors)
(4)	Changes in the supply of money
(5)	Investment in inventories of securities (dealers)

sides of the table. The resulting cost of capital or rate of interest determines the rate of capital formation. This chapter is a synthesis of theory and economic policy.

The main users of the financial and stock index futures are: dealers in government and corporate securities; intermediaries in the housing industry FNMA and GNMA; and intermediaries in the savings-investment process (the institutional investors).

Item 1 is the rate of planned investment, or the supply of risky assets by firms during a time interval. This rate is positively related to the level of security prices relative to the cost of production of new capital goods. I explain how the use of futures by the FNMA reduces the risk premium that it charges to mortgage bankers and savings and loan associations. As a result of the lower risk premium, mortgage interest rates are reduced and planned investment in housing is increased.

Item 3 is savings less the change in the demand for money. This constitutes the savings directed towards risky assets during a time interval. A large part of the savings of the public is managed by institutional investors (pension funds and insurance companies). I show how the use of futures markets by institutional investors improves the trade-off between expected return and risk on their investments. This improvement leads to an increase in the flow of savings directed towards risky assets. Were there no futures markets in Treasury securities and stock market indexes, there would be a lower expected return for a given level of risk available to institutional investors. A greater proportion of current savings would then be directed towards holding money or near money. The lower flow demand for securities would lower the level of security prices (i.e. raise interest rates) which would adversely affect the rate of capital formation.

If there were no securities dealers, item 5, then intra-month or intra-year variations in the government budget deficit or planned investment by firms would have to be absorbed by savings less the change in the demand for money. Since item 3 is not highly responsive to changes in the nominal rate of interest, intra-month variations in the supplies of risky assets (items 1 and 2) would be associated with very large variations in levels of security prices. Such a phenomenon would increase the risks of holding equities and fixed income securities, and would decrease the savings directed towards risky assets (item 3). In this manner, an increase in the variability of interest rates would raise the average level of interest rates. Capital formation would be reduced.

The economic function of dealers is to provide an inventory investment in securities. The greater the elasticity of demand by dealers for investment in inventories of securities, the smaller will be the price (interest rate) variation associated with short-period variations in items 1 to 4. I explain how dealers use futures markets to diversify away risks of changes in market indexes. As a result they have more elastic demands for inventory. This is equivalent to a reduction in the risk premium they must charge their customers via commissions and spreads. The net effect of the dealer's use of futures markets is to lower both the variance of interest rates and the cost of capital to firms. In this manner, futures markets are conducive to capital formation. This is the answer to the questions posed by the Congress.

2

Market-Clearing Futures Prices and Hedging

2.1 Risks of Commercial Firms

Futures markets are used by commercial firms to manage, but not to eliminate, risk. Several examples will motivate the analysis. First, a Maine potato farmer makes a decision in the spring concerning the production to be harvested in the autumn. Costs of input are known, but the price of potatoes in the autumn is unknown when the production decision is made. Inventories of potatoes are not carried from the summer to the autumn. How is the production decision to be made?

In the second example, feeder cattle are purchased when they weigh approximately 600 pounds, they are fed for five to six months and marketed when they weigh about 1100 pounds. At the time that the purchase decision is made, neither the market price six months hence nor the cost of the inputs, primarily corn and protein supplements, during the production period, is known. Even if the inputs are purchased at the beginning of the feeding period, the market price of the final product is still unknown. How many feeder cattle should be purchased, and when should they be marketed?

As a third example, suppose that a foreign firm or a foreign government announces that it is accepting bids on grain to be shipped within four to six months. The quality, quantity and port locations are specified. The American exporter deciding to bid on the sale does not know what will be the market price of the specific grade of grain that he must purchase in fulfillment of the contract. What price should the exporter bid to the foreigner? Too high a price will adversely affect sales or may lead to the rejection of his bid. Too low a price may result in an unprofitable transaction.

Fourthly, suppose that home builders finance their investment in housing by selling mortgages to mortgage bankers and savings and loan associations. In turn, the banks offer both old and new mortgages to the Federal National Mortgage Association (FNMA) and other investors. The FNMA purchases the mortgages as investments in its own portfolio and finances its purchases of mortgages by selling in its own securities in the capital market where they are purchased by institutional investors. In effect, the FNMA buys one type of security and sells another type of security.

Several risks confront the FNMA. At time t, the FNMA is asked to bid for large batches of mortgages offered by banks for forward delivery. Due to the legal documentation required to transfer the mortgages, there is a time lag of several months before the mortgages can be delivered. Moreover, as a rule, the FNMA is only permitted to enter the capital market once a month to sell its debentures, on a date given to it by the Treasury. The rationale for this provision is that the Treasury does not want the FNMA to compete with its own borrowing or with those of the other government agencies. At time t, when the FNMA is asked to bid on mortgages for forward delivery, it does not know at what date it will be permitted to enter the capital market to borrow nor at what prices (interest rates) it will be able to sell its securities. Since October 1979 there have been very large intra-year variations in interest rates.

Profits for the FNMA depend upon two elements: (a) the spread between the sales price of its debentures in the capital market and the forward bid price for mortgages; plus (b) the fees that it receives from the sellers of mortgages. If the FNMA bids too high a price for the forward purchases of mortgages, it faces the risk that the unknown sales price of its own debentures at the unknown subsequent date will be below its forward bid price. Large losses will result. If the FNMA bids too low a forward price for mortgages, it will be unsuccessful in obtaining the mortgages. The question facing the FNMA can be posed in two equivalent ways, because the quantity of mortgages that will be successfully purchased is positively related to the forward bid price. What price should the FNMA bid forward at time t for mortgages? What is the optimum quantity of mortgages to be purchased?

The subject of this chapter and the next is the effect of futures markets when there is a point input–point output problem. An input (output) decision is made at time t and the output (input) will be sold (purchased) at an uncertain price at subsequent date $t + h$. In these cases, there is no investment in inventories. The inventory investment or disinvestment problem, analysed in subsequent chapters, is inherently dynamic and is a development of the present analysis.

A general theoretical analysis is developed in Sections 2.1–2.3 which is used in Section 2.4 to explain where and why futures are useful in risk management. In the present chapter, the subjectively expected prices by the commercial and noncommercial firms are treated as parameters in determining the market-clearing futures price. In Chapter Three, the subjective expected prices are endogenous variables and, using the analysis of Chapter Two, the cash price and level of output by the industry are determined. A summary of the present chapter is reflected in Section 2.4.

The profit calculus of the commercial firm is described by equation (2.1) or (2.8) depending upon whether the risk concerns the sales price or the input price risk respectively.

2.1.1 Risk of Changes in the Output Price

In this section, consider the case where the input costs are known but the sales price is unknown at time t, when the production decisions are made. Commercial firms are denoted by the subscript 1 or 2 and stochastic variables are denoted by an asterisk, unless the context is unambiguous.

It is convenient to refer to the firm in equation (2.1) as the 'producer', even though the main users of futures markets are intermediaries who purchase inputs forward from the original producers at cost $C[s(t+1)]$ and transform these inputs into output $s(t+1)$ which is sold to the final consumers. The theoretical analysis explains why intermediaries are the main users of the futures markets.

Intermediaries face demand rather than production uncertainty. Appendix A discusses the modifications in the analysis that result when there is also production uncertainty.

$$\pi_1^*(t+1) = p^*(t+1)s(t+1) - C[s(t+1)]$$
$$+ [q_T(t) - q_T^*(t+1)]x(t) \tag{2.1}$$

where $\pi_1^*(t+1)$ is the producer profit at $t+1$; $s(t+1)$ is the output at $t+1$; $p^*(t+1)$ is the price at $t+1$; $C(\cdot)$ are the costs at t; $q_T(t)$ is the price at time t of a futures contract maturing at time $T > t$; and $x(t)$ are the sales (+) and purchases (−) at time t of futures contracts maturing at T. Profits at time $t+1$, denoted by $\pi_1^*(t+1)$, consist of three parts. Total receipts are output $s(t+1)$

times the price $p^*(t + 1)$ which is unknown at time t. Total costs $C[s(t + 1)]$ are assumed to be known at time t. In this case there is no production uncertainty. The first two terms are the profits of a firm which does not engage in any hedging or risk management.

Firms can manage risks by using the futures market. Output $s(t + 1)$ and price $p^*(t + 1)$ are location, time of delivery, quality and quantity specific. The commercial firm can sell (+) or buy (−) quantity $x(t)$ of futures contracts for delivery at time T. These contracts are standardized. Each futures contract is identical and calls for the delivery of a fixed amount and quality of the product at a specified location during a given interval of time. The contract specifications are specified by the exchange.[1] Whereas the commercial firms trade heterogeneous commodities in terms of quality, location, delivery period and quantity, the futures trading is in a homogeneous commodity in terms of these four characteristics. It is most unlikely that the commodity $s(t + 1)$ of the commercial firm is the same as $x(t)$ the commodity specified in the futures contract.

At time t when the production decision is made, the commercial firm sells at price $q_T(t)$ quantity $x(t)$ of futures contracts which mature at subsequent date T. When the producer is ready to market his output at time $t + h$, he sells the product at price $p(t + h)$ and repurchases the futures contract at price $q_T(t + h)$. For example, when the FNMA, at time t, bids on a collection of heterogeneous long-term mortgages with a face value of s, it simultaneously sells $x(t)$ dollars of Treasury bond futures at price $q_T(t)$ for delivery at subsequent date T. When the FNMA enters the capital market at time $t + h$, it sells its own debentures at price $p(t + h)$ and repurchases the Treasury bond futures at price $q_T(t + h)$. The underlying 'commodity' in the futures contract is not the same as the underlying 'commodity' sold by commercial firm. The reasons emerge from the theoretical analysis. It is often convenient for theoretical analysis to assume that $T = t + h = t + 1$ so that the analysis is simple and in discrete time. A continuous time analysis is done in chapters concerning inventories.

Equations (2.2) and (2.3) are the crucial relationship: a highly predictable relation exists between the price of the commodity relevant for the commercial firm $p(t + 1)$ and the price $I(t + 1)$ of the standardized commodity defined in the futures contract. A convenient form is

$$p^*(t + 1) = I(t + 1) + \eta^* \tag{2.2}$$

$$E(\eta) = 0 \tag{2.2a}$$

$$E(I, \eta) = 0 \tag{2.2b}$$

Assume (equation 2.2b) that the differential η is independent of the futures price. Price differential η could be a constant plus a stochastic term. It simplifies the exposition if it is assumed (equation 2.2a) that the differential has an expectation of zero. Since the commodities are not identical in terms of quality, location, delivery period and delivery characteristics, there is a variance (denoted var) to η the differential.

The variance of the price differential is equation (2.2c), where r is the correlation between the two prices,[2]

$$\text{var } \eta = (1 - r^2) \text{ var } p \tag{2.2c}$$

Quantity r^2 will be referred to as the *quality of the hedging instrument*, and is a crucial variable in the analysis developed in this chapter.

At the maturity of the contract, the futures price $q_{t+1}(t + 1)$ is equal to the price $I(t + 1)$ of the standardized commodity defined in the futures contract

$$q_{t+1}(t + 1) = I(t + 1) \tag{2.3}$$

Hence, the relation between the price p and the futures price q_{t+1} at maturity is

$$p(t + 1) = q_{t+1}(t + 1) + \eta^* \tag{2.4}$$

Substitution of equation (2.4) into (2.1) leads to equation (2.5): the basic profit equation for a commercial firm which hedges an anticipated sale but carries no inventories

$$\pi_1^*(t + 1) = \{q_{t+1}(t)x(t) - C[s(t + 1)]\}$$
$$\text{deterministic}$$

$$+ \{p^*(t + 1)[s(t + 1) - x(t)] + \eta^*x(t)\} \tag{2.5}$$
$$\text{stochastic}$$

There are two components to the profit equation: a deterministic part

$$q_{t+1}(t)x(t) - C[s(t + 1)]$$

and a stochastic part

$$p^*(t + 1)[s(t + 1) - x(t)] + \eta^*x(t).$$

The decision variables are the quantity $s(t + 1)$ to be produced and the sales (+) or purchases (−) of $x(t)$ of futures contracts.

The subjective expected value of profits of the producers (denoted by 1) is $E\pi_1(t+1)$ in equation (2.6). Variable $E_1p(t+1;t)$ is the subjective expectation taken by the producer (E_1) at time t of the price that will prevail at time $t+1$. For simplicity, the price differential η is assumed (equation 2.2a) to have a zero expectation

$$E\pi_1(t+1;t) = E_1p(t+1;t)[s(t+1) - x(t)]$$

$$+ q_{t+1}(t)x(t) - C[s(t+1)] \tag{2.6}$$

The subjective variance of profit var $\pi_1(t+1)$ of the producer is equation (2.7), using the above equations.[3] The time and firm subscripts from now on will only be used when necessary.

$$\text{var } \pi = (s-x)^2 \text{ var } p + [x^2 + 2x(s-x)] \text{ var } \eta \tag{2.7}$$

This can also be written as (2.7a), which is graphed in Figure 2.1:

$$\text{var } \pi = [r^2(s-x)^2 + (1-r^2)s^2] \text{ var } p \tag{2.7a}$$

The price risk var p is the sum of two risks. First is the risk of variations in the absolute price level of the products produced by the 'industry' var $I = r^2$ var p. This the *absolute price risk*. Second is the risk of variations in the relative price of the firm var $\eta = (1-r^2)$ var p. This is the *relative price risk*. For example, the absolute price risk for FNMA concerns shifts in the level of the Treasury yield curve var I, where I is the price of a Treasury bond. The relative price risk concerns the variations in the price of FNMA debentures relative to that of Treasury securities. Another example concerns traditional commodities. There is a price differential between the price $p(t)$ of a specific grade of corn at Champaign, Illinois and the price $I(t)$ of the contract grade at the delivery point in Chicago. The absolute price risk concerns variations in $I(t)$, the general level of prices, due to variations in crop yields and in foreign demand. The relative price risk concerns variations in the differential between the prices of the two commodities $(p - I)$.

Figure 2.1, based upon equation (2.7a), graphs of variance of profits relative to the price variance var π/var p on the vertical axis as a function of the position x in futures, measured on the horizontal axis. When there is no position in futures $(x = 0)$, the total risk is s^2, the vertical intercept. Total risk is at a minimum, equal to $(1-r^2)s^2$, when all of the output is hedged $(x = s)$. This is the relative price risk, known as the basis risk, which is the second term in equation (2.7a). The absolute price risk is the first term in equation (2.7a), the difference between the total risk and the minimum risk.

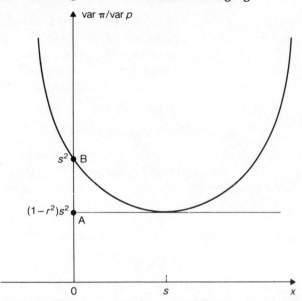

Figure 2.1   The ratio of the variance of profits to the variance of price (var π/var p) is plotted as a function of x, the short (+) or long (−) position in futures. Output is s. The function is a parabola with a minimum of $x = s$. The relative price risk is $(1 - r^2)s^2$ var p, which is the minimum risk. The absolute price risk is $r^2(s - x)^2$ var p, which is the difference between the total risk (var π) and the minimum risk. The maximal percentage risk reduction is the r^2 between the price p relevant to the firm and the price l of the commodity specified in the futures contract.

By using the futures market, the firm can diversify away as much of the absolute price risk $r^2(s - x)^2$ var p that it wants to do. The *maximal percentage reduction in risk possible by just using the futures market is* r^2, the percentage difference between the vertical intercept and the minimum risk point (see Ederington, 1979). A useful contract to the firm is one where r^2, the maximal percentage risk reduction, is high.

2.1.2   Risks of Changes in the Input Price

A dual to equation (2.5) exists when the uncertainty concerns the prices of inputs to be purchased some time after the sales price of output is quoted to the customer. The case of the exporter described at the beginning of the chapter is a good example. Equation

(2.8) describes the alternative to equation (2.5):

$$\pi_2^*(t+1) = R[s(t+1)] - p^*(t+1)s(t+1)$$
$$+ y(t)[q_{t+1}^*(t+1) - q_{t+1}(t)] \tag{2.8}$$

where $R(s)$ is the total revenue from forward sales; s are the inputs purchased; p^* is the uncertain price of inputs; $y = -x$ purchases (+) or sales (−) of futures; and $q_T(t)$ is the price at time t of a futures contract which matures at time T. A firm quotes a forward price at time t for delivery at subsequent time $t+1$. Total revenue from the forward sale is $R(s)$, where s represents the inputs to be purchased. The uncertain price of the inputs is $p^*(t+1)$. Revenues are determined at time t by forward sales, but input costs $p^*(t+1)s(t+1)$ are unknown when the forward sale is made.

Long hedging consists of purchasing (+) quantity $y(t)$ of futures at price $q_T(t)$. The futures contract refers to a specific commodity which is representative of the general level of input prices. The price $p(t+1)$ of the particular input that the firm will purchase at $t+1$ is related to the price $I(t+1)$ of the commodity specified in the futures contract by equation (2.2). In this way, equation (2.4) relates the input price $p(t+1)$ to the futures price $q_{t+1}(t)$.

Substitute equation (2.4) into equation (2.8) to obtain

$$\pi_2^*(t+1) = -\{y(t)q_{t+1}(t) - R[s(t+1)]$$
$$+ p^*(t+1)[s(t+1) - y(t)] + y(t)\eta^*\} \tag{2.9}$$

Equation (2.9) is the negative of equation (2.5), since s is an input in equation (2.9) but an output in equation (2.5). The results obtained from an analysis of equation (2.5) apply to equation (2.9) with reverse signs.

2.1.3 Questions to Be Analysed

The analysis in Chapters Two and Three is designed to answer the following questions. First, what are the optimization equations of, and the interactions among, the agents which ultimately determine the market-clearing futures price and the total quantity of output produced, when no inventories are carried?

Secondly, what determines the futures price? What is its informational content? What is its role in the production process? What determines the variability of the futures price?

The third question is what is the magnitude of the market-clearing volume of hedging, and its ratio to total planned input or output? The determinants of the uses of futures markets by commercial firms are precisely the determinants of the success or failure of futures contracts: under what conditions will they succeed or fail? Pure speculation, unrelated to commercial interests, cannot sustain a futures market.

Fourthly, what are the costs, in terms of sacrificed profits, to producers who use futures markets optimally? In the present chapter, the subjective price expectations $E_i p(t + 1; t)$ of the subsequent period's price by the ith class of agents are treated as predetermined variables. In the next chapter, the analysis is carried further by stressing the endogenous nature of the subjective price expectations of the different classes of agents. The speed of convergence to a Muth rational expectations (MRE) equilibrium is analysed. It is known that there is a diversity in the forecasting ability of producers, professional and amateur futures speculators. This should occur for theoretical reasons and is observed empirically. This leads to the next question. To what extent does the diversity in the forecasting ability of futures speculators simply result in transfers of wealth among themselves and to what extent does it affect the output produced, the price paid by the consumer and the variance of that price?

Lastly, how does the existence of futures markets affect the level of expected production and the variance of the price paid by consumers, relative to situation that would prevail if there were no futures market?

2.2   Optimization by the Firm

2.2.1   *What Is Optimized*

Suppose that the producers are uncertain about their output prices, as described in equations (2.1)–(2.5). There is no uncertainty about production or input prices. There are several reasons why the objective function of the firm is considered to be a function of the expected profits $E_1 \pi(t + 1; t)$ where the subjective expectation is taken at time t, and its variance var π. First, the firm may be a partnership where the appropriate objective function is the expected utility of the partners. Suppose that the utility function of a partner $U(\pi)$ is of the form $U(\pi) = C - \exp(-\alpha \pi)$, where π are profits and C and α are constants. Moreover, suppose that the stochastic variable affecting profits is normally distributed. Then maximizing expected utility is equivalent to maximizing

$$-\exp\{-\alpha[E\pi - (\alpha/2) \text{ var } \pi]\}.$$

This is equivalent to maximizing equation (2.10).

Secondly, if the compensation of the manager of the firm is a concave function of profits, he will behave as if he were maximizing the expected utility of profits $EU(\pi_1)$ described by

$$EU(\pi_1) = E\pi_1(t+1;t) - (\alpha/2)\,\text{var}\,\pi \qquad (2.10)$$

Expected profits are defined in equation (2.6), the variance in equation (2.7) and coefficient α reflects risk aversion by the manager or owner. Large losses are penalized more severely than large profits are rewarded. Bankruptcy is to be avoided at a cost related to coefficient α.

Thirdly, suppose that the manager attempts to maximize expected profits (equation 2.6). The binding constraint is generally the availability of capital. The cost function $C(s)$ contains the cost of obtaining finance. Banks and other lenders charge an interest rate depending upon the risk class of the borrower. Measure the latter (for simplicity) by the variance of profits.[4] Then the expected profits of the firm would be

$$E\pi_1(t+1;t) = E_1 p(t+1;t)[s(t+1) - x(t)]$$
$$+ q_{t+1}(t)x(t) - C[s(t+1), \text{var}\,\pi] \qquad (2.11)$$

Since this equation contains the variance of profits ($C_2 > 0$), the firm can be assumed to maximize a function $EU(\pi_1)$ of expected profits and the variance of profits (equation 2.10). Although equation (2.10) is a traditional expected utility function, for the reasons cited in equation (2.11), the firm could be viewed as maximizing an expected profit function where the cost of capital depends upon the endogenous risk class of the firm. If the firm chooses more risk, the lenders will charge it a higher interest rate.

The analysis is simplified if the cost function $C(s)$ in equation (2.5) is assumed to be quadratic so that marginal costs are linear

$$C(s) = (c/2)s^2 \qquad (2.12)$$

The object of the firm is to select the level of output s and the short (+) or long (−) quantity x of futures to maximize $EU(\pi_1)$ the 'expected utility' of profits. Time indices will only be used when necessary.

2.2.2 Simultaneous Determination of Planned Production and Position in Futures

Joint optimization of planned output and the position in the futures market are given by equations (2.13) and (2.14) respectively, based upon equation (2.10):

$$\frac{\partial E\pi}{\partial s} = \frac{\alpha}{2}\frac{\partial \text{ var } \pi}{\partial s} \qquad (2.13)$$

or

$$\text{MRT}(s) = \frac{\partial E\pi/\partial s}{\frac{1}{2}\partial \text{ var } \pi/\partial s} = \alpha \qquad (2.13a)$$

and

$$\frac{\partial E\pi}{\partial x} = \frac{\alpha}{2}\frac{\partial \text{ var } \pi}{\partial x} \qquad (2.14)$$

or

$$\text{MRT}(x) = \frac{\partial E\pi/\partial x}{\frac{1}{2}\partial \text{ var } \pi/\partial x} = \alpha \qquad (2.14a)$$

Expected return and risk can be traded off against each other in two ways. Output (s) can be varied, given the position in futures. This is the marginal rate of transformation MRT(s) in equation (2.13a) above. Position (x) in the futures market can also be varied, given planned output. This is the marginal rate of transformation MRT(x) in equation (2.14a) above. When the commercial firm optimizes then both of the following two conditions must be satisfied simultaneously: the two marginal rates of transformation must equal each other and the common marginal rate of transformation must equal coefficient α of risk aversion. When these two conditions are jointly satisfied, the firm has optimized its output and position in futures. The second order conditions are satisfied.

Equation (2.15) describes MRT(s) = α; and equation (2.16) describes MRT(x) = α:

$$(\alpha \text{ var } p + c)s - (\alpha r^2 \text{ var } p)x = E_1 p(t + 1; t) \qquad (2.15)$$

$$(\alpha r^2 \text{ var } p)s - (\alpha r^2 \text{ var } p)x = E_1 p(t + 1; t) - q_{t+1}(t) \qquad (2.16)$$

It is apparent that these equations must be solved simultaneously to determine output s and position x in futures. Consider each equation in turn, before their joint solution is examined.

Equation (2.16) for MRT(x) = α states that position $x(t)$ by the commercial firm in the futures market consists of two parts: a hedging element and a speculative element. The *hedging element* is the futures position that would be taken if the futures price were equal to the subjective anticipated price of the producers. Then the short position in futures $x(t)$ would equal planned output $s(t + 1)$. Hedged production is less risky than unhedged production, because there is only a basis risk on the former but an absolute price risk on the latter. If the futures price equalled the subjective expected price of producers, risk could be reduced at no cost to producers by hedging all of the output. To see this decomposition write equation (2.16) for $MRT(x) = \alpha$ as

$$x(t) = s(t + 1) + \frac{[q_{t+1}(t) - E_1 p(t + 1; t)]}{\alpha r^2 \operatorname{var} p} \qquad (2.16a)$$

The *speculative element* is the second term on the right-hand side of equation (2.16a). It would purchase (sell) futures when the futures price is below (above) the firm's subjective expectation. In so far as positive production is planned, the hedging element and the speculative element must be jointly considered.

A simultaneous solution for output and position in the futures market is described by equations (2.17) and (2.18) respectively

optimal output

$$s(t + 1) = \frac{q_{t+1}(t)}{\alpha(1 - r^2) \operatorname{var} p + c} \qquad (2.17)$$

optimal short (+) or long (−) position in futures

$$x(t) = \frac{q_{t+1}(t)}{\alpha(1 - r^2) \operatorname{var} p + c} - \frac{[E_1 p(t + 1; t) - q_{t+1}(t)]}{\alpha r^2 \operatorname{var} p} \qquad (2.18)$$

Write supply equation (2.17) as equation (2.19). This supply equation states that the rate of output produced s is such that marginal cost cs is equal to the futures price q less an endogenous risk premium $\alpha(1 - r^2)s \operatorname{var} p$. The endogenous risk premium is simply the relative price or basis risk $\operatorname{var} \eta = (1 - r^2) \operatorname{var} p$ times coefficient α of risk aversion. The term on the right-hand side of equation (2.19) is the certainty equivalent price

$$cs(t + 1) = q_{t+1}(t) - \alpha(1 - r^2)s(t + 1) \operatorname{var} p \qquad (2.19)$$

marginal cost = futures price − endogenous risk premium

= certainty equivalent price

Potential benefits from the use of futures markets by commercial firms can be seen from equations (2.19) and (2.15), drawn in Figure 2.2. Curve MC is the marginal cost cs of production. If there were no risk or risk aversion ($\alpha \operatorname{var} p = 0$), the firm would

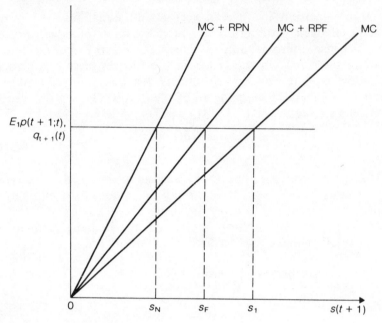

Figure 2.2 The determination of the output of the firm. When it uses the futures market optimally, the supply curve is the sum of the marginal cost MC and an endogenous risk premium RPF which depends on the relative price risk $s(1 - r^2)$ var p. Output s_F occurs where the futures price intersects supply curve MC + RPF. In the certainty case, output s occurs where marginal cost is equal to the expected price Ep. If the firm could not hedge, the supply curve is the sum of the marginal cost MC and an endogenous risk premium RPN which depends upon the total price risk s var p. Output occurs where the expected price intersects supply curve MC + RPN. In this figure expected price is drawn to be equal to the futures price.

produce output s_1 where marginal cost is equal to expected price $Ep(t + 1; t)$.

In so far as there are risk and risk aversion, there are two cases to consider. First, if the commercial firm uses the futures (F) market optimally, an endogenous risk premium

$$RPF = \alpha(1 - r^2)s \text{ var } p$$

is added to the marginal cost curve to determine the supply curve MC + RPF. Given the futures price $q_{t+1}(t)$, the quantity supplied s_F is read off the above supply curve. The sum of the marginal cost and endogenous risk premium is equal to the futures price. This is a graphic interpretation of equation (2.19).

Secondly, if there were no (N) facilities to hedge, the firm must bear the total risk var p of price changes. An endogenous risk premium RPN $= \alpha s$ var p is added to the marginal cost curve to obtain supply curve MC + RPN. This is based upon equation (2.15) when $(x = 0)$ no position is taken in futures. Given the subjectively expected price when there are no futures $E_1 p(t + 1; t)$, the firm produces output s_N read off the relevant supply curve.

If the futures price were equal to the same subjectively expected price that would prevail if there were no facilities to hedge (as drawn in Figure 2.2), then the use of the futures market increases optimal output from s_N to s_F. The reason for the greater output is that the risk premium is reduced, or the certainty equivalent price is raised. When the commercial firm uses the futures market optimally, it diversifies away the absolute price risk and is only left with a relative price risk $(1 - r^2)$ var p. If the firm cannot hedge, it faces an absolute price risk var p. Since the risk to the firm is reduced by its use of futures, its output increases.

Equation (2.19) or Figure 2.2 is not sufficient to answer the question whether the use of futures markets raises output relative to what would occur if there were no facilities to hedge, for several reasons. First, we must explicitly determine what is the relation between the futures price and the subjectively expected price by the producers. Figure 2.2 was drawn on the assumption that they are equal. We know from equation (2.16a) that, in such a case, all of the output would be hedged with sales of futures. That situation generally does not occur. Secondly, we must determine the relation between the subjectively expected price when there is, and when there is not, a futures market. Since production is endogenous, and there is a broad participation in the futures market, there is no presumption that these two subjective expectations are the same. Lastly, the variance of the cash price var p is likely to be different when there is a futures market compared to the situation where there are no facilities to hedge. Chapter Three is concerned with comparing the endogenous output of the industry in these two cases, when the subjective expectations are endogenous variables.

2.2.3 Input Price Uncertainty and Long Hedging

Equation (2.9) concerns the case where the firm faces input price uncertainty, but its revenues from forward sales $R(s)$ are known. The case of the exporter cited above is one example of such a firm. Another example is a miller who has sold flour forward to bakers on a long-term contract and faces uncertainty concerning the level of prices that he will have to pay for the specific type of wheat that must be purchased to produce the specific type of flour sold forward.

The choice problem for the decision-maker is to select a level of input s (i.e. a volume of forward sales) and position y in the futures market to maximize expected utility. Since this problem based upon profit equation (2.9) is the alternative to the problem in profit equation (2.5), the method of analysis is the same.

As a result of optimizing with respect to the level of input s and purchases (+) y of futures, equations (2.20)–(2.22) are derived. They correspond, respectively, to equations (2.19), (2.17) and (2.18). It is assumed that the marginal revenue product derived from forward sales $R'(s) = a - bs$, a declining linear function of the volume of forward sales:

$$R'(s) = a - bs(t + 1) = q_{t+1}(t) + \alpha(1 - r^2)s(t + 1) \operatorname{var} p \quad (2.20)$$
$$\text{MRP} \qquad\quad = \quad \text{MC} \quad + \qquad\quad \text{RPF}$$

Solve explicitly for the level of input and derive

$$s(t + 1) = \frac{a - q_{t+1}(t)}{b + \alpha(1 - r^2) \operatorname{var} p} \quad (2.21)$$

Equation (2.20) can be graphed in a manner analogous to equation (2.19). The level of input s is such that the marginal revenue product (MRP) from forward sales is equal to the futures price, which is the marginal cost MC, plus an endogenous risk premium RPF. The latter depends upon the relative price risk $(1 - r^2) \operatorname{var} p$:

optimal long (+) or short (−) position in futures

$$y(t) = \frac{a - q_{t+1}(t)}{b + \alpha(1 - r^2) \operatorname{var} p} + \frac{E_2 p(t + 1; t) - q_{t+1}(t)}{\alpha r^2 \operatorname{var} p} \quad (2.22)$$

where the first term is the hedging term, equal to the planned input purchases (equation (2.21) and the second term is the speculation based upon the difference between the expected price of the input and the futures price.

2.3　The Market-Clearing Futures Price and Hedging

The market-clearing futures price $q_{t+1}(t)$ and volume of hedging are now determined in the case where no inventories are carried, conditional upon the subjective expectations of the agents. In Chapter Three, the subjective expectations are given economic structure, and the price of output $p(t + 1)$ and quantity of output produced are determined within that structure.

2.3.1 Supply of and Demand for Futures

The net supply of futures and output by the commercial firms (denoted by subscript 1) which face uncertainty in output prices, described by equations (2.18) and (2.17) respectively, are graphed in Figure 2.3a. Output supply curve 0S (equation 2.17) is exactly the curve labelled MC + RPF in Figure 2.2 and it relates the quantity supplied s to the futures price q.

Curve C_1C_1 is the net supply of futures by these commercial firms. As equation (2.18) indicates, all of the planned output would be hedged if the futures price were equal to the subjectively expected price. This is point A_1 (Figure 2.3a). At this point, quantity h_1 represents *short* hedging pressure from the commercial firms facing uncertain output prices.

The supply $X(t)$ of futures by the summation of these firms is less (greater) than the summation of planned output S in so far as the futures price is less (greater) than the subjectively expected price. For example, at futures price q' which is below the subjectively expected price $E_1p(t + 1; t)$, the supply of futures X' is less than planned output S'.

Figure 2.3b describes the commercial firms (denoted by subscript 2) which face uncertain input prices. Curve S_2 is based upon equation (2.21). It relates the quantity of inputs S to be purchased as a declining function of the futures price q. Vertical intercept a is the marginal revenue product of the input, evaluated at the origin.

Curve C_2C_2 is the summation of the net demand for futures by these commercial firms; and is based upon equation (2.22). If the futures price were equal to the subjectively expected price, then all of the planned inputs would be hedged with purchases of futures. This is point A_2 (Figure 2.3b) where quantity h_2 represents the *long* hedging pressure from the commercial firms facing uncertain input prices. The net demand $Y(t)$ for futures is greater (less) than planned input in so far as the futures price is below (above) the subjectively expected price. For example, if the futures price were q'', input demand would be S'' and the quantity of futures demanded would be $Y'' < S''$.

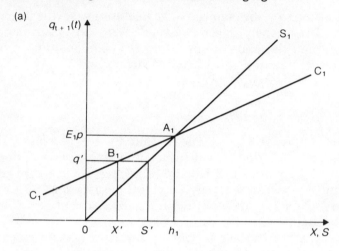

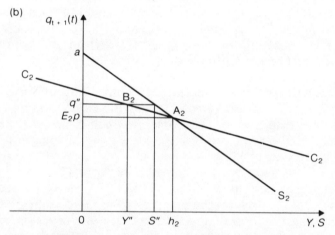

Figure 2.3   (a) The C_1 curve is the supply of futures by firms with output price uncertainty and S_1 is the supply of output. At a futures price $q_{t+1}(t)$ equal to the subjectivity expected price $E_1p(t + 1; t)$ all of the output will be hedged. (b) The C_2 curve is the demand for futures by firms with input price uncertainty and S_2 is their demand for the input. At a futures price $q_{t+1}(t)$ equal to the subjectivity expected price $E_2p(t + 1; t)$ all of the input will be hedged.

Figure 2.4 contains the supply and demand curves C_1C_1 and C_2C_2 by the commercial firms which face uncertain output prices and uncertain input prices respectively. If the only participants in the futures market were the commercial firms, the market clearing

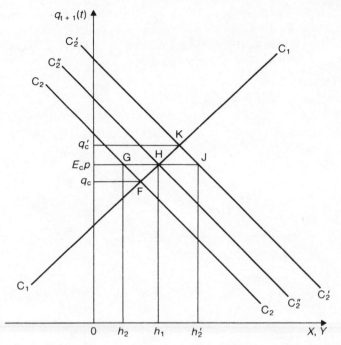

Figure 2.4 The supply of futures by commercial firms facing output uncertainty is C_1, and the demand for futures by commercial firms facing input price uncertainty is C_2 (C_2', C_2''). The commonly subjectively expected price $E_1 p(t+1;t)$ is $E_c p$, by commercial firms. Net hedging pressure $h = h_1 - h_2$ is the excess supply $X - Y$ when the futures price $q_{t+1}(t)$ is equal to the expected price $E_c p$.

futures price q_c would be at point F. Price q_c will be below (above) the commonly expected price $E_1 p = E_2 p = E_c p$ if there is net hedging pressure by the commercial firms which face output (input) price uncertainty.

With curves $C_1 C_1$ and $C_2 C_2$ (Figure 2.4), there is net hedging pressure GH by the firms facing output price uncertainty: $h_1 > h_2$. Then, futures price q_c is below the commonly shared expected price. However, if the marginal revenue product of the input whose price were uncertain should rise, the demand for futures by the commercial firms which face uncertain input prices would rise to $C_2' C_2'$. Then the net hedging pressure by the shorts h_1 is less than that of the longs h_2'. Futures price q_c' is at point K which exceeds the subjectively expected price $E_c p$, because the net hedging pressure $h_1 - h_2' = JH$ is negative.

The excess supply of futures by commercial firms corresponding to these two situations are curves CC and CC' respectively, in Figure 2.5. Vertical intercepts q_c and q'_c in Figure 2.5 correspond to points F and K respectively in Figure 2.4.

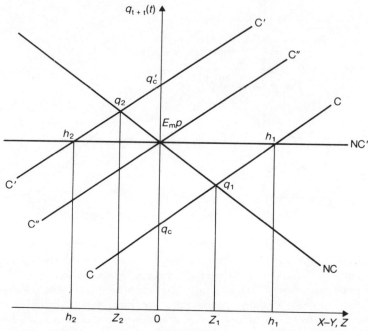

Figure 2.5 The excess supply of futures $X - Y$ by commercial firms is CC (C'C' or C"C")' The excess demand Z for futures by noncommercial firms is NC (NC').

Mathematically, curve CC (or C'C') in Figure 2.5 is the sum $X = \Sigma x$ of equation (2.18) over ξ_1 firms facing output price uncertainty less the sum $Y = \Sigma y$ of the ξ_2 firms facing input price uncertainty. The excess supply of futures by commercial firms $X-Y$ is equation (2.33), which is abbreviated as equation (2.34). In the latter equation, the w_c coefficients reflect risk and risk aversion and the v coefficients mainly reflect cost and demand conditions. It is assumed for analytic simplicity that the commercial firms have the same subjective distributions of the price, the same coefficient of risk aversion and the same relative price risk $(1 - r^2)$ var p, regardless of whether they face input or output price uncertainty.

$$X\text{-}Y = \xi_1 \left[\frac{q}{\alpha(1-r^2)\,\mathrm{var}\,p + c} + \frac{(q-E_cp)}{\alpha r^2\,\mathrm{var}\,p} \right]$$

$$- \xi_2 \left[\frac{(a-q)}{\alpha(1-r^2)\,\mathrm{var}\,p + b} + \frac{(E_cp-q)}{\alpha r^2\,\mathrm{var}\,p} \right] \qquad (2.33)$$

excess supply of futures by commercial firms

$$X\text{-}Y = w_c(q - E_cp) + v_1q - v_2(a - q) \qquad (2.34)$$

CC curve

$$X\text{-}Y = (w_c + v_1)q - w_cE_cp - v_2a$$

speculative coefficient

$$w_c = \frac{\xi_1 + \xi_2}{\alpha r^2\,\mathrm{var}\,p} \qquad (2.34a)$$

output coefficient

$$v_1 = \frac{\xi_1}{\alpha(1-r^2)\,\mathrm{var}\,p + c} \qquad (2.34b)$$

input coefficient

$$v_2 = \frac{\xi_2}{\alpha(1-r^2)\,\mathrm{var}\,p + b} \qquad (2.34c)$$

$$v = v_1 + v_2 \qquad (2.34d)$$

The excess supply of futures by commercial firms $(X\text{-}Y)$ consists of speculative elements with coefficients w_c and hedging elements with coefficients v_1 and v_2. Figures 2.3a and 2.3b illustrate these two elements for the two types of commercial firms.

Futures speculators are defined as noncommercial (NC) firms who do not use futures contracts as adjuncts to their commercial activities, but engage in futures transactions to profit from the difference between the futures price $q_{t+1}(t)$ at time t and its value at maturity $q_{t+1}(t+1)$.

If there were no futures market, potential long speculators would have to acquire, finance and store the commodity, and potential short speculators would have to find parties who are willing to lend them the commodity to sell it short. Since, by definition, these speculators are not commercials, the resulting high transactions costs would effectively prevent them from speculating.

With futures markets, the transactions costs of taking long or short positions are low. Entry into the speculative activity is facilitated. All types of individuals are drawn into the futures market from professionals on the floor of the exchanges to rank amateurs. An analysis of the real effects of the diversity in futures speculators is the subject of Chapter Three. At present the distinction among the types is not stressed.

Each class of speculator has profit function $\pi_i(t + 1)$, the product of his position $z_i(t)$ and the difference $p^*(t + 1) - q_{t+1}(t)$ between the subsequent futures price and the current futures price. Variable $z_i(t)$ is the long $(+)$ or short $(-)$ position of the ith futures speculator:

$$\pi_i^*(t + 1) = [q_{t+1}^*(t + 1) - q_{t+1}(t)]z_i(t) \qquad (2.35)$$

Assume that each futures speculator attempts to maximize the expected utility of profits $EU_i(\pi_i)$ as described by equation (2.36). Parameter β_i is the coefficient of risk aversion. From equation (2.4), the expected value of $q_{t+1}(t + 1)$ is equal to the expected value of the cash price $p(t + 1)$:

$$Ep(t + 1; t) = Eq_{t+1}(t + 1; t) \qquad (2.35a)$$

The variance of the futures price $q_{t+1}(t + 1)$ is equal to the variance of the price of the standard commodity var $I(t + 1)$, from equation (2.3). But the variance of the price of the standard commodity var I is not the same as the variance of the price of any particular cash commodity var p, from equation (2.2). Let the variance var I be a constant times the variance var p. Define β_i in equation (2.36) as the coefficient of risk aversion times this constant:

$$\text{Max}_{z_i} EU_i[\pi_i(t + 1)] = E\pi_i(t + 1; t) - \frac{\beta_i}{2} \text{ var } \pi_i; \qquad i = 1, 2$$

$$(2.36)$$

It was explained in Chapter One why the CAPM or its variants is not useful in explaining the pricing of risky assets (Levy, 1978). In so far as individuals are constrained to hold undiversified portfolios consisting of three or four securities, optimizing theory implies that the CAPM does not apply. These constraints are derived from transactions costs, indivisibilities and ability to borrow. Since a given security is not included in all portfolios, the own variance will have a greater impact upon asset demand than will its beta from the CAPM. Indeed, Douglas (1969) found that the own variance is more important than the beta in explaining returns on risky assets.

Maximization of equation (2.36) implies

$$z_i(t) = [E_i p(t + 1; t) - q_{t+1}(t)]/\beta_i \text{ var } p \qquad (2.37)$$

where z_i is the long (+) or short (−) position of futures speculators.

Let there be ξ_i futures speculators of type i of (noncommercial firms). Then the total demand $Z(t) = \Sigma \, \xi_i z_i(t)$ for futures by speculators is

$$Z(t) = \Sigma \frac{\xi_i}{\beta_i \text{ var } p} [E_i p(t + 1; t) - q_{t+1}(t)] \qquad (2.38)$$

Although the distinctions between the speculators are very important in the next chapter, they are not used in this chapter. Therefore, define the weighted average subjectively expected price by futures speculators as $E_s p(t + 1)$ as defined in

$$E_s p(t + 1) = \Sigma \frac{\xi_i}{\beta_i \text{ var } p} E_i p(t + 1; t)/ \Sigma \frac{\xi_i}{\beta_i \text{ var } p} \qquad (2.39)$$

where ξ_i is the number of futures speculators of type i. Similarly, define the denominator of equation (2.39) as the weighted average sensitivity of futures speculation to the expected profit from futures speculation. It is the change in $Z(t)$ resulting from a change in the expected price less the futures price and it is abbreviated as w_s:

$$w_s \equiv \frac{\xi}{\beta \text{ var } p} = \Sigma \frac{\xi_i}{\beta_i \text{ var } p} \qquad (2.40)$$

Using definitions (2.39) and (2.40) in demand equation (2.38), the demand of futures speculators is equation (2.41). It is graphed as curve NC (noncommercial) in Figure 2.5:

NC curve

$$Z(t) = \frac{\xi_s}{\beta \text{ var } p} [E_s p(t + 1) - q_{t+1}(t)]$$

$$= w_s[E_s p(t + 1) - q_{t+1}(t)] \qquad (2.41)$$

The position in futures is proportional, with weight w_s, to the difference between the weighted average subjectively expected price $E_s p$ and the current futures price q.

Market clearing requires that the futures price $q_{t+1}(t)$ adjust until the excess supply by commercial $X(t) - Y(t)$ is equal to the excess demand by noncommercials:

$$X(t) - Y(t) = Z(t) \tag{2.42}$$

Figure 2.5 describes equations (2.34) and (2.41), and thereby equation (2.42).

Total output produced $S(t + 1)$, the summation of supply equation (2.17) over the set of ξ_1 identical producers, is

$$S(t + 1) = \xi_1 s(t + 1) = v_1 q_{t+1}(t) \tag{2.43}$$

where v_1 is defined in equation (2.34b) above.

2.3.2   The Market-Clearing Futures Price

The market-clearing futures price (Figure 2.5) is q_1 or q_2, depending upon the net hedging pressure h. Curve CC is drawn so there is net hedging pressure h_1 by the commercial firms facing output price uncertainty. At the expected price Ep, there is an excess supply h_1 of futures by the commercials. This corresponds to GH in Figure 2.4. The futures price (Figure 2.5) declines to $q_1 < E_m p$ so that the noncommercials demand $Z_1 = X_1 - Y_1$ of futures. Difference $E_m p - q_1$ is a risk premium.

Curve $C'C'$ describes the net hedging pressure by the commercials who face input price uncertainty. At the expected price Ep, there is an excess demand, h_2 for futures (Figure 2.5), equal to distance HJ in Figure 2.4. The market-clearing futures price rises to $q_2 > Ep$ so that the noncommercials demand $Z_2 = X_2 - Y_2$ (Figure 2.5). Difference $q_2 - Ep$ is a risk premium.

The bias $Ep - q \gtrless 0$ of the futures relative to the expected price depends upon two factors. First is the net hedging pressure $h = h_1 - h_2$ of the commercials. Second is the adequacy of speculation, which depends upon the slope of the NC curve. The slope of the NC curve is $1/w_s = \beta \operatorname{var} p/\xi_s$ in absolute value. This depends upon risk aversion β divided by the numbers ξ_s of futures speculators. As the numbers increase relative to the average risk aversion, the NC curve rotates to the horizontal line NC'. In Figure 2.5 (but not in the algebraic analysis below) it is assumed that all groups have MRE where they know the first two moments of the distribution of the price. Then when β/ξ_s declines, there would be a perfectly elastic supply of or demand for futures at the expected price. The bias would be zero, as w_s becomes infinite. Then the noncommercial demand or supply completely absorbs the net hedging pressure. The net hedging pressure h (equation 2.44) is the excess supply of futures by commercials, when the future price is equal to their expected price $E_c p$.

$$h = [(X-Y)|E_c p = q] = v_1 q - v_2 (a - q) \qquad (2.44)$$

Algebraically, the market-clearing futures price solves equation (2.42), using equations (2.34), (2.44) and (2.41):

$$q_{t+1}(t) = E_m p(t + 1; t) - h/w \qquad (2.45)$$

where

$$E_m p(t + 1; t) = \frac{w_s E_s p(t + 1; t) + w_c E_c p(t + 1; t)}{w_s + w_c} \qquad (2.46)$$

$$w \equiv w_s + w_c \qquad (2.47)$$

Equation (2.45) states that the market-clearing futures price is equal to the average subjectively expected price by the market $E_m p(t + 1; t)$ minus or plus a risk premium h/w. The average subjectively expected price by the market (m) is a weighted average of the subjectively expected prices $E_c p$ and $E_s p$ by the commercials and noncommercials, where the weights w_c and w_s reflect their numbers divided by their relative risk aversions. No assumption is made that the two groups have the same subjective expectations. The net hedging pressure h can be positive or negative at any time.

2.4 Implications of the Analysis

Futures markets are characterized by a few widely traded homogeneous contracts which are used by many different commercial firms for diverse purposes. The commodity specified in the futures contract is a good, but not a perfect, substitute for the products produced by the commercial firms. *Forward* markets, by contrast are characterized by as many contracts as there are specific products produced by commercial firms, because they are simply cash contracts for deferred delivery.

Futures markets are highly liquid. As a rule, no single firm can affect the market price. There are no search costs to find buyers or sellers of these homogeneous contracts, Each party preserves its anonymity, because trading is done by open outcry on organized exchanges and clearing of these homogeneous, widely traded, contracts is done through a clearing house. *Forward* markets are

Table 2.1 Average net hedging and average total hedging 1947–72, 1972–78, for eight commodities

Commodity, period	(1) Average net hedging $(Y - X)$	(2) Average total hedging $(Y + X)$	(3) Ratio (1) to (2) (percentage)
Wheat (millions of bushels)			
1947/48–1971/72	−31.9	87.7	−36
1972/73–1977/78	−15.1	344.5	−4
Corn			
1948/49–1971/72	−31.4	104.6	−30
1972/73–1977/78	7.5	565.7	1
Soybeans			
1951/52–1971/72	−16.2	85.9	−19
1972/73–1977/78	−8.3	298.3	−3
Maine potatoes (1000 contracts)			
1952/53–1974/75	−2.2	3.4	−65
Live cattle			
1972–77	−13.5	19.3	−70
Pork bellies			
1971–77	−0.5	1.3	−38
GNMA certificates			
July 1978–June 1979	−1.5	37.7	−4
90-day Treasury bills			
July 1978–June 1979	−0.9	13.2	−7

Notes: Long hedging is Y and short hedging is X.
Source: Anne Peck, 1979–80, Tables 1 and 2.

thin markets, where price is negotiated between buyers and sellers. There are substantial search costs and parties have the power to affect the price because it is a negotiated price. Forward contracts are not fungible: they are unique.

2.4.1   The Use of Futures Markets by Commercials

The usefulness of the futures markets to commercial firms is reflected by the volume of short X and long Y positions of the commercial firms in the analysis above. At any time, a given contract is used by commercial firms with short positions because they have made forward purchases of a commodity and by commercial firms with long positions because they have made forward sales of a commodity. Table 2.1 describes, for eight commodities: the average net reported hedging $(Y - X)$ long less short positions of firms classified as 'hedgers' in column 1; average total hedging $(X + Y)$ by reported hedgers in column 2; and the ratio $(Y - X)/(X + Y)$ in column 3. The reported figures attempt to separate a firm's 'hedging' position from its 'speculative' position. For example, in Figure 2.3a the hedging position is X' and $S' - X'$ is the speculative position.

Several points should be noted. First, the futures markets are not necessarily used by commercial firms just for short hedging. The ratio of net hedging $(Y - X)$ to total hedging $(X + Y)$ is low except for potatoes and live cattle. Secondly, net hedging in wheat, corn and soybeans has moved closer to zero since 1972. Thirdly, prior to 1972, there were clear seasonal patterns in these three commodities and short hedging dominated most of the year. After 1972, not only was net hedging close to balance, but short hedging did not dominate over the year. Seasonality in commercial hedging has virtually disappeared. The reason for these changes is that there were rapid increases in the volume of exports, and commercial firms are using the futures markets to hedge their uncertain input costs. More commercial users of these futures markets are long hedgers than existed prior to 1972 (Peck, 1979–80).

The dichotomy between one group as hedgers and another as speculators in futures markets is misleading. Commercial firms are simultaneously both hedgers and speculators, as noted in Figure 2.3a and 2.3b at points B_1 and B_2. Since 1972, the net hedging pressure $h_1 - h_2$ by commercial firms, as noted in Figure 2.4, is relatively small, as is indicated by Table 2.1, column 3. This means that noncommercial firms, i.e. pure futures speculators, have become relatively less important since 1972 in determining futures prices.

Figure 2.4 can be used to describe the change that has occurred in wheat, corn and soybeans since 1972. Prior to that date, the supply of futures by the commercials facing uncertain output prices was C_1 and the demand for futures by the commercials facing uncertain input prices was C_2. Net short hedging pressure $h = h_1 - h_2$ by commercials generates a demand for long positions by noncommercials. With the rapid growth in exports, more firms have sold commodities forward in the export market. Their demand for futures shifts to C_2'', because the marginal revenue product of their inputs has increased. Net hedging pressure no longer is significant. At subjectively expected price $E_c p$, there is only a small excess supply of futures by commercial firms. This means that the excess supply of futures X–Y by commercial firms has shifted in Figure 2.5 from C to C″. The market-clearing volume of net hedging X–Y is close to zero, even though there is considerable long and short hedging $X = Y = h$, in Figure 2.4. The role played by noncommercials is considerably reduced, since the market is cleared by commercial firms who are *using the same futures contract for different purposes.*

2.4.2   The Success and Failure of Contracts

The reason why the futures markets are simultaneously useful to both the commercials who are long and those who are short is implied by the analysis of this chapter. The volume of hedging $(X + Y)$ depends upon: (a) the quality of the hedging instrument which enables the commercial firms to diversify away the absolute price risk of the product of the broadly defined industry; and (b) the magnitude of the absolute price risk compared to the risk of changes in the relative price of the firm's output or input. These factors are described by Figure 2.4 and equation (2.4).

The quantitative measure of the usefulness of the futures contract to the commercial firm is the maximal percentage risk reduction (MRR), distance AB divided by distance OB in Figure 2.1. This is equal to the r^2 between the price relevant to the firm p and the futures price q (see Ederington, 1979). The greater is the relative price risk var η/var $p = 1 - r^2$, the smaller will be the MRR $= r^2 = 1 -$ var η/var p.

Two examples of declines in the use of a futures market illustrate the point that the usefulness of a futures market to commercial firms is positively related to the maximal percentage risk reduction. The first example concerns wheat.

In April and early May of 1953, flour mills with long hedges in Kansas City wheat futures (against unfilled flour orders) took substantial losses because soft wheat, unexpectedly drawn to Kansas City for delivery on futures contracts, depressed the price of the May futures relative to the prices of hard wheats needed by the mills to fill their flour orders. The millers promptly petitioned for a revision of the Kansas City futures contract to make it strictly a hard-wheat contract. It had always previously been so in effect, speculators and hedgers thought of it as such, and many members of the exchange had been surprised to learn that delivery of soft wheat was permitted by the contract.

The members of the exchange, however, seem to have been almost unanimous in the belief that the amount of futures business done on the exchange depended on attracting speculators, and the majority held also the common belief that speculators want a broad contract, allowing delivery of more than one class and grade of the commodity. So the exchange refused the plea of the millers for a revision of the contract terms. But in July and August millers took even larger losses, per bushel, on their long hedges, for the same reason as earlier, and this time the losses occurred on a great volume of such hedges, held against recently placed flour orders for milling from the new crop. These new losses caused most millers who had been hedging in Kansas City wheat futures to transfer their hedging business either to Minneapolis, where the hedge was in a hard-wheat contract, or to Chicago, where the hedge ... could be placed and removed more economically. And speculators apparently deserted the market in about the same large proportions as did hedgers. (Working, 1960, p. 189)

Theoretically, var η/var p increased and r^2 decreased because the wheat futures price became a poorer signal of the price of the wheat inputs that the millers would be purchasing at a later date. Maximal risk reduction declined. Using Figure 2.6, Working's example can be explained theoretically.

Let there be a long hedging pressure so that the excess supply of futures by commercials is initially $C'C'$. If the futures price were equal to the expected price Ep, net hedging pressure is h_2 at point A'. At this point, all of the input is hedged. The quantity of input purchased is given by equation (2.20) repeated here. The marginal revenue product (MRP) of the hard wheat input is equal to the futures price $q_{t+1}(t)$ plus a risk premium (RPF).

$$a - bS(t+1) = q_{t+1}(t) + \alpha(1 - r^2)S(t+1) \cdot \text{var } p \qquad (2.20)$$
$$\text{MRP} \quad = \quad \text{MC} \quad + \qquad \text{RPF}$$

The solution for the quantity hedged at A' is the value of $S(t+1)$ when $q = Ep$. This is h_2 in Figure 2.6.

The futures contract is then changed so that either soft or hard wheat can be delivered at the discretion of the seller. Since var η increases, r^2 declines. There is a less predictable relation between the price q of a wheat future and the price p of the type of hard wheat that the miller will purchase. The excess supply of wheat futures shifts to CC in Figure 2.6. At the futures price equal to the expected price, there is a smaller volume of long hedging (Y). The rise in the risk premium RPF, as a result of the decline in r^2, shifts the net hedging pressure point to A from A'; and the new demand for futures curve by the commercials goes through A instead of A'.

The futures price will decline from q_2 to q_3 and the market-clearing volume of net long hedging will decline from Z_2 to Z_3. Both commercial firms who were long hedgers and noncommercial futures speculators will leave the market.

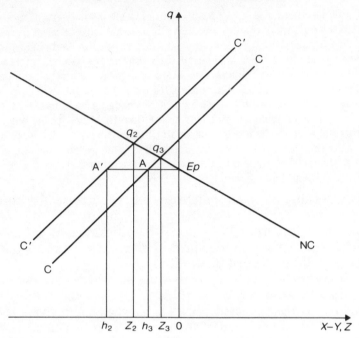

Figure 2.6   The excess supply of futures by commercial firms is CC (C'C'), where there is a balance of long hedging. Net hedging pressure is point A (A'). The excess demand for futures by noncommercial firms is NC. The futures price q_2 exceeds the subjectively expected price. The shift from C'C' to CC occurs because the quality of the hedging instrument r^2 declines.

A second example concerns the GNMA contract (Silber, 1985), and is amenable to the same analysis. Mortgage bankers and savings and loan institutions buy long-term private mortgages forward, assemble them and later sell long-term GNMA pass through certificates to institutional investors. The bankers face a risk concerning their output prices of the GNMA certificates. Alternatively, the mortgage bankers sell long-term GNMA certificates forward to institutional investors and, at a later date, buy and assemble long-term private mortgages. The bankers face a risk concerning their input price of the private mortgages. Bankers hedge their forward positions by taking opposite positions in the futures market.

Initially, the hedging instrument for long-term mortgages was the GNMA future, which was the first interest rate future. There was a close relation between the price of a GNMA future and the average level of long-term mortgage prices. During the first three years, the GNMA future averaged 2000 contracts per day, and traded an average of more than 10 000 contracts per day during the last quarter of 1980. By the last quarter of 1984, the GNMA contract traded an average of 1000 contracts per day.

What happened was similar to Working's wheat example. The cash instrument which motivates the banks to hedge is a long-term mortgage. Several GNMAs can be delivered on the futures contract and the price of the futures is always based upon the instrument which is cheapest to deliver. In recent years, the cheapest to deliver is closer to a two-year rather than to a 30-year mortgage. Variance var η has increased because the relation between the long-term mortgage yield and the two-year mortgage yield is not very close. The value of r^2 or maximal risk reduction declined. In terms of equation (2.20), the risk premium RPF has increased. The analysis is exactly the same for long hedgers as was portrayed in Figure 2.6. An analogous situation would apply to short hedgers. Since r^2 declined, the risk premium rises and net hedging pressure h_1 or h_2 declines. That is why the volume of trading in GNMA futures declined.

2.4.3 Why the Main Commercial Users of Futures are Intermediaries

Dealers in government and corporate securities, institutional investors such as pension funds, the FNMA and mortgage bankers are the main users of interest rate and stock index futures. Very few farmers use agricultural futures.[5] Producers generally sell their output forward to dealers. Processors often purchase their inputs forward from dealers. The dealers are the main commercial users of agricultural futures. Since the main commercial users of futures are intermediaries between the original producer and the ultimate consumer, demand rather than output uncertainty was used in the theoretical analysis in this chapter. The importance of the dealer in commercial hedging can be explained by the theory developed above.

The commodity specified in the futures contract attempts to reflect the 'typical' commodity purchased or sold by the commercial firms. The price $I(t)$ of the deliverable grade should reflect the average price of the various grades in the various locations. Then commercial firms can diversify away the absolute price risk var I by using futures, and are left with the relative price risk var η, reflecting the variance of the price differential.

Let the price of the deliverable grade be equal to the average price. Overall, let there be N grades of a commodity whose average price is I. Let a given commercial firm deal with a subset $n < N$ of grades; and the average price of the subset of n commodities is p_n.

The futures price $q_T(T)$ at maturity is assumed to be the average price $I(T)$. The variance of the futures price is then equal to the variance of the price of the deliverable grade. Call this variance var I which is the variance var q at maturity.

The relative price risk to the commercial firm which deals in $n < N$ grades is the variance of the differential η in equation (2.2):

$$p_n = I + \eta$$

$$\text{var } (p_n - I) = \text{var } \eta \tag{2.2}$$

The variance of the differential is simply the variance of the mean of a sample of size n around the population mean, where there are N elements in the population. It follows that

$$\frac{\text{var } (p_n - I)}{\text{var } I} = \frac{1}{n}\frac{N-n}{N-1} = \frac{\text{var } \eta}{\text{var } I} \tag{2.48}$$

From equations (2.2) and (2.3)

$$\frac{\text{var } \eta}{\text{var } I} = \frac{1-r^2}{r^2} \tag{2.48a}$$

It follows from equations (2.48) and (2.48a) that r^2 is described by equation (2.49). It ranges from 0.5 when $n = 1$ to 1.0 when $n = N$,

$$r^2 = \frac{1}{1 + (1/n)[(N-n)/(N-1)]} \tag{2.49}$$

Firms which handle only a few grades have a low r^2 (close to 0.5) compared to firms which handle many grades. Producers tend to specialize, but dealers purchase output forward from many producers. Dealers handle a substantially larger sample size of grades than do producers, and the former have much higher r^2 or maximal percentage risk reduction by using futures.

As the good is processed and value is added on the way to the consumer, it becomes a more specialized product. The r^2 between the price of a specialized good with a high fraction of value added and the price of the deliverable grade on the futures contract is very low. Most of the risk to the wholesaler is relative price risk. Consequently, the maximal percentage risk reduction from diversification by using futures is low. Commercial firms which have added considerable value to the original product will not be users of futures.

2.4.4 Why There are Few Successful Futures Contracts

It is often asked why there are so few successful futures contracts but an enormous number of specific commodities. Whereas the contingent claims analysis focuses upon a claim to each commodity in the infinitely many states of nature, only 37 traditional commodity futures, five currency futures and ten interest rate plus stock index futures contracts are listed in the *Wall Street Journal.* There is good reason why there can only be a small number of successful futures contracts.

The futures market can only be liquid if the contract is widely traded. Then purchases or sales will have no effect upon market price. To be widely traded, a futures contract must be useful to many firms producing different products. The prices of the output of the k firms using a given futures contract must be linked in the following way:

$$p_i(t) = I(t) + \eta_i(t); \qquad i = 1, 2, \ldots, k \qquad (2.50)$$

Price $p_i(t)$ must be the sum of the industry average price $I(t)$ plus a relative price η_i component and the futures price $q_i(t)$ should be equal to the industry average $I(t)$. The r_i^2 between $p_i(t)$ and $I(t)$ should be high but not unity.

When these conditions are satisfied, the k firms can use the futures contract to diversify away the risk of fluctuations in the industry average price level $I(t)$ but manage its relative price risk. For example, an exporter sells a particular grade of wheat forward but does not know the absolute price that he will have to pay to purchase the wheat when it becomes available at a later date. He does know that the differential η_i, between the price p_i of the grade of wheat that he will purchase and the average price of wheat I, has a small variance, i.e. r^2 is high. He can then use the current futures price plus the mean differential to form an estimate of the price of his inputs. On that basis, he can quote a price to the customer. If the world grain market should tighten when he goes to market at a later date, the futures price will be rising along with the average price of the industry. His only risk concerns the relative price differential and his business acumen consists of managing the relative price risks. Many different firms are related by equation (2.50). Some will be facing input price uncertainty (the exporter who sold forward) and others will be facing output price uncertainty (dealers who purchased forward). Then the futures market will be broad and liquid: firms will be price takers.

If there were as many contracts as there are commodities produced by firms, they would be forward contracts which are
identical to cash contracts. There would be no advantage to using
a forward contract over a cash contract. There would be the same
search costs involved in finding another party to the transaction as
there is in the cash contract. The firm would have the same
power to affect price with either contract. The firm does not have
the ability to separate absolute from relative price risk, nor does it
gain liquidity. It is shown in Chapter Seven why futures are not
used in equity underwriting, although they are used in the underwriting of fixed income securities, for precisely these reasons.
Futures contracts are not Arrow-Debreu securities.

2.4.5   The Bias of the Futures Price and the Risk Premium

The market-clearing futures price in equation (2.45) repeated
here is the sum of the subjectively expected price by market
$E_m p(t + 1; t)$ plus or minus a risk premium:

$$q_{t+1}(t) = E_m p(t + 1; t) - h/w \qquad (2.45)$$

This relation can be seen by comparing q with $E_m p$ in Figure 2.5
above. The risk premium is h/w, where $h = h_1 - h_2$ defined in
equation (2.44) is net hedging pressure and $w = w_c + w_s$ defined
in equations (2.34a) and (2.40) reflect the risk sharing by commercials and noncommercials.

The risk premium is an objective concept here which should
not be volatile. The numerator reflects the excess supply of
futures that would exist if the futures price equalled the subjectively expected price. This is distance h_1 (with curve CC) or h_2
(with curve C'C') in Figure 2.5. The denominator reflects the
slopes of the CC and NC curves in the same figure. If there is a
balance of short hedging, then the numerator will be positive;
and if there is a balance of long hedging, the numerator will be
negative. The magnitude of the bias h/w also depends upon the
denominator: the willingness to take risk or the slopes of the CC
and NC curves.

It is incorrect to equate the deviation between the realized price
$p(t + 1)$ and the futures price $q_{t+1}(t)$ with the 'risk premium'. To
see this, write equation (2.45) as

$$q_{t+1}(t) - p(t + 1) = [E_m p(t + 1; t) - p(t + 1)] - h/w \qquad (2.51)$$

The first term on the right-hand side is the market forecast
error between the subjectively expected price by the market

$E_m p(t + 1; t)$ and the subsequently realized price $p(t + 1)$. The risk premium is h/w. The numerator is measurable theoretically. Qualitatively, it has the same sign as the volume of net hedging and h is not volatile but changes smoothly. It was shown in Table 2.1 above how h has changed over time for traditional commodities as a result of changes in commercial practices, and how it differs among them. Since 1972, the risk premium for agricultural commodities should be relatively small because net hedging h had declined considerably in absolute value.

2.5 Appendix A
Production, Demand and Relative Price Uncertainty

In general, a firm may face demand, output and relative price uncertainty. If the firm does not face input price uncertainty, its profit equation is

$$\pi^*(t + 1) = p^*(t + 1)F[s(t + 1), u^*] - C[s(t + 1)]$$
$$+ x(t)[q_{t+1}(t) - q^*_{t+1}(t + 1)] \qquad (A1)$$

Output $F(s, u^*)$ depends upon planned output $s(t + 1)$ and a stochastic term u^*. Costs depend upon planned output. Equation (A2) is equation (2.2), which relates the price to the firm $p^*(t + 1)$ to the price of the futures at maturity $q_{t+1}(t + 1)$, where the latter is the price of the standard grade which is assumed to be the industry average price. Differential η^* is stochastic:

$$p(t + 1) = q_{t+1}(t + 1) + \eta^*; \qquad E(\eta) = 0, \qquad E(q, \eta) = 0 \qquad (A2)$$

Generally, two types of production disturbances are considered: Additive (A3) and multiplicative (A4),

$$F(s, u) = s(t + 1) + u^*; \qquad Eu = 0 \qquad (A3)$$

$$F(s, u) = s(t + 1)(1 + u^*); \qquad Eu = 0 \qquad (A4)$$

Corresponding profit equations are (A5) and (A6), respectively

$$\pi^* = p^*(s - x) + p^*u^* + x\eta^* + [xq - C(s)] \qquad (A5)$$

$$\pi^* = p^*(s - x) + s(p^*u^*) + x\eta^* + [xq - C(s)] \qquad (A6)$$

The expected profit and variance of profit are (A7) and (A8) respectively, for the additive case, and are (A9) and (A10) respectively, for the multiplicative case. Note that

$$\text{cov}\,(p, \eta) = \text{cov}\,(q + \eta, \eta) = \text{var}\,\eta$$

additive

$$E\pi = (s - x)Ep + E(pu) + [xq - C(s)] \tag{A7}$$

$$\text{var}\,\pi = (s - x)^2\,\text{var}\,p + x^2\,\text{var}\,\eta + \text{var}\,(pu)$$

$$+ 2(s - x)\,\text{cov}\,(p, pu) + 2x(s - x)\,\text{var}\,\eta$$

$$+ 2x\,\text{cov}\,(\eta, pu) \tag{A8}$$

multiplicative

$$E\pi = (s - x)Ep + sE(pu) + [qx - C(s)] \tag{A9}$$

$$\text{var}\,\pi = (s - x)^2\,\text{var}\,p + x^2\,\text{var}\,\eta + s^2\,\text{var}\,(pu)$$

$$+ 2s(s - x)\,\text{cov}\,(p, pu) + 2x(s - x)\,\text{var}\,\eta$$

$$+ 2sx\,\text{cov}\,(\eta, pu) \tag{A10}$$

There are several sources of ambiguity in the covariances. Cov (p, pu) is the covariance between the absolute level of price to the firm p and the change in the value of output pu resulting from the supply disturbance. Presumably, this is negative. Cov (η, pu) is the covariation between the change in the value of output resulting from the supply disturbance pu and the relative price differential η between the producer's price and the price of the standard grade which is the futures price at maturity. If the supply disturbance u is specific to the given producer, then cov (pu, u) is negative. If u is general to the industry, then the cov (pu, η) may be zero.

Optimization equations (2.13) and (2.14) in the text will differ depending upon whether the supply disturbance is additive or multiplicative and also upon the nature of cov (pu, η) and cov (pu, p). The reader can work out the implications of these cases.

Notes

1   See Sandor (1973) for a case study of the development of a futures contract.
2   From equation (2.2), cov $(p, I)/\text{var}\,I = 1$. The definition of r^2 is $r^2 = \text{cov}\,(p, I)^2/\text{var}\,p\,\text{var}\,I$. Since var $\eta = \text{var}\,p - \text{var}\,I$, equation (2.3) follows. Paul, Heifner and Helmuth describe the context of equation (2.3) as follows:

If the futures contract calls for a commodity with a substantially different grade than the commodity the hedger sells on the cash market, or if the delivery locations are different, the prices on the two markets may not be closely tied together and the hedger is subjected to price relationship risk, a 'basis risk'. In general, the basis risk increases with distance from delivery point and with departures in quality from the delivery grade. (Paul, Heifner and Helmuth, 1976, p. 5)

3 The derivation is as follows. From equations (2.4) and (2.5):

$$\operatorname{var} \pi = (s-x)^2 \operatorname{var} p + x^2 \operatorname{var} \eta + 2x(s-x) \operatorname{cov}(p, \eta) \qquad (a)$$

From (2) and (3):

$$\operatorname{cov}(p, \eta) = \operatorname{cov}(q + \eta, \eta) = \operatorname{var} \eta = (1 - r^2) \operatorname{var} p \qquad (b)$$

since $E(q, \eta) = 0$. Hence:

$$\operatorname{var} \pi = (s-x)^2 \operatorname{var} p + [x^2 + 2x(s-x)](1 - r^2) \operatorname{var} p \qquad (c)$$

$$x^2 + 2x(s-x) = s^2 - (s-x)^2 \qquad (d)$$

Using (d) in (c):

$$\operatorname{var} \pi = (s-x)^2 \operatorname{var} p + [s^2 - (s-x)^2](1 - r^2) \operatorname{var} p \qquad (e)$$

This implies equation (2.7a) in the text.

4 The correct measure should be the probability of bankruptcy, but the analysis here will be kept as simple as possible.

5 See the evidence cited in Chapter One. The main reasons farmers do not use futures are that futures markets are too risky and their size was too small to warrant using futures contracts. However, cooperatives and dealers are much more frequent users of futures. See Anderson and Danthine (1983).

3

Effects of Futures Markets Upon Expected Output and Price Variance

Futures markets lower the cost of entry into a speculative activity and thereby attract a diversity of types of speculators. If there were no futures markets, finance costs, transactions costs and risk of default would effectively exclude all but commercial firms from speculation. Consider a potential long speculator: a noncommercial which expects to profit from a rise in prices. He would have to locate a producer, contract to purchase the latter's output, arrange for financing, arrange for storage, locate potential customers and arrange for subsequent delivery. A potential short speculator, a noncommercial, which expects to profit from a decline in prices would have to locate an owner of the commodity who was willing to lend it to him for short sale, locate potential customers, arrange for delivery and then make arrangements for the subsequent repurchase of the commodity to return to the lender.

The financing of the speculative operations for noncommercials would be extremely difficult to obtain due to the high probability of default on the loans. In addition, the high search and transactions costs for noncommercials would offset the potential profits from price changes. For these reasons, it is not feasible for noncommercials to speculate in the physical commodity itself.

With futures markets, entry into speculative activity is cheap and easy. Financing costs simply consist of margin requirements. They are less than 10 per cent of the contract price, and are simply designed to protect the clearing-house from defaults. These margins are in the nature of performance bonds. The 'mark to market' process in effect means that each futures contract is re-settled daily. The financing problem, which excludes noncommercials from speculating in the physical commodity, is not a serious constraint when futures markets exist.

With futures markets, transactions costs are simply the commissions and spreads involved in purchasing or selling the futures contracts, and there are no transactions costs involved in the handling of the physical product. There is perfect liquidity so that purchases and sales can be executed instantly at a known market price. When there are futures markets, there are no search costs for the best price.

In so far as the financing and transactions costs of speculation are reduced to negligible amounts as a result of futures markets, large and small speculators are attracted to the market. The distinction between large and small speculators is closely related to the distinction between professional and amateur futures speculators. The most interesting set of questions for an economist concerns the real effects of the existence of a heterogeneity of futures speculators, whose knowledge of the ultimate determinants of the price $p(t+1)$ when the output is sold to consumers may be more or less than that of the commercial firms. To what extent does the diversity in the forecasting ability of futures speculators simply result in transfers of wealth among themselves, and to what extent does it affect the allocation of resources and flow of final consumption?

Several fundamental questions were left unanswered in the previous chapter. What determines the subjectively expected prices $E_i p(t+1; t)$ of the agents when production decisions are made at time t? What determines the variance of price var p, which is the source of risk to producers? Only when these questions are answered can one compare price $p(t+1)$ and output $S(t+1)$ when there are and when there are no futures markets. These questions are answered in the present chapter, which is a continuation of the preceding chapter.

Section 3.1 explains the theoretical determinants of the diversity of price expectations among agents. The forecast error ϵ_i of the ith agent between the subjectively expected price $E_i p(T; t)$ and the subsequently realized price $p(T)$ can be written as the sum of two elements:

$$\epsilon_i(T) = E_i p(T; t) - p(T)$$
$$= [E_i p(T; t) - Ep(T)] + [Ep(T) - p(T)]$$
$$= \qquad y_i(t) \qquad + \qquad \eta$$

The first element $y_i(t)$ is a *Bayesian error* which reflects the inability of the ith agent to locate the mean of the distribution of prices $Ep(T)$. The second element η is the deviation between the mean price and the particular realization $p(T)$. This is an *unavoidable error* which reflects the fact that demand is not always at its mean value.

The Muth rational expectations (MRE) hypothesis assumes that the Bayesian error in the market is zero: the subjective estimate of the mean price is indeed correct. I prove that the variance of the Bayesian error is positively related to the variance of the objective distribution of prices and inversely related to the total number of samples that an agent has taken from the information set. Agents who have taken larger samples have smaller variances of the Bayesian error than do agents who operate on a small scale. As time continues and repeated samples are taken by each agent, the variance of the Bayesian error declines. However, the variance of the Bayesian error for those that operate on a large scale converges at a faster rate to MRE than for those who operate on a smaller scale. I call this process asymptotically rational expectations (ARE) whose limit is MRE.

Section 3.2 considers an extreme case where two types of noncommercials (i.e. futures speculators) are attracted by the futures markets. Rational speculators and commercials have no Bayesian errors, i.e. they have MRE. Irrational speculators use irrelevant systems to forecast prices. Their Bayesian errors have such a high variance that their excess demand for futures can be considered a random variable with a zero mean and a strictly positive variance. The questions answered are what are the effects upon expected output and price variance of changing: (a) the ratio of irrational to rational agents and (b) the total number of all types of noncommercials? With the development of futures markets, there may be an increase in both (a) and (b). The two factors operate in different ways upon expected output and price variance. The analysis in Section 3.2 is relatively easy to follow and intuitive explanations can be given for all the results.

Section 3.3 considers the general case of ARE developed in Section 3.1. Commercials and both types of noncommercials have Bayesian errors. However, amateur speculators have larger variances of Bayesian errors than do either the commercials or the professional speculators.

My conclusions are as follows. First, futures markets change the structure of the model by changing the supply of output equation. This changes both the expected price and price variance. Secondly, there is an optimum ratio of professional to amateur speculators to minimize the variance of the market forecast error. The optimal ratio of the position of professional to amateurs is equal to the ratio of the variance of the forecast error of amateurs to that of professionals. Thirdly, even though the observed *composition* of speculation is not optimal, given the parameter estimates, as long as the variance of the market forecast error of amateurs is less than six times that of producers, the entry of amateur speculators will not increase the variance of the market forecast error. Lastly, a large total volume of speculation can be expected to lower the expected price, primarily through risk sharing.

3.1 Formation and Diversity of Price Expectations

3.1.1 *The Underlying Source of Uncertainty*

In the model considered in Chapters Two and Three, the demand for the final product is the underlying source of the uncertainty. There is no production uncertainty and, in this model, no inventories are carried. Production decisions are made at time t and total output $S(T)$ is available for consumption at subsequent date T.

The inverse consumer demand is equation (3.1), where total output $S(T) = \Sigma s(T)$ the sum of the individual producers' output, and $u(T)$ is the unknown variable parameter of demand which is the underlying source of the uncertainty:

$$p^*(T) = u^*(T) - bS(T) \tag{3.1}$$

Term $u(T)$ has a mean of W and a variance of var u. The latter reflects variations in domestic and foreign incomes, foreign supply conditions and relative prices at home and abroad. The consumers are the international market and the producers are a minor subset of the consumers. Consequently, in Marshallian fashion, the income effect of price received by the producers upon market demand is ignored.[1]

3.1.2 *Theoretical Determinants of the Diversity of Bayesian Errors*

Price expectations are crucial in determining the futures price which, in turn, determines production (see equations 2.17 and 2.45). The subject of this section is what determines the subjectively expected prices $E_i p(T; t)$ of the members of the ith group.

Agents know that the parameter of demand u is stochastic but they do not know its mean value W. There is no reason why the distribution of u should be constant, because it contains all of the variables other than price which determines the quantity demanded: foreign supply and demand, domestic income and relative prices. These variables change over time in ways that are difficult to predict.

Assume that parameter u is normally distributed with an unknown mean W and (for simplicity) a known precision (i.e. reciprocal of the variance) $r = 1/\text{var } u$:

$$u \sim N(W, r) \qquad r = 1/\text{var } u \tag{3.1a}$$

Since agents do not know the value of the unknown mean W, they form subjective estimates W^* of the unknown mean, in terms of the following probability distribution:

$$W^*(t) \sim N[\mu(t), \tau'(t)] \tag{3.1b}$$

At time t, the mean of the subjective distribution is $\mu(t)$ and its precision is $\tau'(t)$. Precision $\tau'(t)$ reflects the confidence that the agent has that $\mu(t)$ is indeed the unknown mean W.

Associated with each realized value of parameter $u(T)$ is a realized price $p(T)$. The mean value of the price $Ep(T)$ is associated with the mean value of the demand parameter W. The precision (reciprocal of the variance) is $s = 1/\text{var } p$. Since W is unknown to the agents so is $Ep(T)$. In so far as the agent has a subjective expectation $\mu(t)$ of unknown parameter W, he has a subjective expectation $E_i p(T; t)$ of the unknown mean price $Ep(T)$:

$$p(T) \sim N[Ep(T), s]; \qquad s = 1/\sigma^2 \tag{3.2a}$$

$$Ep^*(T) \sim N[E_i p(T; t), \tau(t)] \tag{3.2b}$$

Precision $\tau(t)$ reflects the confidence that $E_i p(T; t)$ is indeed the unknown mean $Ep(T)$.

Alternatively, define the forecast error $\epsilon_i(T)$ of the ith group as equation (3.3a), the difference between the subjectively expected price and its actual realization at subsequent time T:

$$\epsilon_i(T) = E_i p(T; t) - p(T) \tag{3.3a}$$

The popular MRE hypothesis assumes that this error has a zero expectation and has no structure, for example, it is not serially correlated.[2] Such an assumption is not grounded in economic theory and cannot explain why amateur speculators consistently lose to professional speculators, as is shown in Chapter Five. A more satisfactory explanation of price expectations can be derived by using a Bayesian analysis.[3]

The forecast error can be written as a sum of elements,

$$\epsilon_i(T) = [E_i p(T; t) - E p(T)] + [E p(T) - p(T)];$$

$$i = 0, 1, 2 \qquad (3.3b)$$

abbreviated as

$$\epsilon_i(T) = y_i(t) \qquad\qquad + \eta \qquad (3.3c)$$

The first term in brackets $y_i(t)$ is the difference between the subjective and objective expectations. It will be called the Bayesian error. The second term in brackets η is the difference between the actual price and the objective mean of the distribution. From this point of view, the forecast error of the ith agent consists of two parts: (a) the Bayesian error $y_i(t)$ in locating the objective mean of the distribution and (b) the deviation η of any price from the objective mean of its distribution. For simplicity, assume that the variance σ^2 of the objective normal distribution is specified. In Bayesian analysis, it is convenient to work with the precision $s = 1/\sigma^2$, the reciprocal of the variance of a normal distribution. The questions are first, what is the relation between the prior or subjective distribution of the unknown mean and the objective mean? Secondly, how quickly does the subjective or prior distribution of the mean converge to the objective mean? Thirdly, why will the subjective distributions of some agents converge at different rates to the objective mean? These specific questions concern the characteristics of the first term $y_i(t)$ in equations (3.3b) or (3.3c) of the forecast error.

At each time t, each agent takes a sample from the available information set of elements which determines the price which will prevail at later date T. It is impossible for any agent at time t to know all the information which determines $p(T)$. Therefore, a sample of size n is taken at each time by an agent. He receives n useful bits of information at time t concerning the determinants of the the price at time T. Agents differ in terms of their size, access to information, understanding of the price determination process, speed at which the information is obtained and processsed correctly. Subsume all of these factors under n, the sample size or number of relevant bits of information obtained by an agent. The mean, obtained from a sample of size n, concerning $p(T)$ is denoted by $\bar{x}(t)$.

For example, suppose that dealers want to estimate the demand for their product. At time t, a dealer calls n of his customers to determine their values of u and obtains a sample $u_1, u_2, \ldots, u_n$.

Each value implies a price $p_1, p_2, \ldots, p_n$. The mean value of these n prices is $\bar{x}(t)$. The dealer also has a subjective prior estimate of the mean price $E_i p(T; t)$ as well as a subjective prior precision $\tau(t)$.

The subsequent analysis rests upon a fundamental theorem of Bayesian inference concerning the prior and posterior distributions (see De Groot, 1970, pp. 166–68). The prior distribution at time $t - 1$ of the subjectively expected mean is revised on the basis of the sample of information obtained at $t - 1$. A new expectation of the mean is formed: it is the posterior estimate of the mean. Equation (3.4a) described how the prior or subjective expectation is revised, and equation (3.4b) describes how the prior or subjective precision is revised, from $t - 1$ to t:

$$E_i p(T; t) = \frac{E_i p(T; t-1)\tau(t-1)}{\tau(t-1) + ns} + \frac{\bar{x}(t-1)ns}{\tau(t-1) + ns} \qquad (3.4a)$$

$$\tau(t) = \tau(t-1) + ns = \tau(0) + nst \qquad (3.4b)$$

Equation (3.4a) states that the subjective expectation at time t is a weighted average of the subjective expectation at time $t - 1$ and the sample mean obtained at $t - 1$. The weights are the prior precision $\tau(t-1)$ of the subjective distribution and $ns = (\sigma^2/n)^{-1}$, the precision of the distribution of sample means around the population mean.

On the basis of the known theorems of Bayesian inference (equations 3.4a and 3.4b), I obtain a formula concerning the speed of convergence of the subjective expectation $E_i p(T; t)$ to the objective expectation $Ep(T)$. Theorem I expresses the result[4] and is graphed in Figure 3.1.

Theorem I
For very low initial precisions, $\tau(0)$ is small, the variance of $y_i(t)$ the difference between the subjective expectation and objective expectation is equal to σ^2/nt, where n is the sample size, t is the number of samples taken and $\sigma^2 = 1/s$ is the variance of the objective distribution.

The main steps of the proof are as follows (a full derivation is in Appendix B). Variable $y(t)$, called the Bayesian error, was defined as the difference between the prior or subjective expectation and the objective expectation (the first term in brackets in equation 3.3b). Subtract $Ep(t)$ from both sides of equation (3.4a) and use

$$y(t) \equiv E_i p(T; t) - Ep(T) \qquad (3.5)$$

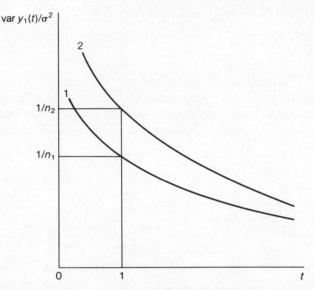

Figure 3.1 The variance of the Bayesian error which is the difference between the subjective and objective expectations is inversely proportional to the product of the sample size n and number of samples t taken by an agent, and directly proportional to the variance σ^2 of the underlying distribution. Agent 1 has the larger sample size. The variance of $y(t)$ is equation (3.10) when the initial precision is close to zero.

to obtain

$$y(t+1) = y(t)\frac{\tau(t)}{\tau(t)+ns} + [\bar{x}(t) - Ep(T)]\frac{ns}{\tau(t)+ns} \qquad (3.6)$$

It is a difference equation in the difference between the subjective and objective expectations. By induction on t, the closed form solution of equation (3.6) is

$$y(t) = \frac{\tau(0)}{\tau(0)+nst}y(0) + \frac{ns}{\tau(0)+nst}\sum_{h=0}^{t-1}[\bar{x}(h) - Ep(T)] \qquad (3.7$$

The expectation of Bayesian error $y(t)$ is

$$Ey(t) = \frac{\tau(0)}{\tau(0)+nst}y(0) \qquad (3.8)$$

because the sample mean $\bar{x}$ is an unbiased estimate of the population mean. The variance of Bayesian error $y(t)$ is obtained directly from equation (3.7) and (3.8); and is

$$\text{var } y(t) = \frac{nst}{[\tau(0) + nst]^2} \tag{3.9}$$

Equation (3.9) is what is being sought: the dispersion of the prior or subjective expected price around the objective mean of the distribution. A slight simplification of this is the content of Theorem I. Let the initial precision $\tau(0)$ be close to zero, then equation (3.9) is

$$\text{var } y(t) = 1/nst = \sigma^2/nt \tag{3.10}$$

$$\tau(0) \to 0$$

which proves Theorem I.

The implications of Theorem I are crucial for understanding the formation of expectations and the role of futures markets. They will be used repeatedly in explaining the empirical phenomena.

1   The variance of Bayesian error $y(t)$, the difference between the subjective and objective expectations, is positively related to the variance of the objective distribution of prices σ^2 and inversely related to nt, the number of bits of relevant information (the product of the sample size n and number t of samples taken). There are advantages to size in obtaining information. Agents who take larger samples have smaller variances of the Bayesian error: the difference between the subjective and objective expectations. The two curves in Figure 3.1 reflect two different sample sizes $n_1 > n_2$, in equation (3.10), taken by different agents. At time $t = 1$ agent 1 has a more precise estimate of the mean of the objective distribution than does agent 2. As time continues and repeated samples are taken by each agent, the variance of Bayesian error $y(t)$ declines. Each agent's subjective expectation converges to the objective expectation, i.e. var $y(t)$ and $Ey(t)$ converge to zero as nt grows. However, the subjective expectations of the agents that operate on a large scale converge at a faster rate than to those who operate on a smaller scale.

2   The Bayesian errors $y(t)$ of each agent between the subjective and objective distributions are serially correlated. This is explicit from equation (3.6).

3   The expected Bayesian error $Ey(t)$ described by equation (3.8) above is a multiple $\tau(0)/\tau(0) + nst$ of the initial error $y(0)$. The multiplier goes to zero as more and more samples are taken.

The curves in Figure 3.1 can also be used to represent either the expected error (equation 3.8) or its variance (equations 3.9 or 3.10).

4 At time T when the futures contract matures, the process starts again. There may be a new set of demand conditions and a new unknown objective distribution of prices.

Theorem I and the above implications prove that, in the absence of futures markets, the MRE hypothesis (which states that the subjective distributions are equal to the objective distributions) is theoretically deficient. The MRE cannot be correct unless nt, the number and size of samples, become very large and the objective distribution is stationary. Equations (3.8)–(3.10) should be viewed as general equations, of which MRE is a special case.

The forecast error ϵ_i (equation 3.3b or 3.3c) is the sum of *Bayesian error* $y_i(t)$ and *unavoidable error* η. These two errors should be relatively independent, for the first reflects the differential ability of an agent to locate the true mean and the second results from the distribution of demand around its mean value. Bayesian errors differ among agents but the unavoidable error is common to all.

On the basis of the above analysis, the forecast error ϵ_i of the professional and amateur speculators and the producers can be taken to have the following structure:

$$\text{var } \epsilon_i = \sigma^2/n_i t + \sigma^2 = \sigma^2(1 + 1/n_i t); \qquad i = 0, 1, 2 \qquad (3.11)$$

The first term is equation (3.10) and the second term is the variance σ^2 of the objective distribution of prices. It is often convenient to write the variance of the Bayesian error of the ith agent as equation (3.12a), a multiple k_i (defined in equation 3.12b) of the underlying variance in demand var u:

$$\text{var } y_i = k_i \text{ var } u \qquad (3.12a)$$

$$k_i = 1/n_i t \qquad k_a > k_s \qquad (3.12b)$$

At time t, when the production decisions are made, the variance of the forecast error is negatively related to the n_i bits of relevant information available to each agent. Professional futures speculators ($i = s$) and commercial firms ($i = c$) operate on a larger scale than do amateurs ($i = a$). The first two groups trade continuously in large volume from geographically dispersed customers and receive many bits of information during any interval of time. This is formally equivalent to drawing many samples where each is of a large size. The amateurs, described briefly in Chapter Five, operate on a small scale, are not in the market continuously, do not devote their full time to this activity and experiment with different forecasting schemes. Hence the k_a of amateurs is greater than the k_s of the professionals.

Define the quality Q of the forecasting ability of the professionals $(i = s)$ to that of the amateurs $(i = a)$ as the ratio of the Bayesian error variance of the amateurs to that of the professionals. Using equation (3.12a) or (3.12b), variable Q can be expressed as:

$$Q = \text{var } y_a/\text{var } y_s = k_a/k_s > 1 \qquad (3.13)$$

If the distribution of u, the parameter of demand, is stationary then Theorem I states that each k_i converges to zero as the process is repeated year after year (i.e. $n_i t$ becomes unbounded). It is realistic to focus upon the case where the distribution of demand disturbance u changes over time. At each decision period, when the quantity to be produced must be determined, the agents must learn the new distribution by combining their priors with samples of current information.

The number of speculators in group i to the number of producers is ξ_i, and the absolute risk aversion of group i is β_i. Define the composition or relative weight of professional to amateur futures speculators as ω defined in

$$\omega = \frac{(\xi_s/\beta_s)}{(\xi_a/\beta_a)} \qquad (3.14)$$

The relative number ξ_i is adjusted for the relative risk aversion β_i. An object of inquiry is to determine the real effects of variations in the composition ω of speculation. It will emerge in Section 3.3 that ratio $(Q - \omega)$, the difference between the relative quality Q of the forecasts of the professional speculators and their relative weights ω, is quite important concerning the real effects of futures markets.

3.2   Rational and Irrational Noncommercials

3.2.1   The Model

For simplicity assume that there is no long hedging pressure and that the hedging instrument is almost perfect (r^2 is close to unity).

Commercials and professional speculators are assumed to have MRE, but there are amateur speculators whose positions are based upon irrelevant systems.

Equation (3.15) is the excess supply of futures X by commercials. It is equation (2.34) when $v_2 = 0$ and MRE are assumed. Equation (3.1) is the inverse demand for the product. Equation (3.17) is the excess demand for futures Z by noncommercials. The excess demand of the professional speculators with weight w_s is the first term. It is equation (2.41) when MRE is assumed. This group has no Bayesian error. The excess demand by amateurs is the second term with weight w_a, where ϵ_a is a random variable with a zero mean and a positive variance. Amateur speculators use irrelevant systems to speculate and have very high variances of Bayesian errors. Equation (3.18) is the futures market-clearing equation.

The five equations in Table 3.1 can be solved for variables: X, Z, S, p and q. The market-clearing futures price q is

$$q = \frac{w}{v_1 + w} Ep + \frac{w_a}{v_1 + w} \epsilon_a \tag{3.19}$$

Variable $w \equiv w_c + w_s$. Let λ in equation (3.20) denote the relative weight of the amateur to the rational participants,

$$\lambda = w_a/w \tag{3.20}$$

If there are no amateur (i.e. irrational) speculators $w_a = 0$ and $\lambda = 0$. Or if the weight of the professional speculators $w_s = \xi_s/\beta_s$ var p were infinitely great, then $\lambda = 0$. This special case has been extensively used in the literature but it is an arbitrary assumption.

Table 3.1 Model with rational and irrational participants

$X = v_1 q + w_c(q - Ep)$	$w_c = \xi_c/\alpha$ var p	(3.15)
$S = v_1 q$	$v_1 = 1/c$	(3.16)
$p = u^* - bS$	$E(u) = W$	(3.1)
$Z = w_s(Ep - q) + w_a \epsilon_a^*$	$w_s = \xi_s/\beta$ var p; $E(\epsilon_a) = 0$	(3.17)
$X = Z$		(3.18)

Symbols: X, excess supply of futures by commercials; q, futures prices; Ep, rationally expected price: S, output; p, price; Z, excess demand for futures by noncommercials; $w \equiv w_c + w_s$, weight of the rational participants.

Parameter λ is exogenous to the model and merely describes the mix of agents drawn into speculation. There is no natural selection. These amateurs resemble the flow of people into the casinos at Las Vegas: when one is forced out by losses another optimist replaces him.

Variable M in equation (3.21) represents the total weight of rational participants in the market: the commercials plus the professional speculators.

$$M = \left(\frac{\xi_c}{\alpha} + \frac{\xi_s}{\beta_s}\right) = (w_c + w_s) \operatorname{var} p = w \operatorname{var} p \qquad (3.21)$$

where ξ represents the number and (α, β_s) represents absolute risk aversion.

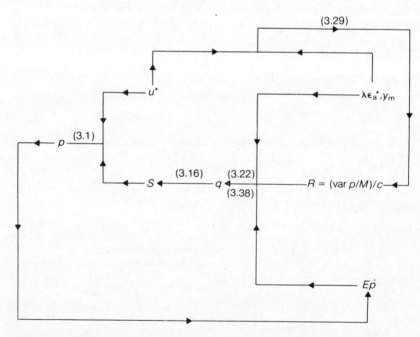

Figure 3.2 Flow chart describing the basic structure of the model. Demand equation (3.1) determines the price p as a function of output S and stochastic variable u. Equation (3.16) determines output as a function of the futures price q. The market-clearing futures price is determined by equation (3.22) or (3.38) as a function of the expected price, risk premium R and the demand of amateur speculators or the market Bayesian error.

Using definitions (3.20) and (3.21) in equation (3.19), the market-clearing futures price can be written as

$$q_T(t) = \frac{Ep(T;t)}{1 + \dfrac{\text{var } p/M}{c}} + \frac{\lambda \epsilon_a}{1 + \dfrac{\text{var } p/M}{c}} \tag{3.22}$$

Figure 3.2 describes the basic structure of the model. Demand equation (3.1) determines the price p as a function of output S and stochastic variable u. Equation (3.16) determines output as a function of the futures price q. The market-clearing futures price is determined in equation (3.22) as a function of the expected price, Ep, the demand of the amateur speculators $\lambda \epsilon_a$ and risk premium (var $p/M)/c$.

Figure 3.3 describes why the futures price and output are negatively related to var p/M, risk divided by the weight of the

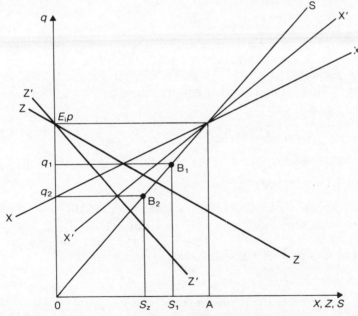

Figure 3.3   The futures price q and output S are negatively related to the var p/M risk divided by the number of participants who are rational. The excess supply curve of futures by commercials is XX. The supply curve of output is 0S. The excess demand for futures by the professional speculators is ZZ. The average position of irrational speculators in this figure is zero. A rise in var p/M shifts the market-clearing futures price from q_1 to q_2.

rational participants. The excess supply curve of futures by commercials is the XX curve, equation (3.15). The supply of output is the OS curve, equation (3.16). The excess demand for futures by the professional (rational) speculators is curve Z, the expected value of equation (3.17). Initially, the market-clearing futures is q_1 and the net hedging pressure is OA.

Let the noisiness of the system increase as reflected by a rise in the variance of the price. Then the XX curve rotates to X'X'. At any futures price below the expected price, there will be a greater supply of futures by commercials. Similarly, the Z curve rotates from Z to Z' at any futures price below the expected price, professional speculators demand a smaller quantity of futures. As a result of the increased risk, the price of futures declines to q_2. This is the meaning of equation (3.22). Moreover, the decline in the futures price reduces the quantity supplied along the OS curve from S_1 to S_2.

3.2.2   Expected Output

The expected supply curve ES in Figure 3.4 relates the expected quantity produced *ES* to the rationally expected price *Ep*. It is derived by substituting futures price equation (3.22) into the supply curve equation (3.16) and taking expectations over stochastic variable ϵ_a. The resulting supply curve is

$$ES = \frac{1}{c + \operatorname{var} p/M} Ep \tag{3.23}$$

or, in inverse form,

$$Ep = (c + \operatorname{var} p/M)ES \tag{3.24}$$

The expected supply curve ES in Figure 3.4 is the sum of the marginal cost curve cS plus a risk premium $(\operatorname{var} p/M)S$.

The expected demand curve ED in Figure 3.4 relates the expected quantity demanded to the expected price.

$$Ep = W - bES \tag{3.25}$$

is derived by taking the expectation of equation (3.1) over stochastic variable, *u*. Where expected supply equation (3.24) and expected demand equation (3.25) are equal, the solution for the expected output *ES* is

$$ES = \frac{W}{b + c + \operatorname{var} p/M} \tag{3.26}$$

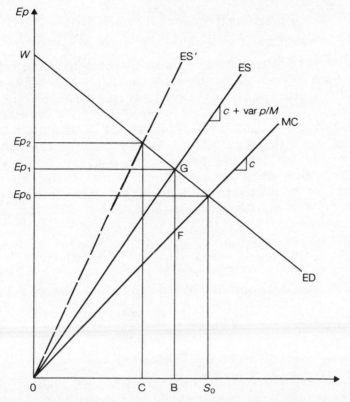

Figure 3.4   The solution for expected output and expected price. The expected demand is ED and the sum of the marginal cost curves is MC. The expected supply curve ES depends upon the risk premium var p/M. The real effects of futures markets manifest themselves through the determination of var p/M, which is endogenous.

The real effects of futures markets are subsumed under this equation.

The real effects of futures markets are subsumed under this equation.

The reason why expected output is negatively related to risk premium var p/M can be understood by jointly considering Figures 3.3 and 3.4. Given any expected price, a rise in the risk var p/M lowers the futures price from q_1 to q_2 in Figure 3.3. A decline in the futures price leads to a decline in the quantity produced from S_1 to S_2 in Figure 3.3 along the OS curve. This means that the expected supply curve in Figure 3.4 rotates from ES to ES' when the risk premium var p/M rises. *This is the crucial point of the analysis.*

3.2.3   *Price Variance and the Risk Premium*

3.2.3.1   *Price Variance*

The effects of futures markets upon expected price and expected output are determined by the expected supply curve ES in Figure 3.4. The latter is equal to the marginal cost curve MC plus a risk premium FG/BF which is the ratio of the price variance var p divided by the weight M (numbers divided by absolute risk aversion) of the rational participants. It is apparent from Figure 3.4 that the higher the risk premium var p/M, the lower will be expected output and the higher will be the expected price. A solution for the price variance is the subject of this section.

Based upon equations (3.1), (3.16) and (3.22), the realized price $p(T)$ is

$$p(T) = u(T) - \frac{b[Ep(T; t) + \lambda \epsilon_a(t)]}{c + \text{var } p/M} \tag{3.2}$$

The difference between the realized and the expected price is

$$p(T) - Ep(T; t) = [u(T) - W] - \frac{b\lambda \epsilon_a(t)}{c + \text{var } p/M} \tag{3.28}$$

Expectations are taken over $u(T)$ and $\epsilon_I(t)$.

The variance of the price is

$$\text{var } p = \text{var } u + \left(\frac{b\lambda}{c + \text{var } p/M} \right)^2 \text{var } \epsilon_a \tag{3.29}$$

The expectations are taken over $u(T)$ and $\epsilon_a(t)$. These two stochastic variables are independent because the amateurs are making Bayesian errors.

There are two sources of price variation. The first is var $u = E[u(T) - W]^2$ which is the inherent variation in demand resulting from unpredictable foreign excess supply, level of domestic income and relative prices. This source of variation would exist even if all participants had MRE (i.e. $\lambda = 0$). The second is var ϵ_a which results from the 'noise' introduced by the amateur speculators. They do not know the mean demand, so that their excess demands for futures $w_a \epsilon_a(t)$ should be viewed as random variables. These speculators use irrelevant systems, i.e. misinformation, to determine their purchases or sales of futures. Thus var ϵ_a is an additional source of noise.

If there were such a large weight w of rational participants that the average rational participant is effectively risk neutral, then

$\lambda = 0$. Graphically, this condition can be described as follows in terms of Figure 3.3. Either the excess demand for futures by the rational noncommercials, the Z curve, is perfectly elastic at $q_T(t) = Ep(T; t)$, or the excess supply of futures by the rational commercials, the X curve, is perfectly elastic at $q_T(t) = Ep(T; t)$. Then, the random excess demands by the amateurs would be absorbed by the rational participants with no effect upon the futures price. Variable $\lambda^2 \, \text{var} \, \epsilon_a$ would be zero and the price variance would be var u.

However, if the rational participants are risk averse and their relative weight were bounded, parameter λ is not zero. Random variations in the excess demand for futures by the irrationals produce parallel shifts in the Z curve. The futures price would have to change until the rational participants are induced to take offsetting positions. The smaller the weight M of the rational participants, the larger will be the variations in the futures price. Figure 3.2 indicates how variations in both u and ϵ_a affect the futures price q which affects output S which affects price p.

3.2.3.2 The Risk Premium

The crucial variable which determines the real effects of futures speculation is risk premium $R \equiv \text{var} \, p/M$, because it determines the expected supply curve relative to the marginal cost curve in Figure 3.4. This endogenous risk premium, R, can be determined from equation (3.29). Divide both sides of equation (3.29) by M to obtain

$$R = \frac{\text{var} \, u}{M} + \frac{1}{M}\left(\frac{b\lambda}{c+R}\right)^2 \text{var} \, \epsilon_a; \qquad (3.30)$$

$$R \equiv \text{var} \, p/M$$

This equation is solved graphically for R in Figure 3.5. The 45 degree line is the left-hand side of equation (3.30) and the curve RHS is the right-hand side. There are two components to the RHS. The first var u/M is the risk-sharing element, and is the horizontal asymptote. If M were infinitely large, the average rational participant acts as if he were risk neutral. No risk premium is added to marginal cost to determine expected supply. The futures price would be equal to expected price Ep_o and output would be S_o in Figure 3.4. Deviations of the actual price from Ep_o would result from deviation $(u - W)$. If the noncommercials were as rational as the commercials then the introduction of futures would increase M and lower risk premium var u/M. Futures

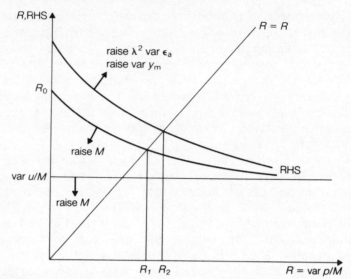

Figure 3.5   The endogenous determination of risk premium R, var p/M. Variance u is inherent in the system. The variance of the Bayesian errors of the irrational speculators is var ϵ_a in Section 3.2. The variance of the market Bayesian error is var y_m in the model of Section 3.3. The higher either var ϵ_a or var y_m is, the higher the risk premium. The greater participation of all types in the market raises M and lowers the risk premium.

markets would rotate the expected supply ES in Figure 3.4 towards the marginal cost curve MC. Expected output would rise towards S_o and expected price would decline to Ep_o. This is the traditional conclusion in the literature.

The second component on the right-hand side of equation (3.30) is the risk premium produced by the inflow of amateur speculators into the futures markets. The greater the ratio λ, (i.e. the relative weight of amateurs to rational participants), the higher is the right-hand side. A rise in the right-hand side, due to a rise in λ, raises risk premium R from R_1 to R_2. Consequently, the expected supply curve in Figure 3.4 rotates counterclockwise to ES'. Expected output declines to 0C and expected price rises to Ep_2.

3.3   Asymptotically Rational Expectations and Diverse Precisions

The previous assumption that commercial firms and professional speculators have MRE but amateur speculators are totally irrational is a polar case. It is better theory to model the groups as having different variances of Bayesian errors, $y_i(t) \equiv E_i p(T; t) - Ep(T)$, as a result of differential information. Amateur speculators have higher variances of Bayesian errors than do the large commercial firms and professional speculators. If the distribution of stochastic parameter of demand u were stationary, then all Bayesian errors converge to zero, i.e. parameter k_i in equation (3.12a) or (3.32) converges to zero. When the distribution of u has changed, the variances of the Bayesian errors are given by equation (3.9) or (3.10).

Denote the three groups by 'c' standing for commercials, 's' for professional speculators and 'a' for amateur speculators. The subjective expectation of the price can be written as

$$E_i p(t + 1; t) \equiv Ep(T) + y_i(t); \qquad i = c, s, a \tag{3.31}$$

The model is a modification of that used in Section 3.2 and is summarized by equations (3.32)–(3.37) in Table 3.2. Equation (3.12a) is repeated here as equation (3.32). Equation (3.33) is the same as demand equation (3.1); and equation (3.34) is the same as supply equation (3.16). Equation (3.35) is the excess supply of futures by commercials. It is the same as equation (2.34) when there is no long hedging and definition (3.31) is used. Equation (3.36) is the excess demand for futures by noncommercials. It is the same as equation (2.41) when definition (3.31) is used. Market-clearing equation (3.37) is the same as equation (3.18) above.

Table 3.2   Model with diverse precisions

var $y_i(t) = k_i$ var u $(k_c, k_s) < k_a$	(3.32)
$p(t + 1) = u^* - bS(t + 1)$	(3.33)
$S(t + 1) = v_1 q_{t+1}(t)$	(3.34)
$X(t) = S(t + 1) + w_c[q_{t+1}(t) - Ep(t + 1) - y_c(t)]$	(3.35)
$Z(t) = w_s[Ep(t + 1) + y_s(t) - q_{t+1}(t)] + w_a[t + 1] + y_a(t)$	
$\qquad - q_{t+1}(t)]$	(3.36)
$X(t) = Z(t)$	(3.37)

Symbols: p, price; *S*, output; *q*, futures price; *X*, excess supply of futures by commercials; *Z*, excess demand for futures by all noncommercials; y_i, Bayesian error.

The market-clearing futures price is

$$q_{t+1}(t) = \frac{Ep(t+1) + y_m(t)}{1 + \operatorname{var} p/Mc} \tag{3.38}$$

It is a discounted value of the sum of the *objectively* expected price $Ep(t+1)$, and the market Bayesian error, $y_m(t)$. Variable $y_m(t)$ is a weighted average of the Bayesian errors of the three groups, as defined in

$$y_m(t) = \Sigma w_i y_i(t)/\Sigma w_i \qquad i = \text{c, s, a}$$

$$= \Sigma \gamma_i y_i(t) \qquad \gamma \equiv w_i/\Sigma w_i \tag{3.39}$$

Variable M defined in

$$M \equiv \xi_c/\alpha + \xi_s/\beta_s + \xi_a/\beta_a = (\Sigma w_i) \operatorname{var} p \tag{3.40}$$

is the sum of the number of participants divided by their coefficients of risk aversion. Discount factor $\operatorname{var} p/Mc$ is the risk premium resulting from net short hedging pressure. If $\operatorname{var} p/Mc$ is small, then the risk is spread thinly; there is very little discounting for risk.

The supply curve of output is equation (3.41), derived by substituting the market-clearing futures price equation (3.38) into supply equation (3.34). It is drawn as the curve ES in Figure 3.4, which is the same as equation (3.24) when the expected Bayesian error Ey_m is zero.

$$S(t+1) = \frac{Ep(t+1) + y_m(t)}{c + \operatorname{var} p/M} \tag{3.41}$$

or, in inverse form,

expected supply

$$Ep(t+1) = (c + \operatorname{var} p/M)ES(t+1) \tag{3.42}$$

Expected demand curve is

expected demand

$$Ep(t+1) = W - bES(t+1) \tag{3.43}$$

repeated here as equation (3.43), and is graphed as curve ED in Figure 3.4. The expected value of demand parameter u is W. The solution for expected supply is equation (3.44). It has the same form as equation (3.26) but $\operatorname{var} p/M$ is not the same as it was in Section 3.2:

$$ES(t + 1) = \frac{W}{(b + c) + \operatorname{var} p/M} \tag{3.44}$$

Futures markets have real effects, i.e. affect expected output, if and only if they change risk premium $\operatorname{var} p/M$. Variable M is taken as a parameter, but price variance $\operatorname{var} p$ is endogenous. The next step is to analyse the determinants of $\operatorname{var} p$ when the participants have different precisions.

3.3.1 Price Variance and the Variance of the Market Bayesian Error

Price variance $\operatorname{var} p$ is derived as follows. Price $p(t + 1)$ in equation (3.45) is obtained by substituting output supplied (equation 3.41) into demand (equation 3.33):

$$p(t + 1) = u^* - \frac{b[Ep(t + 1) + y_m]}{c + \operatorname{var} p/M} \tag{3.45}$$

Take the expectation of equation (3.45) over u and y_m and derive equation (3.46), since $Eu = W$ and $Ey_m = 0$:

$$Ep(t + 1) = W - \frac{bEp(t + 1)}{c + \operatorname{var} p/M} \tag{3.46}$$

Subtract equation (3.46) from equation (3.45) to obtain

$$p(t + 1) - Ep(t + 1) = (u - W) - \frac{by_m}{c + \operatorname{var} p/M}$$

Price variance $\operatorname{var} p$ is

$$\operatorname{var} p = \operatorname{var} u + \left(\frac{b}{c + \operatorname{var} p/M} \right)^2 \operatorname{var} y_m \tag{3.47}$$

where the expectations are taken over *independent* stochastic variables u and y_m. Variable u is the demand parameter and y_m is the market Bayesian error which results from the failure of the market participants to locate the objective mean of the distribution. It was shown in equation (3.9) or (3.10) above that, if the distribution of demand parameter u is stationary, the Bayesian errors eventually converge to zero.

Variance $\operatorname{var} u$ is an *unavoidable* variance. It would exist in a world of MRE because the parameter of demand u is stochastic. Variance of the Bayesian error $\operatorname{var} y_m$ is due to insufficient information concerning the objective *mean* of the distribution of the prices. If the agents drew upon larger samples of relevant information of what determines price, their Bayesian errors would be smaller and less variable. The entry into the futures markets of amateur speculators with very little relevant information adds Bayesian error y_a to the market Bayesian error. Hence, var y_m is *avoidable* variance. This distinction between avoidable and unavoidable variance is used in the welfare analysis in Chapter Six.

3.3.2 Futures Markets and Avoidable Variance

When there are futures markets, the weighted number M of participants (equation 3.40) increases due to the inflow of professional and amateur speculators. Each group comes with its Bayesian errors and thus contributes to var y_m. The question examined here is: how does the introduction of futures markets affect the avoidable variance in the market var y_m compared to the avoidable variance of the commercials var y_c?

Avoidable variance var y_m is equation (3.48), based upon equation (3.39). The Bayesian errors of the three groups are assumed to be independent:

$$\text{var } y_m = \gamma_c^2 \text{ var } y_c + \gamma_s^2 \text{ var } y_s + (1 - \gamma_c - \gamma_s)^2 \text{ var } y_a \qquad (3.48)$$

Define two variables Q and ω. Variable Q is the relative *quality* of the forecasts of professionals to amateurs. It is the ratio of the precisions (reciprocals of variance) of professionals to amateurs. Thus Q is the variance of the Bayesian error of the amateurs to that of the professionals.

$$Q = \text{var } y_a/\text{var } y_s > 1 \qquad (3.49)$$

measures differences in forecasting ability. If the distribution of u is stationary, then var y converges to zero and there is only unavoidable variance. I am dealing with the case where full convergence has not occurred.

The relative *weight* of professional to amateur speculators in the market is variable ω, defined as

$$\omega = w_s/w_a = \gamma_s/\gamma_a = (\xi_s/\beta_a)/(\xi_a/\beta_a) \qquad (3.50)$$

It represents the ratio of the excess demands for futures if both groups had the same subjective expectations of the price.

Using definitions (3.49) and (3.50) in equation (3.48), the variance of the market Bayesian error var y_m relative to the Bayesian error of the commercials var y_c is

$$V = \frac{\text{var } y_m}{\text{var } y_c} = \gamma_c^2 + \left(\frac{1 - \gamma_c}{1 + \omega}\right)^2 (\omega^2 + Q) \frac{\text{var } y_s}{\text{var } y_c} \qquad (3.51)$$

This is a rational function of ω (i.e. it is a ratio of polynomials). Ratio V is graphed in Figure 3.6 as a function of ω, the ratio of amateur to professional speculation, and has a maximum equal to V_o when all futures speculators are amateur ($\omega = 0$). Ratio V is at a minimum equal to V_Q (defined in equation 3.53) when $\omega = Q$:

optimal composition

$$\omega = Q \qquad (3.52)$$

$$V_Q = \gamma_c^2 + (1 - \gamma_c)^2 \frac{\text{var } y_s}{\text{var } y_c} \frac{Q}{1 + Q} \qquad (3.52)$$

The variance of the market Bayesian error V is at a minimum when the relative weight ω of the professionals is equal to the relative quality Q of their forecasts. *This is the optimal composition of futures speculation.*[5]

If the initial weight ω of professional to amateur speculators were W_1 (Figure 3.6) then ratio V would be V_1. An inflow of amateur speculators which lowered the weight to W_2 would lower the ratio V to V_2, even though the amateurs have poorer forecasting abilities than do the professionals.

A priori it is not possible to know whether the composition of the futures speculators ω will lower or raise V, the variance of the market Bayesian error var y_m relative to the variance of the Bayesian error of the commercials var y_c. It is useful to obtain quantitative estimates of equation (3.51), in order to evaluate the likelihood that futures speculation will increase or decrease the variance of the Bayesian error. Ratio $V = \text{var } y_m / \text{var } y_c$ is less than unity if

$$Q < \left(\frac{1 + \gamma_c}{1 - \gamma_c}\right)(1 + \omega)^2 \frac{\text{var } y_c}{\text{var } y_s} - \omega^2 \qquad (3.53)$$

An estimate of ω is the ratio of net commitments of large speculators to those of small traders. On average from 1947 to 1965 large speculators' holdings were less than one-fifth of the value of small traders' holdings (Rockwell, 1967, p. 178) hence $\omega = 0.2$. An estimate of γ_c is the fraction of output not hedged by the commercials.[6] Assume that $\gamma_c = 0.6$. Moreover, assume that professional speculators and commercials have equal forecasting ability so that var y_c/var y_s is unity. Then var y_m will be less than

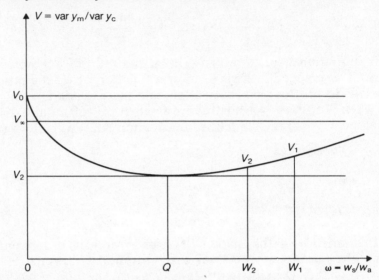

Figure 3.6   The ratio V of the variance of the market Bayesian error var y_m to the Bayesian error of the commercials var y_c, is the curve. The quality of the professionals relative to the amateurs is $Q = $ var y_a/var y_s. The weight of the professionals to the amateurs is $\omega = w_s/w_a$. The minimum market Bayesian error to that of the commercials occurs when $Q = \omega$. This is the optimal composition of speculation.

var y_c (i.e. $V < 1$ in equation 3.51) if $Q = $ var y_a/var y_s is less than 5.72. As long as the variance of the Bayesian error of amateurs is less than six times that of the professionals (equal to that of the commercials), then futures speculation lowers the variance of the Bayesian error.

3.3.3   The Real Effects of Futures Speculation

The real effects of futures speculation can be determined in the case where the agents have diverse precisions. Expected output (equation 3.44) depends upon the risk premium $R \equiv $ var p/M because the latter determines the position of the expected supply curve ES relative to the marginal cost curve MC in Figure 3.4.

Risk premium $R \equiv $ var p/M is derived from equation (3.47) and is

$$R = \frac{\text{var } u}{M} + \frac{1}{M}\left(\frac{b}{c + R}\right)^2 \text{var } y_m \qquad (3.54)$$

which is graphed in Figure 3.5. The vertical intercept R_o is

$$R_o = \frac{\text{var } u}{M} + \frac{1}{M}\left(\frac{b}{c}\right)^2 \text{var } y_m \qquad (3.55)$$

The curve, which is the right-hand side of equation (3.54), is asymptotic to var u/M.

The introduction of futures markets exerts two effects upon the risk premium R. Firstly, it raises M, the total participation or sharing of risk. Since the risk is shared among more people, the average risk premium R declines. The rise in M shifts the right-hand side downwards and decreases the risk premium R. Expected output will then rise because it is negatively related to the risk premium:

$$ES(t+1) = \frac{W}{(b+c)+R} \qquad (3.44a)$$

Secondly, the inflow of both amateur and professional speculators affect the variance of the market Bayesian error var y_m. The curve RHS in Figure 3.5 shifts up or down with var y_m. We do not know *a priori* how the composition of speculators affects the variance of the market Bayesian error. On the basis of the previous analysis in equation (3.53) and estimates of parameters, it is likely that var y_m will decline as all types of futures speculators are drawn into the market. In that case, the curve RHS declines unambiguously thereby reducing the risk premium R. Consequently, the expected supply curve ES in Figure 3.4 rotates closer to the marginal cost curve. Expected output will rise and expected price will decline.

3.3.4 Conclusion

Figure 3.2 summarizes the models used in this chapter and describes the interactions among agents. It is intuitively appealing to believe that the variance of the cash price can be reduced only if the speculators have superior forecasting abilities than producers. If there were an inflow of amateur speculators with poorer forecasting abilities than producers, it seems 'reasonable' to believe that the variance of the cash price would increase, and there would be a less efficient allocation of resources.

I prove that these conjectures are not correct. Continue to analyse the case where no inventories are carried, then the variance of the cash price *can* be reduced and expected output *can* be increased by the entry of amateur speculators with poorer fore-casting abilities than producers.

There are two counterbalancing effects of the diversity of futures speculators. First, in so far as there are more futures speculators of all types, they share the risks with the producers. As a result of the decline in the average risk premium, expected output is increased and the expected cash price is lowered. Secondly, the negative effect whereby expected output is lowered, results from the higher variance of the forecast error of the amateurs relative to that of the producers. The higher variance of the Bayesian forecast error of the amateur speculators var y_a raises the variance of the futures price var q which, in turn, raises the variance of output var S. The resulting greater variance of the cash price var p induces more short hedging by producers and decreases the demand by futures speculators. The resulting increase in the excess supply of futures lowers the futures price q. As a result, the quantity produced S decreases and the cash price p paid by con-sumers rises. The larger the variance or the more numerous are the amateur speculators, the more important will be the negative effect relative to the positive effect. *A priori*, it cannot be decided which effect dominates.

A formula is derived concerning the effects of futures specula-tion upon the variance of the market forecast error. Given esti-mates of parameters, as long as the variance of the forecast error of the amateur speculators is less than six times that of the pro-ducers, the introduction of futures markets can be expected to lower the variance of the market forecast error. Then unambigu-ously, expected price to the consumer will decline and expected output will rise.

3.4   Appendix B
Properties of the Bayesian Error

The detailed steps in the derivation of theorem I are presented here. First, show by induction on t how equation (3.7) is derived from equation (3.6).

For $t = 1$,

$$y(1) = y(0)\frac{\tau(0)}{\tau(0) + ns} + [\bar{x}(0) - Ep(T)]\frac{ns}{\tau(0) + ns} \tag{B1}$$

which satisfies equation (3.7). Suppose that equation (3.7) is true for $y(t)$, show that it is true for $y(t + 1)$.

From equation (3.4a), assuming it is true through time t:

$$y(t+1) = \frac{\tau(t)}{\tau(t)+ns}\left\{\frac{y(0)\tau(0)}{\tau(t-1)+ns} + \frac{ns}{\tau(t-1)+ns}\right.$$

$$\left. \sum_{h=0}^{t-1}[\bar{x}(h)-Ep(T)]\right\} + \frac{ns}{\tau(t)+ns}$$

$$\times [\bar{x}(t)-Ep(T)] \qquad \text{(B2)}$$

Using equation (3.4b) for $\tau(t) = \tau(t-1) + ns$ and doing the summation,

$$y(t+1) = y(0)\frac{\tau(0)}{\tau(t)+ns} + \frac{ns}{\tau(t)+ns}\sum_{h=0}^{t}[\bar{x}(h)-Ep(T)] \qquad \text{(B3)}$$

which is equation (3.7) in the text, just advanced a period.

Secondly, derive the variance explicitly:

$$\text{var } y(t) = E[y(t)-Ey(t)]^2 \qquad \text{(B4)}$$

Using equations (3.7) and (3.8),

$$E\left\{\left[\frac{ns}{\tau(0)+nst}\right]\sum_{h=0}^{t-1}[\bar{x}(h)-Ep(T)]\right\}^2 = \text{var } y(t) \qquad \text{(B5)}$$

$$\text{var } y(t) = \left[\frac{ns}{\tau(0)+nst}\right]^2\frac{t}{ns} \qquad \text{(B6)}$$

since the t samples are independent and each one has a variance of $1/ns = \sigma^2/n$.

Notes

1   This effect is important in Britto (1984).
2   See Muth (1961), equation (5.7).
3   Alternative approaches which yield similar conclusions are in Grossman and Stiglitz (1980) and Stein (1984).
4   I have benefited from discussions with Yukio Takahashi of Tohoku University in connection with this theorem.
5   This was first noted by Figlewski (1982) in a pure exchange model.
6   From equations (3.35)–(3.37):

$$S(t+1) = w_c(Ep+y_c-q) + w_s(Ep+y_s-q) + w_a(Ep+y_a-q)$$

The total stock is held unhedged by commercials $w_c(Ep+y_c-q)$ or in long positions by the noncommercials

$$\sum_{a,s} w_j(Ep + y_j - q)$$

$$1 = \frac{w_c(Ep + y_c - q) + \sum\limits_{a,s} w_j(Ep + y_j - q)}{\sum\limits_{c,a,s} w_i(Ep + y_i - q)}$$

If all groups had similar expectations,

$$1 = \gamma_c + \gamma_s + \gamma_a$$

represents the distribution of the holdings. Coefficient $\gamma_c = w_c / \Sigma w$ is then the fraction of stock not hedged by the commercials.

4

Dynamic Stock-Flow Interactions in Futures Markets with Continuous Inventories

This chapter is concerned with storable commodities, where production and consumption are continuous. The focus is upon dealers who are intermediaries between producers and consumers. They stand ready to purchase at their bid and sell at their ask prices. Investment in inventories is equal to purchases from producers less sales to consumers. The dealers' main risks arise from fluctuations in the value of their inventories. Dealers are the main users of futures markets which help them to manage the risks of holding inventories.

' There are four parts to this chapter. First, optimization equations of dealers are derived. These equations, as well as the market clearing futures price, are practically identical to those developed in Chapter Two. Secondly, the market-clearing cash price and desired level of inventories are derived in the general case. This is the fundamental change from the previous chapters. The cash price equates production with the sum of consumption and the desired rate of change of inventories. The desired level of inventories, however, depends upon the cash price. A dynamic process inevitably results.

In the previous chapter, I discussed the effects of Bayesian errors of the commercials and noncommercials upon the expected cash price and output when no inventories are carried. Since the continuous inventories case is more complicated, the exposition is facilitated by just focusing upon the case where Muth rational expectations (MRE) always prevails, whether or not there are futures markets. Chapter Five, however, shows that a necessary but not sufficient condition for MRE is the existence of well-developed futures markets. Hence, the contribution of futures markets is underestimated in the exposition of the present chapter.

Thirdly, I derive a rational expectations dynamic solution for the evolution of the cash price and level of inventories over time when there are developed futures markets. Three methods of solution are presented.

1   The standard MRE solution (Muth, 1961; Turnovsky, 1983) is tersely outlined.
2   A more revealing method of solution, which focuses upon the interaction of a rational expectations stock demand function and endogenous rate of change of inventories (Beckmann, 1965; Stein, 1979, 1980) is the prime method of analysis used in this chapter.
3   A simple graphic derivation of the above solution (inspired by Keynes) conveys the essential economics of the Beckmann–Stein solution in a nontechnical manner.

Fourthly, the implications of Section 4.3 are as follows. The expected cash price converges asymptotically to the flow equilibrium price P_e, defined as the price where current production is equal to current consumption. This is described in Figure 4.4. The speed of convergence depends positively upon three elements: the average price elasticity, a, of current production and current consumption; the slope, c, of the marginal carrying cost function; and the risk premium, R, which depends negatively upon the degree of speculation by noncommercials. A rise in the risk premium lowers the current cash price but increases its rate of change to the flow equilibrium price. The trajectory is changed from $p_0 E$ to $p'_0 E'$ in Figure 4.4.

A change in the flow equilibrium price produces an immediate corresponding change in the cash price. The variance of the change in the cash price is equal to $[(c + R)/a]$ var u, where var u is the variance of the sum of the intercepts of supply of current production and demand for current production.

The variance of the change in the futures price relative to the change in the cash price is negatively related to the distance to maturity of the futures contract. The longer the distance to maturity, the relatively smaller the variance of the change in the futures price.

4.1   Dealer Optimization and the Clearing of the Futures Market

When the commodity is storable, the focal point of the analysis of the role of futures markets is the dealer who is the intermediary between the original producers and the final consumers. At time t, the dealer purchases $S(t)$ of the commodity at price $p(t)$. He charges the sellers and buyers commissions $V[S(t)]$ which constitute the nonspeculative income of the dealer. Storage, financing and distribution costs are $\phi[S(t)]$. At time $t + h$ the dealer's inventory is worth $p^*(t + h)S(t)$, which he may either sell or continue to hold.

A dealer may sell $x(t)$ futures contracts at price $q_T(t)$ for delivery at time T. At time $t + h$, the value of the futures contract is $q_T^*(t + h)$. Equation (4.1) is the profit equation of the dealer, where $\pi^*(t + h)$ represents profits:

$$\pi^*(t + h) = [p^*(t + h) - p(t)]S(t) + \{V[S(t)] - \phi[S(t)]\}$$
$$+ x(t)[q_T(t) - q_T^*(t + h)] \qquad (4.1)$$

where $\pi^*(t + 1)$ are the profits, $S(t)$ is the inventory at time t, $p(t)$ is the cash price at time t, $x(t)$ are sales $(+)$ and purchases $(-)$ of futures at time t, $q_T(t)$ is the price at t of a futures maturing at T, $V(\cdot)$ is the revenue from commissions and fees, $\phi(\cdot)$ are the storage, financing and distribution costs and * is the stochastic variable.

If there were no change in prices, the dealer's profit would be the second term in brackets: total revenue from commissions less costs. This would be the standard deterministic equation of the theory of the firm. Marginal revenue is $V'(S)$ and marginal cost is $\phi'(S)$. The quantity of the commodity purchased for inventory would be such that marginal revenue is equal to marginal cost. It is convenient for the subsequent analysis to write marginal revenue less marginal cost as a linear function:

$$V'(S) - \phi'(S) = v - cS \qquad (4.2)$$

At low levels of stock $S(t)$, marginal revenue exceeds marginal cost and the reverse occurs at high levels of stock. If prices were constant, net purchases of the dealer for inventory would be:

$$S_e = v/c \qquad (4.3)$$

Parameter v, the vertical intercept of the marginal revenue curve corresponds to what has been called the 'convenience yield'. Quantity S_e is the equilibrium level of stocks.

It is convenient to consider a simplified version of the analysis in Chapter Two where there is no basis risk, so that there is perfect convergence of cash and futures price. Using

$$q_{t+h}(t + h) = p(t + h) \qquad (4.4)$$

in equation (4.1), the profit equation of the dealer is

$$\pi^*(t + h) = p^*(t + h)[S(t) - x(t)] + x(t)q_{t+h}(t) - p(t)S(t)$$
$$+ \{V[S(t)] - \phi[S(t)]\} \tag{4.5}$$

The risk to the dealer concerns the value of the unhedged inventory: the first term in equation (4.5). Using utility function (equation 2.10) and profit equation (4.5) above, the optimum purchases of stock for inventory $S(t)$ is derived. The aggregate inventory demanded by all dealers is equation (4.6) or (4.7), where the number of dealers has been normalized at unity. At present, assume that $h = 1$ so that the futures contract matures at $t + 1$.

$$q_{t+1}(t) - p(t) = cS(t) - v \tag{4.6}$$

$$S(t) = \frac{q_{t+1}(t) - p(t) + v}{c} \tag{4.7}$$

A unit of the commodity is purchased for $p(t)$ and marginal cost is $\phi'(S)$. It is sold at the futures price $q_{t+1}(t)$ and marginal revenue $V'(S)$ is obtained from commissions and fees. Equation (4.6) states that the level of inventory is such that total marginal revenue $q + V'$ is equal to total marginal cost $p + \phi'$. The desired level of inventory is positively related to the difference between the futures price and the current cash price (equation 4.7). If the futures price were equal to the current cash price, then the equilibrium level of stock S_e would be held. Positive stocks would be held even though the futures price were equal to the current cash price, because the dealer earns commissions from his purchases and sales – his normal source of income.

The market-clearing futures price is exactly equation (2.45) derived in Chapter Two, when there is no long hedging by commercials ($Y = 0$). The supply of futures by commercials $X(t)$ is equal to the demand $Z(t)$ by noncommercials. The futures price $q_{t+1}(t)$ is a weighted average of the subjectively expected prices $E_m p(t + 1, t)$ less an endogenous risk premium $\operatorname{var} p/M \cdot S(t)$ resulting from net hedging pressure.[1]

$$q_{t+1}(t) = E_m p(t + 1; t) - \frac{\operatorname{var} p}{M} \cdot S(t) \tag{4.8}$$

$$M = \frac{\xi_s}{\beta} + \frac{\xi_c}{\alpha} \tag{4.8a}$$

Parameter M reflects risk sharing. The larger M, the lower will be the endogenous risk premium R defined as

$$R = \text{var } p/M \qquad (4.8b)$$

Substitute the market clearing futures price from equation (4.8) into the demand for inventory equation (4.7) and obtain equation (4.9):

$$gS(t) - v = E_m p(t+1; t) - p(t) \qquad (4.9)$$

$$g = c + R \qquad (4.9a)$$

Equation (4.9) is the stock demand function of dealers when the futures market has cleared. It is the first of the three basic equations of the dynamic model.

4.2 The Market-Clearing Cash Price

The investment in inventories during period t, $S(t) - S(t-1)$, is equal to current production $Q(t)$ less current consumption $C(t)$,

$$S(t) - S(t-1) = Q(t) - C(t) \qquad (4.10)$$

This can be viewed as the equation which determines the current cash price $p(t)$ because it can be written as

$$S(t) + C(t) = S(t-1) + Q(t) \qquad (4.10a)$$

The available supply consists of current production $Q(t)$ plus the inventories held at the end of the period $S(t-1)$. The total demand consists of current consumption $C(t)$ plus the stocks that the dealers want to carry during period t.

Assume that there is no lag in production so that producers produce output $Q(t)$ where marginal cost of production is equal to current price $p(t)$. Production supply[2] is

$$Q(t) = a_0 + a_1 p(t) + u_1(t) \qquad (4.11)$$

where $u_1(t)$ represents transitory supply disturbances.

Consumption $C(t)$, where $u_2(t)$ represents transitory demand disturbances, is

$$C(t) = b_0 - b_1 p(t) + u_2(t) \qquad (4.12)$$

The excess supply of current production is

$$Q(t) - C(t) = u(t) + a[p(t) - P_e] \qquad (4.13)$$

equal to equation (4.11) less (4.12), where

$$u(t) = u_1(t) - u_2(t); \qquad Eu = 0 \qquad\qquad (4.13a)$$

and

$$a = a_1 + b_1 \qquad\qquad (4.13b)$$

The *flow equilibrium price* P_e is defined as the price which would prevail on average if production were always equal to consumption:

$$P_e = [p(t) : EQ(t) = EC(t)]$$

$$P_e = (b_0 - a_0)/(a_1 + b_1) \qquad\qquad (4.14)$$

Using equation (4.13) in (4.10), the supply of inventory investment is

$$S(t) - S(t-1) = a[p(t) - P_e] + u(t) \qquad\qquad (4.15)$$

the second of the three basic equations of the dynamic model.

A graphic solution of equations (4.9) and (4.15) indicates the basic determinants of the cash price $p(t)$ and the inventory that

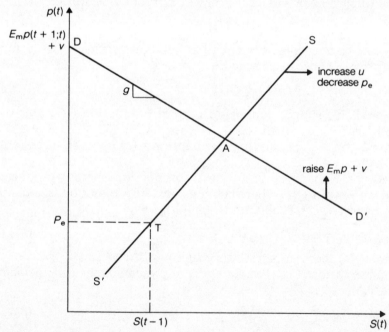

Figure 4.1   The determination of the cash price $p(t)$ and level of inventories $S(t)$. Curve SS′ is the supply of inventories (equation 4.15) and curve DD′ is the demand for inventories (equation 4.9). Here, the initial level of inventories $S(t-1)$ and expected price, $E_m p(t+1;t)$ are predetermined.

dealers want to hold during period t. Equation (4.9) can be viewed as the demand for inventory by dealers. It is graphed as curve DD′ in Figure 4.1. The quantity demanded is negatively related to the cash price, relative to the price expected to prevail during the next period.

Equation (4.15) can be viewed as the supply of inventory, graphed as curve SS′ in Figure 4.1. The quantity of inventory supplied is positively related to the current price relative to the flow equilibrium price, given the previous level of inventory. A rise in $p(t) - P_e$ raises production and decreases consumption. More goods are available for inventory investment. If the price were P_e then, on average, production would equal consumption and inventories would not change (point T).

Figure 4.1 (equations 4.9 and 4.15) permits us to analyse the impact effects of changes in predetermined variables upon the cash price and level of inventories. Inspection of these equations reveals their inherent dynamic nature, because they contain the variables $S(t-1)$ and $E_m p(t+1; t)$. Given the expected price and initial level of stocks, the subsequent level of stocks and current price are determined. In turn, this generates a new price and level of stocks. The process is inherently dynamic.

4.3 Rational Expectations Solutions of the Dynamic Model

There are several ways to solve the model described by equations (4.9) and (4.15), graphed in Figure 4.1. Solve equation (4.9) explicitly for $S(t)$, the stock demanded during period t:

$$S(t) = \frac{E_m p(t+1; t) - p(t) + v}{g} \tag{4.16}$$

A similar expression is derived for $S(t-1)$, the stock demanded during period $t-1$. Subtract the latter from the former and thereby obtain $S(t) - S(t-1)$, the demand for inventory investment. This is the left-hand side of equation (4.17). The supply of inventory investment $Q(t) - C(t)$ is equation (4.15), which is the right-hand side of

$$\frac{1}{g} [E_m p(t+1; t) - p(t)] - \frac{1}{g} [E_m p(t; t-1) - p(t-1)]$$

$$= a[p(t) - P_e] + u(t) \tag{4.17}$$

Equation (4.17) is the market-clearing equation which determines the price $p(t)$ when the stocks are endogenous. *This is a general equation which is compatible with any theory of price anticipations.*

The MRE assumption is that there are no Bayesian errors. The subjective and objective price expectations are the same:

$$E_m p(t+1; t) = Ep(t+1; t) \qquad (4.18)$$

There are several ways to solve the MRE system. The first is the standard method (Muth, 1961; Turnovsky, 1983). The second is one where a rational expectations stock demand equation is used in conjunction with the excess supply of current production (Beckmann, 1965; Stein, 1979, 1980). The third is a simple graphic solution inspired by Keynes (1930, pp. 140–2) which implies the Beckmann–Stein solution. The reader who is not interested in the mathematical techniques of the solution may skip directly to Section 4.3.3 where an intuitive solution is derived very simply. They all yield identical results, but the second two methods are more revealing.

4.3.1　*The Standard MRE Solution*

The standard way to solve the MRE system (equations 4.17 and 4.18) is as follows. At time $t-1$, the agents know the model described by equation (4.17) and want to forecast the evolution of prices. Each one takes the expectation of the price to prevail at t and $t+1$. Equation (4.19) is derived where E is the expectations operator at time $t-1$:

$$Ep(t) - Ep(t-1) + ag[Ep(t) - P_e] = Ep(t+1) - Ep(t) \quad (4.19)$$

The agents solve this second-order difference equation for the expected prices, which they then use in deriving their stock demand functions (equation 4.9). There are two roots to the solution[3] of equation (4.19), which must satisfy

$$r^2 - (2 + ag)r + 1 = 0 \qquad (4.20)$$

One root is stable (r_s) and the other is unstable. The agents are assumed to select the stable root in forming their price expectations. Under these assumptions, the expected price is

$$Ep(t+h) - P_e = [p(t) - P_e]r_s^h \qquad (4.21)$$

The derived expected price, equation (4.21), is substituted into the market-clearing equation (4.17) and the current price is determined.

4.3.2 A Rational Expectations Stock Demand Function and the Excess Supply of Current Production

The graphic solution, Figure 4.1, uses a demand for inventories which depends upon the current price and its expected price at a later date. The rational expectations approach developed here derives a stock demand function where the expected price and stocks are endogenous.

Postulate the (inverse) rational expectations stock demand function as

$$p(t) = V_0 + V_1 S(t) \tag{4.22}$$

The object of the analysis is to solve for coefficients V_0 and V_1 which relate the desired stock $S(t)$ to the current price $p(t)$.

At time t, the price expected to prevail at time $t + h$ is

$$Ep(t + h; t) = V_0 + V_1 ES(t + h; t) \tag{4.23}$$

This is derived directly from equation (4.22). Subtract equation (4.22) from (4.23) and derive

$$Ep(t + h; t) - p(t) = V_1 [ES(t + h; t) - S(t)] \tag{4.24}$$

The stock at time $t + h$ is the stock at time t plus the accumulated sum of production less consumption $Q(t) - C(t)$ over the interval of length h. Using equation (4.15), the stock at time $t + h$ is equation (4.25), where $p(\tau)$ is the average price during the interval $(t, t + h)$:

$$S(t + h) = S(t) + \{a[p(\tau) - P_e] + u(\tau)\}h;$$
$$t + h \geqslant \tau \geqslant t \tag{4.25}$$

Take the expectation[4] of equation (4.25) where $Eu = 0$, substitute equation (4.22) for $p(\tau)$ to obtain

$$ES(t + h) - S(t) = a[V_0 + V_1 S(\tau) - P_e]h \tag{4.26}$$

Using equation (4.26) in (4.24), the expected price change is

$$Ep(t + h; t) - p(t) = aV_1 [V_0 + V_1 S(\tau) - P_e]h \tag{4.27}$$

Equation (4.9), the desired stock demand function, can be written as

$$Ep(t + h; t) - p(t) = [gS(\tau) - v]h \tag{4.28}$$

Equate equation (4.27) to (4.28) and let h go to zero. *Identity* (4.29) is derived:

$$gS(t) - v \equiv aV_1^2 S(t) + aV_1(V_0 - P_e) \tag{4.29}$$

Parameters V_0 and V_1 of the desired stock demand function (4.22) must satisfy equation (4.28) *identically*. The solutions are:

$$V_1 \equiv \pm\sqrt{g/a} \tag{4.30}$$

and

$$V_0 \equiv P_e + v/\sqrt{ag} \tag{4.31}$$

A negatively sloped stock demand function is sought. Therefore the negative root of V_1 is selected. Alternatively, if the dynamic system is to be stable, the negative root of V_1 must be chosen.

The resulting rational expectations stock demand is

$$p(t) = P_e + \frac{v}{\sqrt{ag}} - \sqrt{g/a}\, S(t) \tag{4.32}$$

It relates the current price $p(t)$ to the desired level of inventory $S(t)$ that firms want to carry during period t. This is graphed in Figure 4.3a.

The equilibrium stock S_e was defined to be the inventory that will be held if the dealers do not expect the price to change. From equations (4.3) or (4.9) above:

$$S_e = v/g \tag{4.3}$$

Using the concept of the equilibrium stock in equation (4.32), the rational expectations stock demand function is equation (4.33). In continuous time, difference equation (4.15) is written here as differential equation (4.34).

Rational expectations dynamic system

$$p(t) = P_e - \sqrt{g/a}[S(t) - S_e] \tag{4.33}$$

$$DS(t) = a[p(t) - P_e] + u(t); \qquad D \equiv d/dt \tag{4.34}$$

Differentiate equation (4.33) with respect to time and substitute equation (4.34) for $DS(t)$. Differential equation (4.35) is derived when the flow equilibrium price P_e and equilibrium level of stocks S_e are constant:

$$D[p(t) - P_e] = -\sqrt{ag}[p(t) - P_e] - \sqrt{g/a}\, u(t)$$

or

$$Dx(t) = -\sqrt{ag}\, x(t) - \sqrt{g/a}\, u(t)$$

Variable $x(t) \equiv p(t) - P_e$ is defined here as the deviation of the price from the flow equilibrium price. This is the basic rational expectations differential equation to be used in the subsequent analysis.

4.3.3 An Intuitive Derivation of the Rational Expectations Solution[5]

The economic content of the technical mathematical rational espectations solution in the previous section can be more easily understood by the following simple analysis. Figure 4.2 facilitates the derivation.

Let $C(t)$ represent the flow demand curve of current consumption (equation 4.12) and $Q(t)$ the flow supply curve of current production (equation 4.11). In Figure 4.2, these curves are drawn at their normal values where u_1 and u_2 are zero. The normal flow equilibrium price P_e is defined as unity. At this price, normal production is equal to normal consumption which is also normalized at unity. Measure the current price $p(t)$ as a percentage

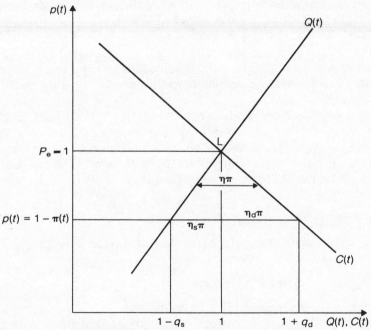

Figure 4.2 The flow equilibrium $P_e \equiv 1$ equates consumption CC to current production QQ. At price $p(t) \equiv 1 - \pi(t)$, the rate of decline in inventories is $q_d + q_s = \pi(\eta_d + \eta_s)$, where η_i is the price elasticity. The time T to work off $s(t)$ of inventories is $T = s(t)/\eta\pi$ where $\eta = \frac{1}{2}(\eta_d + \eta_s)$ is the average elasticity.

deviation denoted by $\pi(t)$ from the flow equilibrium price $P_e \equiv 1$ so that $p(t) = 1 - \pi(t)$.

At time t, let there be excess stocks denoted by $s(t) \equiv S(t) - S_e$, where the equilibrium stock S_e is defined in equation (4.3) above. At the equilibrium stock S_e, the marginal revenue from commissions is equal to the marginal cost plus the endogenous risk premium.

Stock demand function (4.9) can be written as equation (4.36). Let T be the time required to absorb the redundant stock $s(t) \equiv S(t) - S_e$ and restore the price to the normal flow equilibrium price $P_e = 1$. The required rate of return must equal the marginal carrying costs plus risk premium $gs(t)$. The rate of return is the percentage change in price $\pi(t)$ per unit of time T.

$$\frac{\pi(t)}{T} = gs(t) \tag{4.36}$$

where $\pi(t) = 1 - p(t)$. Equation (4.36) is the stock demand function (4.9) in two unknowns: percentage $\pi(t) = 1 - p(t)$ and time T. Another equation is required to solve the system, i.e. to derive a rational expectations stock demand function.

When the price $p(t)$ is $\pi(t)$ per cent below normal, consumption will be q_d per cent above normal, and production will be q_s per cent below normal (Figure 4.2). The decline in inventories per unit of time, as a fraction of normal consumption, is $(q_d + q_s)$ as shown in Figure 4.2.

As the price rises from $p(t) = 1 - \pi(t)$ to its normal level of unity, the decline in inventories per unit of time goes from $(q_d + q_s)$ to zero. On average, the decline in inventories per unit of time is $1/2(q_d + q_s)$ relative to normal consumption. Let η_i $(i = d, s)$ be the absolute value of the price elasticity of demand or supply:

$$q_s = \pi\eta_s; \qquad q_d = \pi\eta_d \tag{4.37}$$

Then, on average, the rate of decline in inventories per unit of time is

$$\tfrac{1}{2}(q_d + q_s) = \tfrac{1}{2}(\eta_d + \eta_s)\pi = \eta\pi$$

where η is the *average* of the two elasticities.

The time T required to work off the redundant stock is derived from equation (4.38). Rate $\eta\pi$ of inventory disinvestment multiplied by time T equals excess stock $s(t)$. This is the second equation:

$$\eta\pi T = s(t) \tag{4.38}$$

Time T, required to work off the redundant stock, is

$$T = \frac{1}{\eta} \frac{s(t)}{\pi(t)} \tag{4.39}$$

Substitute time T from equation (4.39) into the stock demand equation (4.36) to derive

$$\pi(t)^2 = (g/\eta)s(t)^2 \tag{4.40}$$

The solution for the price is equation (4.41), which is the rationally expected stock demand function:

$$\pi(t) = \sqrt{g/\eta}\,s(t) \tag{4.41a}$$

or

$$p(t) = 1 - \sqrt{g/\eta}\,[S(t) - S_e] \tag{4.41b}$$

$$T = 1/\sqrt{g\eta} \tag{4.41c}$$

Equation (4.41b) is precisely the Beckmann–Stein equation (4.33) above.

The analysis (in Sections 4.3.2 and 4.3.3) explains how price is determined when stocks are held. First, price $p(t)$ does not equate the flow of production $Q(t)$ to the flow of consumption $C(t)$, but produces a portfolio balance. When there are redundant stocks $s(t)$, then the market price is below the normal flow equilibrium price $P_e = 1$. The owners of the stocks can expect a rate of return $gs(t)$ from the appreciation of the price. Secondly, at a market price below the normal price, production is less than consumption and stocks are reduced. Thirdly, the magnitude of the price decline below the normal price is directly related to the magnitude of the redundant stocks. Therefore the crucial variable that the market participants must observe to determine the trajectory of price is the level of stocks relative to normal consumption. Fourthly, the (absolute value of the) slope of the stock demand function $\sqrt{g/\eta}$ depends positively upon the slope of the marginal cost function and the risk premium, and negatively upon the average elasticity of production and consumption.

4.4 Implications of the Theory

4.4.1 The Trajectory of the Cash Price

The dynamical system equations (4.33) and (4.34) can be portrayed by Figure 4.3a and b; and the resultant pattern of the expected price is portrayed in Figure 4.4.

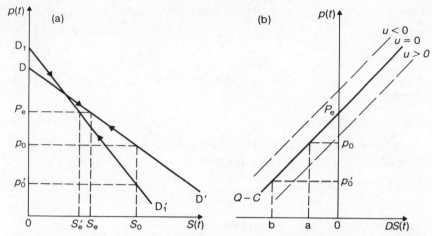

Figure 4.3   The cash price $p(t)$ in (a) is determined by the rational expectations stock demand function which equates the stock demanded to the stock in existence $S(t)$. Along the demand curve, the expected change in price is equal to the sum of the marginal net carrying cost and marginal risk premium. Given this price $p(t)$ the production less consumption $Q(t) - C(t)$ determines the rate of change of stocks in (b). The new level of stock is $S(t) + DS(t)$ and the process is repeated.

The normal flow of production less consumption is equation (4.15) or Figure 4.3b, and the flow equilibrium price is P_e. At time $t = 0$ let there be an abnormally large excess supply of current production: for example, the main harvest in the case of staple products or the main export season in the case of foreign exchange. Initial stocks are S_0 in Figure 4.3a. The rational expectations stock demand equation (4.34) is curve DD' in Figure 4.3a. The market clearing rational expectations price is p_0 when the initial stock is S_0. At this price, the rationally expected rise in price is equal to the marginal net carrying costs plus the endogenous risk premium (equation 4.9).

When the price is p_0 then on average ($u = 0$) consumption will exceed production by 0a in Figure 4.3b. Stocks will be drawn down at this rate, in the direction of the arrows in Figure 4.3a.

The closed-form solution for the price is derived by solving differential equation (4.35) or (4.35a) whose solution is equation (4.42) or (4.42a) where $x(t) \equiv p(t) - P_e$:

$$p(t) = P_e + [p(0) - P_e] \exp(-\sqrt{ag}\, t) - \sqrt{g/a}$$

$$\times \int_{\tau=0}^{t} \exp[-\sqrt{ag}(t - \tau)]u(\tau)d\tau \qquad (4.42)$$

$$x(t) = x(0) \exp\left(-\sqrt{ag}\, t\right) - \sqrt{g/a}$$

$$\times \int_{\tau=0}^{t} \exp\left[-\sqrt{ag}(t-\tau)\right] u(\tau)d\tau \tag{4.42a}$$

The first term in equation (4.42a) is the price deviation from the flow equilibrium price expected at time zero to prevail at subsequent date t, i.e. $Ex(t; 0)$. The expected price $Ep(t; 0)$ is graphed in Figure 4.4 as curve p_0E. Price $p(t)$ is expected to converge asymptotically to flow equilibrium price P_e at rate $\sqrt{ag}$. The 'half life' T in equation (4.43) is the length of time when half of the initial deviation has been eliminated. It satisfies the equation $Ex(T; 0)/x(0) = 0.5$; hence

$$T = -\frac{\ln 0.5}{\sqrt{ag}} = 0.69/\sqrt{ag} \tag{4.43}$$

The speed of convergence $\sqrt{ag}$ is positively related to the slope of the marginal cost function, risk and risk aversion and the average elasticity of current production and current consumption.

The second term of equation (4.42) or (4.42a) is the weighted sum of the stochastic disturbances to the excess supply of current production less current consumption $Q - C$.

4.4.1.1 Change in the Risk Premium

To understand the effects of futures markets upon the trajectory of the cash price, as well as the economics underlying the dynamical system, consider the effects of variations in the parameters.

Coefficient g is described by equation (4.9a) repeated here as

$$g = c + \operatorname{var} p/M \equiv c + R \tag{4.44}$$

Term c is the slope of the marginal cost curve. Risk premium $R = \operatorname{var} p/M$ is the subjective measure of risk and risk aversion. Term M represents the risk sharing.

Suppose that risk premium R rises so that g increases to g'. Graphically, the stock demand curve in Figure 4.3a shifts from DD' to D_1D_1'. There is a decline in the equilibrium stock to $S_e' = v/g'$ and the absolute value of the slope rises to $\sqrt{g'/a}$. Given an initial stock S_0, the price declines to p_0'. A larger difference must exist between the current price and the flow equilibrium price, in order to induce the market to hold the same level of stocks.

When the price declines to p_0', there is a rise in current consumption less current production. Inventories are drawn down at rate 0b (in Figure 4.3b) which exceeds 0a. The decline in inventories raises the price along D_1D_1' in the direction of the arrows at a faster rate than before.

Price trajectory $p(t)$ shifts from p_0E to $p_0'E'$ in Figure 4.4. The initial price declines, but it converges at a faster rate than before because the stocks are being drawn down at a faster rate. As equation (4.43) shows, the half life is reduced as the risk premium rises. For an agricultural commodity, a rise in the risk premium would mean that immediate post-harvest price would be lower (p_0' is less than p_0). A rise in g would increase the intra-seasonal price variance.

4.4.1.2 Change in the Flow Equilibrium Price

Suppose that at time θ during the period, the market learns that the flow equilibrium price P_e has increased to P_e'. Both the stock demand curve (Figure 4.3a) and the flow of the excess supply of current production $Q - C$ (Figure 4.3b) will shift upwards.

The trajectory of the cash price is described in Figure 4.5. From time $t = 0$ to $t = \theta$, the price rises along the curve OLD from p_0 to

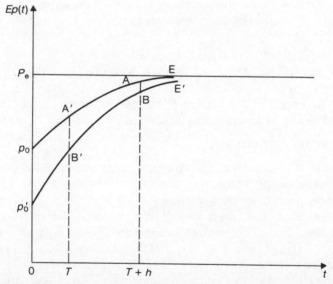

Figure 4.4 The trajectory of the expected cash price $p(t)$ to the flow equilibrium price depends upon the risk premium and the slope of the marginal cost curve, as well as the average price elasticity of current production and current consumption. The rise in the risk premium changes the trajectory from p_0E to $p_0'E'$.

p_1. At time θ, when the market learns that the new flow equilibrium price is P'_e, the cash price jumps from p_1 to p_2. From time θ on, the expected cash price moves along the NEW curve towards P'_e at the same rate $\sqrt{ag}$ as before.

These trajectories are the expected trajectories (the first term in equation (4.42a). In fact the price will also contain the weighted sum of the stochastic terms (the second term in equation (4.42a).

4.4.2   Variance of the Cash Price

It was shown above (Figures 4.3a and 4.4) that a rise in the risk premium increases the intra-seasonal variability of the cash price. An exact equation is derived here for the variance of the change in the cash price.

The change in the cash price relative to the flow equilibrium price is equation (4.35a), repeated here:

$$Dx(t) = -\sqrt{ag}\, x(t) - \sqrt{g/a}\, u(t); \qquad x(t) \equiv p(t) - P_e \qquad (4.35a)$$

Coefficient g is the sum of the slope c of the marginal cost curve plus risk premium R (equation 4.44). It is convenient to treat the risk premium as a parameter.

The expected change in the price is equation (4.45), based upon equations (4.35a) and (4.44). It is the slope of the curve in Figure 4.4 evaluated at a given price deviation $x(t)$:

$$E[Dx(t); x(t)] = -\sqrt{a(c + R)}\, x(t) \qquad (4.45)$$

which is conditional upon the current price deviation $x(t)$.

The variance of $Dx(t)$, conditional upon $x(t)$, is

$$\text{var } Dx = E[Dx(t) - EDx(t)]^2 = \frac{c + R}{a} \text{ var } u \qquad (4.46)$$

which is graphed in Figure 4.6.

The price is expected to rise smoothly along stock demand curve DD' from p_0 to P_e (Figure 4.3a) as inventories decline according to the expected excess flow supply curve $u = 0$ in Figure 4.3b. The variance of the change in the cash price results from shifts in the $Q - C$ curves in Figure 4.3b. At price p_0, the expected decline in inventories is 0a. But the $Q - C$ curve could be $u < 0$ or $u > 0$ at any time. Hence, the decline in inventories, associated with any given price deviation $x(t) \equiv p(t) - P_e$, is stochastic. For this reason, the trajectory of the cash price $p(t)$ to the flow equilibrium price P_e is also stochastic. The trajectories in

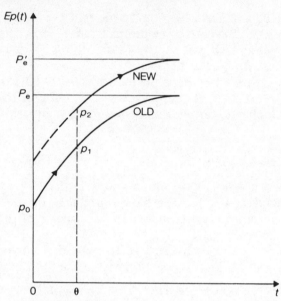

Figure 4.5   The flow equilibrium price rises from P_e to P_e'. The market learns of this change at time θ.

Figures 4.4 and 4.5 represented expected trajectories not the actual trajectories.

The variance of the change in the cash price stems from the variance of u. The magnitude of the variance of the change in the cash price (equation 4.46) also depends upon the steepness of the stock demand function $\sqrt{(c + R)/a}$.

Figure 4.6 indicates the four determinants of the variance of the change in the cash price. If the degree of futures speculation 'M' by noncommercials were very large, then the risk premium R would be driven down to zero. Then the variance of the change in the cash price would be driven down to (c/a) var u.

In this chapter, unlike Chapter Three, it was assumed that MRE prevails regardless of the existence of a futures market. The only difference produced by a futures market is in M, the degree of risk sharing. As a result of the greater risk sharing resulting from futures markets, the risk premium declines from R_0 to R_1 (Figure 4.6). Thereby, the variance of the change in the cash price is reduced from V_0 to V_1.

It is shown in Chapter Five that MRE does not occur without futures markets. Consequently, the benefits of futures markets are greater than the reduction in the variance of the change in the cash price.

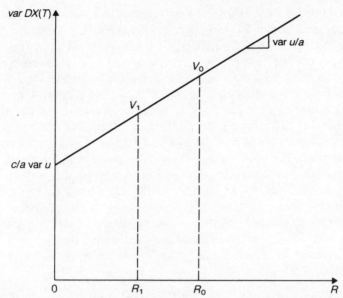

Figure 4.6   The variance of the change in the cash price, conditional upon its current level, depends upon the underlying parameter variance var u, the risk premium R, the slope of the marginal cost function c and the average price elasticity a of current production less current consumption.

4.4.3   The Variance of the Change in the Futures Price

Two issues that have been discussed in the literature of efficient markets are what is the expected change in the price of a futures contract and what determines the variance of the change in the futures price? These questions can be answered by using the theory developed above.

The price at time t of a futures contract maturing at subsequent date $T = t + h$, based upon equation (4.8), is

$$q_T(t) = Ep(T; t) - RS(t) \tag{4.47}$$

where $R = \text{var } p/M$ is the risk premium resulting from inadequate rational speculation.

The expected cash price $Ep(T; t)$ is equation (4.48), based upon equation (4.42), which is trajectory p_0E in Figure 4.4:

$$Ep(T; t) = P_e + [p(t) - P_e] \exp[-\sqrt{ag}(T - t)] \tag{4.48}$$

The change in the futures price $Dq_T(t)$, the sum of two components, is

$$Dq_T(t) = DEp(T; t) - RDS(t); \qquad D \equiv d/dt \tag{4.49}$$

The first component $DEp(T; t)$ corresponds to variations along the stock demand curve DD′ in Figure 4.3a, resulting from stochastic variations u in the stock. In Figure 4.4 it is the shift in the trajectory p_0E of the expected cash price. The second component $RDS(t)$ is the change in the risk premium whereby the futures price is below the expected price. If there were no risk premium ($R = 0$), then $q_T(t) = Ep(T; t)$ and the only reason for the change in the futures price would be shifts in the trajectory of $Ep(T; t)$ to P_e: for example, from p_0E to $p_0'E'$ in Figure 4.4. When there is a risk premium $RS(t)$ whereby there is a deviation between $q_T(t)$ and $Ep(T; t)$, the futures price will converge to the trajectory of the expected price (p_0E) as the stocks are driven to their equilibrium level.

A formal derivation of the answers to the questions above is followed by an economic explanation of the results.

The change in the futures price, based upon equations (4.49), (4.34) and (4.35), is

$$Dq_T(t) = -\sqrt{g/a} \exp \left[-\sqrt{ag}(T - t) \right] u(t)$$
$$- Ra[p(t) - P_e] - Ru(t) \qquad (4.50)$$

The *expected* change in the futures price, where the expectation is taken over stochastic variable u, is

$$EDq_T(t) = -Ra[p(t) - P_e] \qquad (4.51)$$

If there were no risk premium, then the futures price $q_T(t)$ equal to $Ep(T; t)$ is given by trajectory p_0A' in Figure 4.4. The expected price rises towards the flow equilibrium price because there are positive marginal carrying costs (parameter $g = c$ in equation 4.9 or 4.33). If there is a risk premium, then $q_T(t) = Ep(T; t) - RS(t)$. The expected change in stocks is $a[p(t) - P_e]$ and the expected change in the differential $Ep(T; t) - q_T(t)$ is $Ra[p(t) - P_e]$. This is the meaning of equation (4.51).

The variance of the change in the futures price is

$$\text{var } Dq_T(t) = E[Dq_T(t) - EDq_T(t)]^2$$
$$= \text{var } u \left[\sqrt{(c + R)/a} \exp \left[-\sqrt{a(c + R)}(T - t) \right] + R \right]^2$$
$$\qquad (4.52)$$

The variance of the change in the futures price is most easily understood by considering a special case where there is no risk premium. This could occur because there is a large amount of rational speculation (M is very large) or because hedging by commercials is balanced (see Chapter Two). Then equations (4.51) and (4.52) become equations (4.53) and (4.54) respectively.

$R = 0$

$$EDq_{t+h}(t) = 0 \qquad\qquad\qquad\qquad\qquad h = T - t \quad (4.53)$$

$$\operatorname{var} Dq_{t+h}(t) = \operatorname{var} u(c/a) \exp(-2\sqrt{ac}\, h) \qquad\qquad (4.54)$$

The variance of the change in the futures price results solely from shifts of the trajectory $p_0 E$ or $p_0' E'$ in Figure 4.4. These shifts occur because of $u(t)$, the disturbances to the excess supply of production $Q(t) - C(t)$ in Figure 4.3b. A positive u increases the stocks and the cash price falls to p_0' from p_0 in Figure 4.4. The magnitude of the price change depends upon c, the steepness of marginal carrying costs.

The expected trajectory to the flow equilibrium price will be $p_0' E'$ instead of $p_0 E$. The magnitude of the variance of the change in the near futures price depends upon the steepness of the stock demand function in Figure 4.3a.

An interesting implication of this analysis concerns the ratio of the variance of the change in the futures price to the variance of the change in the cash price.[6] This is equation (4.55) when $R = 0$. It is based upon equations (4.54) and (4.46):

$$\frac{\operatorname{var} Dq_{t+h}(t)}{\operatorname{var} Dp(t)} = \exp(-2h\sqrt{ac}) \qquad\qquad (4.55)$$

The variance of the change in the futures price is inversely related to the distance h to maturity. Far futures fluctuate less than near futures. An intuitive explanation of this result can be seen from Figure 4.4, when there is no risk premium.

The expected cash price will converge asymptotically to the flow equilibrium price P_e, regardless of the initial condition $p(0)$. Since there is no risk premium, the futures price $q_{t+h}(t)$ is $Ep(t + h; t)$; given by trajectory $p_0 E$.

Disturbance $u(t)$ affects the stock $S(t)$ and hence the magnitude of the marginal carrying costs $cS(t)$. A transitory rise in $u(t)$ raises the stocks which raises the marginal net carrying costs. As a result, the cash price $p(t)$ must decline relative to the flow equilibrium price. Trajectory $p_0' E'$ is produced instead of $p_0 E$ (Figure 4.4). The expected price $Ep(T; t)$ declines from A$'$ to B$'$ when the initial cash price declines from p_0 to p_0'. The expected price $Ep(T + h; t)$ declines from A to B. If h is sufficiently large then, on either trajectory, the expected price is close to P_e the flow equilibrium price. Hence, the movement from A to B is very small relative to the movement of the cash price from p_0 to p'_0. This is the intuitive explanation of equation (4.55), that the variance of the change in the futures price relative to that of the cash price is negatively related to distance to maturity.

This completes the theory of futures markets when there are continuous inventories.

Notes

1   From equations (2.17), (2.44) and (2.45) when $\xi_c = 1$, there is no long hedging $v_2 = 0$ and no basis risk $r^2 = 1$,

$$q_{t+1}(t) = E_m p(t + 1; t) - \frac{S(t)}{w_s + w_c}$$

From equation (2.40) $M = (\Sigma w_i) \operatorname{var} p$. It follows that $q = E_m p - (\operatorname{var} p / M)S$. The risk premium per unit of S is $R = \operatorname{var} p / M$.

2   Let total costs of producers be

$$TC = \frac{1}{2a_1} Q^2 - \left(\frac{a_0 + u_1}{a_1}\right) Q$$

Then marginal cost MC is

$$MC = \frac{1}{a_1} Q - \left(\frac{a_0 + a_1}{a_1}\right)$$

When MC is equal to price, equation (4.11) is derived. Recall that there is no production lag.

3   Let $Ep(t) = Kr^t$ be the solution. Substitute this into equation (4.19) and solve for the roots r.

4   $EX(s; t)$ is the expectation taken at time t of the value of variable X at subsequent time s. If there is no ambiguity, it will be written $EX(s)$.

5   This derivation was inspired by Keynes, 1930, pp. 140–142.

6   See Stein, 1979, pp. 252–253; Samuelson, 1976.

5

Anticipations, Hypotheses and Empirical Evidence

Four main issues have been studied in connection with futures markets. First, to what extent do commercial firms pay a risk premium to futures speculators for the transfer of the risk of price changes? Secondly, are the subjective expectations of the subsequent price held by the market participants equal to the objective expectation? The efficient market hypothesis, or the Muth rational expectations (MRE) hypothesis consists of two parts.

1   The subjective expectation assessed at time t by the market $E_m p(t + 1; t)$ of the subsequent price is equal to the objective expectation at time t, denoted by $Ep(t + 1; t)$.
2   The difference $\epsilon(t + 1)$ between the objective expectation at time t and the subsequent realization $p(t + 1)$ is a noise term which has no structure.

Combining 1 and 2, the MRE hypothesis is

$$E_m p(t + 1; t) - p(t + 1) = \epsilon(t + 1), \qquad \text{'noise'} \qquad (5.1)$$

The subjective expectation differs from the subsequent realization by a pure noise term. Is this hypothesis consistent with the empirical evidence?

Thirdly, how do futures markets affect the relation between the subjective and objective expectations? If the MRE hypothesis were correct, then the two expectations would always be equal. Then; futures markets would not affect the relation between the subjective and objective expectations. An alternative point of view is that the futures markets speed the convergence of the market's subjective expectation to the objective expectation. Unless the underlying distribution of prices has been stationary for a long time, without futures markets the MRE hypothesis is unlikely to be correct.

Fourthly, to what extent does the existence of futures markets change the structural equations which determine the quantity produced and the price paid by the consumer?

The aim of this chapter is to address these questions, by relating the theoretical analyses of Chapters Two to Four to several important empirical studies. Since all of the above questions are interrelated, a concluding section draws together the separate parts of the chapter.

5.1 Profits of Commercial Firms and Speculators

The average profits of commercial firms ($i = 0$) and all futures speculators ($i = s$) are important for several reasons. First, a formula is derived (equation 5.9) which relates the expected profits of all speculators *vis-à-vis* commercial firms to the optimal amount of price discovery that can be generated by futures markets. Hence, an objective measure of the price discovery process can be derived. Secondly, the magnitude of expected profits of various groups enables me to evaluate the importance of the diverse precisions hypothesis developed in Chapter Three.

5.1.1 The Data Set

There are four important studies of the source of profits in futures markets. Two are based upon aggregated data and two are based upon data of particular firms. The former are studies by Hendrik Houthakker (1957) and Charles Rockwell (1967). The latter are studies by Blair Stewart (1949) and Michael Hartzmark (1984).

Houthakker and Rockwell utilized data reported to the Commodity Exchange Authority (CEA) predecessor of the Commodity Futures Trading Commission (CFTC). Traders whose commitments in any one futures contract exceeded the reporting limit had to report their entire position to the CEA, which classified these futures commitments as hedging or speculative. A given firm could have some of its commitments classified in both categories. The unit of analysis is a speculative or hedging position. Contract holdings were contained in month-end reports. The reported (i.e. large) hedging and speculative positions are held by professionals. The nonreporting (i.e. small) commitments constituting the open interest are those of small traders who are believed to be amateur speculators.

Houthakker's study is the classic analysis, with respect to the techniques used, of aggregate data. To estimate profits and losses it was assumed that the commitments of a group of traders that existed at the end of the month were opened at the average price during that month and closed out at the average price during the following month. The profit or loss of the position is the product of the end of the month position and the change in the average price. Rockwell followed Houthakker's approach but had a broader coverage. While Houthakker had 324 monthly observations on three markets from 1937–40 and 1946–52, Rockwell had 7900 semi-monthly observations covering 25 markets from 1947–65. He did not have positions cross-classified, as Houthakker had for corn and wheat, so Rockwell used for all of his commodities the same method that Houthakker used for cotton. The percentage distribution of open commitments among futures contracts was assumed to be the same for all traders.

Stewart was primarily concerned with the trading behaviour of small speculators in grain futures. Statistics were analysed on the futures operations of nearly 9000 traders during 1924–32 and involving more than 400 000 individual futures transactions.

Hartzmark utilized a data base from the CFTC reports on the end of the day positions of large traders, during the period 1 July 1977 to 31 December 1982. He had a daily history of traders, identified by code number, from the first time the trader reached a reportable level. If the trader's hedge position dominated, Hartzmark classified the trader as a *commercial trader*. If the trader's speculative position dominated, Hartzmark classified the firm as a *noncommercial trader*. He followed each firm over the entire period. There are two main differences between the data set used by Hartzmark and that used by Houthakker and Rockwell. Hartzmark focuses upon types of traders (commercial, noncommercial) over time, whereas Houthakker and Rockwell focus upon types of positions over time. Hartzmark uses profits or losses using a daily data base, whereas Houthakker and Rockwell use end of the month positions.

5.1.2 Theoretical Analysis

The empirical studies are analysed in terms of the theory developed in Chapters Two to Four. First, profit functions are derived for commercial firms and noncommercial firms, which correspond to the commercial firms ($i = 0$) and all futures speculators ($i = s$) in Chapter Two. This facilitates an analysis of Hartzmark's data.

Secondly, profit functions are derived for professional ($i = 1$) and amateur ($i = 2$) speculators, when there is no net hedging pressure by producers. These two approaches permit an analysis of the empirical studies.

Profits of futures speculators π_s are described by

$$\pi_s(t + 1) = [p(t + 1) - q_{t+1}(t)]Z(t) \tag{5.2}$$

the product of the position $Z(t)$ and the difference

$$p(t + 1) - q_{t+1}(t)$$

between the cash price at $t + 1$ and the futures price at time t of a $t + 1$ contract. A positive (negative) $Z(t)$ corresponds to a long (short) position. The position $Z(t)$ is derived from optimizing behaviour (equation 2.41), and is repeated as

$$Z(t) = w_s[E_s p(t + 1; t) - q_{t+1}(t)] \tag{5.3}$$

The market-clearing futures price is equation (5.4) (based upon equations 2.45–2.47), a discounted value of a linear combination of the subjectively expected prices by commercials ($i = 0$) and futures speculators ($i = s$):

$$q_{t+1}(t) = (1 - \delta) E_m p(t + 1; t) \tag{5.4a}$$

$$q_{t+1}(t) = (1 - \delta)[\gamma_0 E_0 p(t + 1; t)$$
$$+ (1 - \gamma_0) E_s p(t + 1; t)] \tag{5.4b}$$

The term in brackets is the subjectively expected price by the market $E_m p(t + 1; t)$, which is a weighted average of the prices subjectively expected by the two groups ($i = 0, s$).

Discount factor δ reflects the bias or backwardation resulting from a risk premium (see equations 2.44–2.47) and γ_0 is the weight of the producers in determining the futures price:

$$\delta \equiv \frac{h/w}{E_m p(t + 1; t)} \gtreqless 0 \tag{5.4c}$$

$$\gamma_0 \equiv \frac{w_c}{w_c + w_s} \tag{5.4d}$$

In Figure 2.5, quantity $(1 - \delta)$ is $q_1/E_m p$ or $q_2/E_m p$, depending upon the net hedging pressure when the demand for futures by noncommercials is NC. In that figure, it is assumed that all groups have the same subjective expectations of the mean price $E_m p$.

As explained in Chapter Three, there are two components of the forecast error ϵ_i between the subjectively expected price by the i group and the realized price. The first component is the Bayesian error y_i between the subjective and objective expectations. The second component is the unavoidable error η between the objective expectation and the realization. Equations (3.3a)–(3.3c) are repeated here as equations (5.5a)–(5.5c):

$$\epsilon_i(t+1) = E_i p(t+1; t) - p(t+1) \qquad\qquad i = 0, 1, 2 \quad (5.5a)$$

$$\epsilon_i(t+1) = [E_i p(t+1; t) - E p(t+1)] + [E p(t+1) - p(t+1)]$$

$$s = 1 + 2 \qquad (5.5b)$$

$$\epsilon_i(t+1) = \qquad\qquad y_i(t) \qquad\qquad + \qquad \eta. \qquad (5.5c)$$

To remind the reader of the distinction between the two components of the error, consider the following statistical problem. A large urn contains many numbers, where the mean number is Ep and there is a variance σ^2 to the numbers. A person is asked at time t to predict the number to be drawn at time $t + 1$. He has a subjective estimate $E_i p(t+1; t)$ of the mean number, based upon whatever information or misinformation that he has at time t, and hence predicts that number $E_i p(t+1; t)$ will be drawn. When a drawing is made, number $p(t+1)$ results.

Forecast error $E_i p(t+1; t) - p(t+1)$ can be considered to be the sum of two errors. One component is $(E_i p - E p)$, the difference between the prior subjective belief of the mean and the objective mean. This is the Bayesian error $y_i(t)$ whose statistical properties were analysed in Chapter Three. Equation (3.6) showed that these Bayesian errors are serially correlated, and equation (3.10) showed that the variance of the Bayesian error is positively related to the variance σ^2 and is inversely related to the cumulative number of items sampled. The second component of the forecast error is $[Ep - p(t+1)]$, the deviation between the mean number in the urn and the actual number drawn. This is an unavoidable error due to the variance σ^2.

Using equations (5.5a) in equations (5.3) and (5.4), and substituting the result in equation (5.2), the profits of the noncommercials (futures speculators s) is

$$\pi_s(t+1) = [\delta p(t+1) - (1-\delta)\epsilon_m] w_s [\delta p(t+1)$$

$$+ \epsilon_s - (1-\delta)\epsilon_m] \qquad (5.6)$$

The expected profits $E_s \pi(t+1)$ of the noncommercials (i.e. futures speculators) are now derived. The stochastic variables are the forecast errors ϵ_m and ϵ_s, and the realized price is normalized at unity. That is, corresponding to any realized price $p(t+1)$, the futures price $q_{t+1}(t)$ and the subjectively expected prices $E_i(t + 1; t)$ are stochastic.

Equation (5.6) can be written as

$$\pi_s(t + 1) = w_s[\delta - (1 - \delta)\epsilon_m]^2 + w_s\epsilon_s[\delta - (1 - \delta)\epsilon_m] \quad (5.6a)$$

when $p(t + 1) = 1$.

It is convenient to assume that, on average, the forecast error is zero $E(\epsilon_i) = 0$. Then the expected profits of the noncommercials (i.e. futures speculators s) are

$$E\pi_s = w_s[\delta^2 - (1 - \delta)E(\epsilon_m, \epsilon_s) + (1 - \delta)^2 \text{var } \epsilon_m] \quad (5.7)$$

The economic implication of this equation emerges clearly, if the following relation is used. Parameter b in equation (5.8) is the slope of the linear relation between the forecast error ϵ_s of the non-commercials (speculators) and the market forecast error ϵ_m (see Figure 5.1):

$$b = \text{cov } (\epsilon_m, \epsilon_s)/\text{var } \epsilon_m = E(\epsilon_m, \epsilon_s)/\text{var } \epsilon_m \quad (5.8)$$

since the mean errors are assumed to be zero.

Using equation (5.8) in (5.7), the expected profits of the non-commercials s are derived:

$$E\pi_s = w_s\delta[\delta - (1 - \delta) \text{var } \epsilon_m] + (1 - \delta)w_s(1 - b) \text{var } \epsilon_m \quad (5.9)$$

This is the basic equation of the analysis.

There are two components of the expected profits $E\pi_s$ in equation (5.9). The first component is the risk premium paid by the commercials to the noncommercials, s, due to net hedging pressure. This is reflected by distances $(E_m p - q_1)$ or $(q_2 - E_m p)$ in Figure 2.5. The second term arises from differential forecasting ability, resulting from the diverse precisions discussed in Chapter Three.

Since the expected profits of all noncommercials (speculators) $E\pi_s$ are equal to the expected losses of the commercials, the expected profits of the commercials on their operations in futures $E\pi_0$ are $-E\pi_s$:

$$E\pi_0 = -E\pi_s \quad (5.10)$$

This relation is used in subsequent analysis.

Figure 5.1 is helpful in understanding the returns to differential forecasting ability.

5.1.2.1 Diverse Precisions
If there were no risk premium due to net hedging pressure, the expected profits of noncommercial firms are

$$E\pi_s(\delta = 0) = w_s(1 - b) \text{ var } \epsilon_m \qquad (5.11)$$

using equation (5.9) when $\delta = 0$.

Consider Figure 5.1. Regress the error

$$\epsilon_s(t + 1) = E_s p(t + 1; t) - p(t + 1)$$

of the futures speculators upon the market forecast error

$$\epsilon_m(t + 1) = E_m p(t + 1; t) - p(t + 1).$$

Slope b of the regression is equation (5.8) above. When b is less (greater) than unity, the regression is FF' (GG') in Figure 5.1. When there is no bias ($\delta = 0$) equation (5.4a) states that the futures price is equal to be subjectively expected price by the market:

$$q_{t+1}(t) = E_m p(t + 1; t)$$

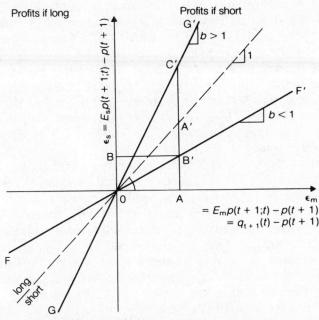

Figure 5.1   Lines FF' and GG' represent linear regressions between the forecast errors of speculators (noncommercials) and those of the market. When there is no bias (backwardation), the 45 degree line represents the futures price. When the market forecast error ϵ_m is positive (negative), profits are made by being short (long) futures. If the speculators' error is described by FF' (GG'), they will be short (long) futures. Therefore expected speculative profits (losses) will be made if the regression line is FF' (GG').

when $\delta = 0$. Then, the market forecast error $\epsilon_m(t+1)$ is

$$\epsilon_m(t+1) = q_{t+1}(t) - p(t+1)$$

The horizontal axis plots the market forecast error ϵ_m, the deviation of the futures price from the subsequently realized price. The 45 degree line maps the futures price deviation on the horizontal axis to the vertical axis. When the market forecast error $\epsilon_m(t+1)$ is positive (negative), profits would be made by being short (long). This is noted in Figure 5.1.

Futures speculators will be short (long) depending upon the difference between the futures price and their subjectively expected price (see equation 5.3). The futures price is the 45 degree line, and the subjectively expected price is the regression line FF' (GG') in Figure 5.1, both measured as deviations from the subsequently realized price. If the futures price were 0A = AA', the subjectively expected price by the futures speculators implied by line FF' which has a slope of less than unity would be AB' < AA'. Since $E_s p(t+1;t) - q_{t+1}(t) = (AB') - (AA') < 0$, futures speculators would be short futures. This is precisely the profitable position when the market forecast error is 0A. A similar argument applies when the market forecast error is negative. *Consequently, when b is less than unity, futures speculators profit from their differential forecasting ability.*[1] *These profits arise from making a smaller forecast error than does the market as a whole (i.e. $1 > b$), because the market determines the futures price.*

Similarly, suppose that b exceeded unity so that the subjectively expected price $E_s p(t+1;t)$ were described by line GG'. When the futures price is 0A = AA', the speculators have a subjectively expected price of AC'. They are therefore long futures (equation 5.3). But, when the market error $\epsilon_m = 0A$, profits are made by being short futures. That is why expected profits are negative. When b exceeds unity, futures speculators have poorer forecasting ability than the market; and they lose on average. If b were equal to unity, then all groups are similar in forecasting ability; and no expected profits are made in the absence of net hedging pressure.

A more explicit analysis of equation (5.11), the source of profits from differential forecasting ability is based upon the analysis in Chapter Three.

The forecast errors ϵ_i are sums of Bayesian errors y_i and unavoidable errors η as described by equations (5.5a)–(5.5c) above. Therefore, coefficient b in equation (5.8) can be written as

$$b = \frac{\text{cov} \, (\epsilon_s, \epsilon_m)}{\text{var} \, \epsilon_m} = \frac{\text{cov} \, [y_s + \eta, \, \gamma_0(y_0 + \eta) + (1 - \gamma_0)(y_s + \eta)]}{\text{var} \, [\gamma_0(y_0 + \eta) + (1 - \gamma_0)(y_s + \eta)]}$$

in terms of the basic sources of error: unavoidable error η and Bayesian errors (y_0, y_s0.

The crucial quantity $(1 - b) \, \text{var} \, \epsilon_m$ in equation (5.11) is then described by

$$(1 - b) \, \text{var} \, \epsilon_m = \gamma_0^2 \, \text{var} \, y_0 - \gamma_0(1 - \gamma_0) \, \text{var} \, y_s$$
$$+ \gamma_0\{[2(1 - \gamma_0) - 1] \, \text{cov} \, (y_0, y_s)$$
$$+ \text{cov} \, (y_0 - y_s, \eta)\} \tag{5.12}$$

A simplifying assumption which makes economic sense is that the term in braces involving covariances is very small relative to the first two terms. Hence, equation (5.12a) is an approximation to equation (5.12):

$$(1 - b) \, \text{var} \, \epsilon_m = \gamma_0^2 \, \text{var} \, y_0 - \gamma_0(1 - \gamma_0) \, \text{var} \, y_s \tag{5.12a}$$

Define the quality Q of the forecasting ability of the noncommercials (speculators) to that of the commercials as the ratio of the variance of the Bayesian errors of the commercials to that of the noncommercials:

$$Q = \text{var} \, y_0 / \text{var} \, y_s \tag{5.13}$$

Define the relative weight of the noncommercials as ω where

$$\omega = \frac{1 - \gamma_0}{\gamma_0} = \frac{w_s}{w_c} \tag{5.14}$$

Then equation (5.12a) can be expressed as

$$(1 - b) \, \text{var} \, \epsilon_m = \gamma_0^2 \, \text{var} \, y_s \cdot (Q - \omega) \tag{5.15}$$

Therefore, using equation (5.15) in (5.11), the expected profits of the noncommercials, when there is no bias resulting from net hedging pressure, is

$$E\pi_s(\delta = 0) = w_s \delta_0^2 \, \text{var} \, y_s \cdot (Q - \omega) \tag{5.16}$$

The sign of $(1 - b)$ is the same as the sign of $(Q - \omega)$. When there is no bias resulting from net hedging pressure, profits are made by the group whose quality of forecasting Q exceeds their relative weight in the market. Coefficient b will be less than unity for the noncommercials (i.e. line FF' in Figure 5.1) if their Q exceeds their relative weight ω.

Consider a different decomposition of market agents. Suppose that the futures market just contains professional ($i = 1$) and amateur ($i = 2$) speculators who are trading with each other in a zero sum game. This would correspond to the situation in Chapter Three where $\gamma_0 = 0$ and $\gamma_1 + \gamma_2 = 1$. The futures price would be determined by the condition that the excess demand for futures by all futures speculators is zero. It is shown in Appendix C that, in such a case, the expected profits of the professionals $E\pi_1$ (equal to the losses of the amateurs $-E\pi_2$) is

$$E\pi_1 = \frac{(1 - \gamma_1)^2}{\beta_1 \operatorname{var} p} (Q - \omega) \operatorname{var} \epsilon_1 \tag{5.17a}$$

where

$$Q = \operatorname{var} y_2/\operatorname{var} y_1 > 1 \tag{5.17b}$$

and

$$\omega = \gamma_1/(1 - \gamma_1) = w_1/w_2 = (\xi_1/\beta_1)/(\xi_2/\beta_2) \tag{5.17c}$$

Expected profits of the professionals are proportional to quantity $(Q - \omega)$, where Q is the forecasting ability of professionals relative to amateurs (equation 5.17b) and ω is the relative weight of the professionals to that of the amateurs in determining the futures price. Expected profits of the professionals will be positive if their relative forecasting ability exceeds their relative weight in determining the futures price.

5.1.2.2   Optimal Price Discovery

Optimal price discovery is a situation where the Bayesian error $y_m(t) = E_m p(T; t) - Ep(T)$ converges to zero. In a stochastic system, the convergence is measured by the variance. Hence, optimal price discovery is a situation where the variance of the market Bayesian error is minimal. It was shown in Chapter Three that, in the limit when the objective mean $Ep(T)$ is unchanged, the expectation of the Bayesian error is zero. I now show that optimal price discovery occurs when $Q - \omega$.

At any time, the variance of the market Bayesian error depends upon the composition and forecasting abilities of the various groups (i, j) in the market:

$$\operatorname{var} y_m = \operatorname{var} [\gamma_i y_i + (1 - \gamma_i) y_j] \tag{5.18}$$

If the Bayesian errors of the two groups are independent, then the variance of the market Bayesian error is

$$\text{var } y_m = \gamma_i^2 \text{ var } y_i + (1 - \gamma_i)^2 \text{ var } y_j \qquad (5.19)$$

This variance is at a minimum with respect to composition γ_i when equation (5.20) is satisfied:

$$\frac{\text{var } y_j}{\text{var } y_i} = \frac{\gamma_i}{1 - \gamma_i} \qquad (5.20)$$

$$Q = \omega \qquad (5.20a)$$

The left-hand side is the quality Q of the forecasting ability of group i relative to group j. The right-hand side is the weight of group i relative to that of group j. The dichotomy (i, j) could be (a) noncommercials $(i = s = 1 + 2)$ and commercials $(j = 0)$; (b) professional $(i = 1)$ and amateur $(j = 2)$ speculators.

The conclusion of this section is that, in the absence of a bias resulting from net hedging pressure, expected profits are made by the group whose quality of forecasting Q exceeds its relative weight ω. The optimal price discovery occurs when $Q = \omega$ so that there are no expected profits.

5.1.2.3 *Sources of Profits to Noncommercials*
A view of the futures market that frequently appears in the literature[2] is as follows. Producers are net short hedgers who are willing to pay a premium to avoid risk. Futures speculators and producers both have MRE, i.e. have equal forecasting ability because they have the same knowledge of the objective distribution of the subsequent cash price. Commercial firms are willing to pay a risk premium to equally knowledgeable speculators by selling a futures contract to them below the commonly shared MRE subsequent cash price. Futures speculators therefore gain on average at the expense of producers by the amount of bias or backwardation. Denote this as the *'Backwardation MRE' hypothesis.*

A different and more general point of view is implied by equations (5.9) and (5.15), which can be written as

$$E\pi_s = w_s \delta[\delta - (1 - \delta) \text{ var } \epsilon_m] + w_s (1 - \delta)\gamma_0^2 \text{ var } y_s, (Q - \omega)$$

$$\underset{\text{bias}}{\phantom{E\pi_s = w_s \delta[\delta - (1 - \delta) \text{ var } \epsilon_m]}} \quad \underset{\text{diverse precisions}}{\phantom{+ w_s (1 - \delta)\gamma_0^2 \text{ var } y_s, (Q - \omega)}}$$

$$(5.21)$$

which is drawn in Figure 5.2. There are several interesting implications of this equation. First, the expected profits of all futures

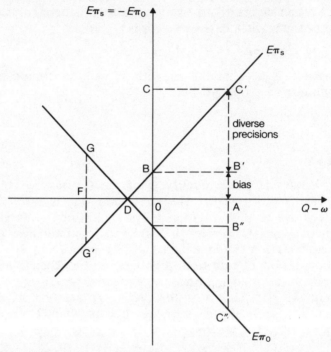

Figure 5.2   The expected profits of speculators (commercials) are $E\pi_s(E\pi_0)$. They consist of two parts. Quantity OB comes from backwardation or bias. The rest arises from differential forecasting ability resulting from diverse precisions. Quantity $Q = \text{var } y_0/\text{var } y_s$ represents the relative forecasting ability of the speculators and $\omega = w_s/w_0$ represents their relative weight in the market. If $(Q - \omega) = 0A$, then expected profits will be $0C = 0B + BC$. The backwardation yields OB of profits and BC arises from superior forecasting ability.

speculators *vis-à-vis* producers consists of two parts. One part arises from the assumption of risk (first term) and the other part arises from their differential forecasting ability (second term). Secondly, the profits to speculators resulting from the differential forecasting ability are positively related to quantity $(Q - \omega)$, where Q is the variance of the forecast error of commercials relative to that of all futures speculators, and ω is the relative weight of futures speculators to commercials in determining the futures price. Thirdly, the intercept term (OB in Figure 5.2) reflects the expected profits of the noncommercials if there were no Bayesian errors. The Backwardation MRE hypothesis is that the expected profits of the futures speculators are given by the first term in equation (5.21) which is the intercept term in Figure 5.2. Graphically, this source of profits is described in Figure 2.5. All groups have the same expectations (i.e. have MRE) but the futures price differs from $E_m p$ according to the direction and magnitude of net hedging pressure. Thus the expected profits of the noncommercials are $(E_m p - q_1)Z_1$ or $(q_2 - E_m p)Z_2$ in Figure 2.5, equal to $w_s(E_m p - q)^2$. Fourthly, when there is no net hedging pressure by producers, the expected profits of the professional speculators are proportional to quantity $(Q - \omega)$, where Q is the variance of the forecast error of amateurs relative to that of the professionals and ω is the weight of the professionals to the amateurs in determining the futures price. Expected profits of the professionals arise from the differential forecasting ability. Fifthly, the variance of the market forecast error relative to that of producers is at a minimum when the expected profits of futures speculators is zero. Call this view the *'diverse precisions hypothesis'* or *asymptotically rational expectations* (ARE) hypothesis. The Backwardation MRE hypothesis is a special case of the ARE hypothesis.

5.1.3   An Interpretation of the Empirical Studies

In this section, the four main empirical studies (cited in Section 5.1.1) are interpreted on the basis of the equations in Section 5.1.2. It is shown that the Backwardation + MRE hypothesis is inconsistent with the evidence whereas the 'diverse precisions' or ARE hypothesis is consistent with the data.

Houthakker's seminal study can be summarized in Table 5.1. It relates the profits (losses) of large hedgers, large speculators and small traders (who are primarily speculators) to the distance from maturity of futures contracts in corn and wheat.

The main findings are as follows. In terms of total profits, large speculators gain, large hedgers lose and small speculators lose. On nearby contracts (one to six months to maturity), large speculators gain and small speculators lose. Large hedgers make small losses in corn and large profits in wheat. Thus we can say that small speculators lose to the professionals (speculators and hedgers) on nearby contracts. On distant contracts (seven to eleven months to maturity) small speculators gained and large hedgers lost. Large speculators lost in corn and gained in wheat. Houthakker concludes that professional speculators show definite evidence of forecasting skill and that amateur speculators have no skill in forecast-

Table 5.1 Net profits and losses of three categories of traders by distance from maturity of futures contracts ($ million)

Months from maturity	Corn			Wheat		
	Large hedgers	Large speculators	Small traders	Large hedgers	Large speculators	Small traders
1	−2.59	+4.37	−1.78	−1.04	+4.57	−3.53
2	−1.47	+5.29	−3.82	+8.90	+4.03	−12.93
3	+0.59	−0.23	−0.36	+16.01	+4.13	−20.14
4	+3.85	−1.25	−2.61	−3.32	+5.25	−1.93
5	−0.54	+2.57	−2.02	+5.73	+1.72	−7.44
6	−2.63	+3.13	−0.50	−9.45	+5.00	+4.45
7	−1.87	+0.48	+1.39	−5.68	+1.82	+3.86
8	−0.84	−1.08	+1.92	−8.26	+1.33	+6.93
9	−0.56	−0.60	+1.16	−9.06	+0.67	+8.39
10	−0.03	−0.77	+0.80	−0.16	−0.71	+0.86
11	−0.01	−0.27	+0.28	+0.06	−0.67	+0.61
Total	−6.09	+11.62	−5.53	−6.28	+27.16	−20.88
1–6	−2.79	+13.88	−11.09	+16.82	+24.71	−41.53
7–11	−3.30	−2.26	+5.56	−23.09	+2.45	+20.65

Source: Houthakker, 1957, Table 6

ing prices on nearby contracts. They do much better in the more distant contracts where they profit from backwardation.

Variable $(Q - \omega)$ relative forecasting ability of the professionals to the amateurs determines the expected profits of the professional speculators. In terms of Table 5.1, quantity $(Q - \omega)$ is positive. Houthakker suggests the following explanation for the superior results of the professionals on nearby compared to distant contracts.

The price behavior of the near futures depends to a large extent on the magnitude and ownership of deliverable stocks at the relevant terminals (Chicago, Kansas City, and Minneapolis for wheat, Chicago for corn), and this is a matter on which nonprofessionals cannot easily inform themselves. Price movements in the more distant contracts, on the other hand, are influenced mainly by basic supply and demand factors such as crop prospects, the general economic outlook, or government policy. In evaluating the latter factors the professionals have no particular comparative advantage. Indeed it is often profitable for them to use their superior knowledge by taking a long or short position in the near futures, at the same time taking an opposite position in the more distant deliveries in order to limit their risks .... By taking the other side of the distant half of these spreads the small traders may then earn a risk premium from the professionals; the other side of the near half is more likely to be taken by the hedgers, who rarely go into distant futures. (Houthakker, 1957)

In the nearby contract, the professional speculators have many more bits of information concerning the distribution of the sub-sequent cash price than do the amateurs. Professionals are in the market continually, purchase and sell from diverse parties who are spread over wide geographical areas and have up-to-date informa-tion. Amateurs[3] purchase or sell sporadically, obtain their informa-tion from brokers or newspapers, use technical analysis or other chartist techniques and hence have obsolete information or are misinformed.

According to equation (3.10), the variance of the difference between the subjective, $E_i p(T; t)$, and objective, $Ep(T; t)$, expecta-tions of the subsequent cash price, var $[E_i p(T; t) - Ep(T; t)]$, is inversely related to the product, N_i, of the sample size taken each time and the number of samples, and is positively related to the variance, σ^2, of the cash price:

$$\text{var } [E_i p(T; t) - Ep(T; t)] = \sigma^2/N_i \qquad i = 0, 1, 2$$

Therefore, the variance of the difference between the subjective and objective means of amateurs $(i = 2)$ relative to professionals $(i = 1)$ is N_1/N_2. The forecast error ϵ_i (given by equation 5.5b) is

$$\epsilon_i(T) = [E_i p(T; t) - Ep(T)] + [Ep(T) - p(T)]$$

Then the variance of the error (given by equation 3.11) is

$$\text{var } \epsilon_i = \sigma^2 \left(1 + \frac{1}{N_i}\right)$$

where N_i is the product of the sample size and number of samples. Consequently, parameter $Q = \text{var } \epsilon_2/\text{var } \epsilon_1$ is directly related to $N_1/N_2 > 1$. Since Q is greater than unity, the smaller ω the weight of professional to amateur speculators, the greater will be the profits of the professional speculators.

Houthakker's explanation of the lower profits, or even losses, of the large speculators in the distant future is that professional speculators limit their risks by spreading. A group of professional speculators take long $(+)$ or short $(-)$ positions $Z(t)$ in the nearby contract which matures at time $t + 1$ and an opposite position in the more distant contract which matures at time $t + 2$. Their profits are

$$\pi^*(t+1) = \{[q^*_{t+1}(t+1) - q_{t+1}(t)]$$
$$- [q^*_{t+2}(t+1) - q_{t+2}(t)]\}Z(t) \qquad (5.22)$$

A nearby contract is purchased at price $q_{t+1}(t)$ and a distant contract is sold at price $q_{t+2}(t)$, at time t. These positions will be reversed at time $t+1$ at prices $q^*_{t+1}(t+1)$ and $q^*_{t+2}(t+1)$ respectively.

Define the spread $b(t)$ as the difference between the more distant and nearer future:

$$b(t) = q_{t+2}(t) - q_{t+1}(t) \qquad (5.23a)$$

$$b^*(t+1) = q^*_{t+2}(t+1) - q^*_{t+1}(t+1) \qquad (5.23b)$$

Using the definition of the spread, the profit of the speculator is equation (18):

$$\pi^*(t+1) = [b(t) - b^*(t+1)]Z(t) \qquad (5.24)$$

A spread is sold at time t at price $b(t)$ and is expected to be repurchased at $t+1$ at price $b^*(t+1)$. If the speculator chooses position $Z(t)$ to maximize the expected utility of profits (equation 2.37), then the optimum spread position is

$$Z(t) = \frac{b(t) - Eb(t+1; t)}{\beta \, \text{var} \, b} \qquad (5.25)$$

Position $Z(t)$ is proportional to $b(t) - Eb(t+1; t)$. Profits will be made on a long spread $Z(t) > 0$ if the spread narrows: $b(t+1)$ is less than $b(t)$. Risk is subsumed under the variance of the spread var b, which is substantially less than the variance of the absolute price var $q_T(t)$. It is irrelevant if there are losses on one leg of the spread, as long as the total on both legs is profitable. Houthakker's results are easily understood by writing equation (5.25) in full as

$$Z(t) = \frac{[Eq_{t+1}(t+1) - q_{t+1}(t)] - [Eq_{t+2}(t+1) - q_{t+2}(t)]}{\beta \, \text{var} \, b}$$

$$(5.25a)$$

Profits on a long position in the nearby future are the first term in brackets. Losses on a short position in the more distant future are the second term in brackets. Houthakker showed that: (a) in corn, profits were made on the nearby which exceeded the losses on the more distant future; (b) in wheat, profits were made on both the nearby and the distant future. The conclusion is that large speculators are better able to forecast price than can the market as a whole. In terms of equation (5.8) or Figure 5.1 coefficient $b = \text{cov}\,(\epsilon_s, \epsilon_m)/\text{var}\,\epsilon_m$ is less than unity: the professional speculators make smaller forecasting errors than does the market.

Rockwell's study enables us to estimate the sources of profits of the professional speculators. In terms of the theory developed in equation (5.21) above, his results imply that the profits of the professional speculators are primarily due to their superior forecasting ability, and only a small part is due to backwardation.[4] This again contradicts the Backwardation MRE hypothesis. If total profits of futures speculators are OC in Figure 5.2, then OB due to backwardation (first term in equation 5.21) is small relative to quantity BC which is due to differential forecasting ability. The latter corresponds to the second term in equation (5.21). A detailed analysis of Rockwell's results follows (Table 5.2).

Total profits of large speculators, large hedgers and small traders must sum to zero; therefore, only two groups need be

Table 5.2 Annual profits of large speculators, large hedgers and small traders in all markets and small markets 1947–65 ($n = 18$)

		Large speculators	Large hedgers	Small traders
All markets				
1	Total 10^6	178.80	−176.60	−3.40
2	Mean (m)	9.94	−9.82	−0.18
3	Standard deviation (s)	11.24	35.43	25.20
4	t_1	3.75**	−0.85	−0.03
5	Percentage profitable	83 (15/18)	56 (10/18)	39 (7/18)
6	t_2	2.83**	0.69	−0.94
Small markets				
1	Total 10^6	61	6.50	−69.50
2	Mean (m)	3.40	0.37	−3.84
3	Standard deviation (s)	4.38	14.85	11.46
4	t_1	3.30**	0.11	−1.42
5	Percentage profitable	83 (15/18)	56 (10/18)	28 (5/18)
6	t_2	2.83**	0.69	−1.89**

Notes: The value of $t_1 = m/(s/\sqrt{n})$ concerns the distribution of sample means. The value of $t_2 = (m - np)/\sqrt{npq} = (m - n/2)/\sqrt{n/4}$ concerns the number of profitable years, where p is the probability of a profitable year. The null hypothesis is that $p = 0.5$. Significant at 1 per cent (**) or 5 per cent (*) level.
Source: Rockwell, 1967, Tables 4 and 5

studied together. Rockwell examined three large markets (wheat at Chicago, cotton at New York and soybeans) and 23 small markets. In all markets combined, the large speculators gain at the expense of large hedgers and small traders lose small amounts. The profits of the large speculators are significantly positive in two senses.

1   The mean profit per year is significantly greater than zero at the 1 per cent level. Row 4 contains the value of $t_1 = m/(s/\sqrt{n})$ of the distribution of the sample mean m around a population mean hypothesized to be zero.

2   Profits were made in 15 out of the 18 years, row 5. We can reject at the 1 per cent level (**) the hypothesis that the probability of a profitable year is one half. This is shown by t_2, row 6, where $t_2 = (m - n/2)/\sqrt{n/4}$. In all markets combined, the losses of the small trader are not significantly different from zero.

In the small markets, the hedgers' profits were positive but not significantly different from zero in the two senses indicated in rows 4 and 6. The mean profit was not significantly different from zero and the fraction of profitable years was not significantly different from one half. Large speculators made significant profits in small markets. The mean profit was significantly different from zero at the 1 per cent level and the fraction of profitable years was significantly greater than one half. In the 23 small markets, the profits of the large speculators were at the expense of the small speculators. Speculative profits in these markets could not have been produced by backwardation because hedging positions were not unprofitable. In terms of the theory, speculative profits occurred because $(Q - \omega)$ was positive. The value of $Q = \text{var}\,\epsilon_2/\text{var}\,\epsilon_1$, the variance of the forecast error of amateurs to that of the professionals, exceeded the weights of the professionals to amateurs in determining the futures price.

Table 5.3 converts the profits into a rate of return R_i ($i = 0, 1, 2$) in large, small and all markets. This is derived by dividing the ratio of gross profits by the dollar value of contracts held. This is a gross underestimate of both positive and negative rates of return for the following reasons cited by Rockwell

Omission of commisions causes a serious upward bias in the results for all groups. This bias is apt to be strongest for nonreporting traders who have the greatest relative overlap of long and short positions and who are least likely to own a seat on the exchange. However, the use of the value of the contract in the denominator introduces a gross understatement of the true return.

Actual margin requirements are only five or ten per cent of the contract value and, even after allowing for a one-to-one 'safety reserve', the true rate of return would be five to ten times larger than that measured here. (Rockwell, 1967)

Table 5.3 Division of rate of return by groups according to market and source

Group	Large markets	Small markets	All markets
1 Hedgers			
(a) Trend	−2.1	−0.7	−1.0
(b) Special	−0.9	0.8	−0.6
(c) Total R_0	−3.0	0.1	−1.7
2 Large speculators			
(a) Trend	2.2	0.7	1.3
(b) Special	5.0	3.9	4.8
(c) Total R_1	7.2	4.6	6.1
3 Small traders			
(a) Trend	0.7	0.0	0.4
(b) Special	−0.1	−1.2	−0.4
(c) Total R_2	0.6	−1.2	−0.0

Source: Rockwell, 1967, Table 8

If any backwardation existed, it would have to arise in the large markets because hedgers did not lose in the small markets, where their return was $R_0 = 0.1$ per cent. They did lose in large markets, where their return $R_0 = -3$ per cent. Consequently, the next question is what was the magnitude of the bias or backwardation?

Backwardation or bias is the return which the speculator receives from taking a position opposite to the hedgers. Rockwell calculated the return on the total long open interest. If backwardation exists it should be positive when hedgers are short and negative when hedgers are long. Table 5.4 contains the returns on the long open interest.

Row 1 indicates that in large markets there is a return from backwardation when hedgers are net short. This does not occur in small markets. Row 2 indicates that there is no return from backwardation, in either large or small markets, when hedgers are net long. Instead of negative returns on the long open interest there are positive net returns when hedgers are net long. An analysis of the rate of return from backwardation (Rockwell, 1967, Chart 2)

Table 5.4   Return on the long open interest

		Large markets	Small markets	All markets
1	When hedgers are net short	6.1	−0.4	3.7
2	When hedgers are net long	6.3	4.0	5.7
3	Rate of backwardation	4.0	−0.8	2.3
4	Rate of backwardation divided by return to large speculators	56	−17	37

Notes: Row 4 is row 3 divided by row 2c in Table 5.3.
Source: Rockwell, 1967, Tables 7 and 8

indicates that: (a) in the 23 smaller markets the return is distributed around zero; (b) it is positive in the three larger markets but it only results when hedgers are net short.

A comparison of row 3, Table 5.4, with the returns R_1 to large speculators in row 2c of Table 5.3 indicates the fraction of the total return to speculators due to backwardation (row 4 in Table 5.4). Backwardation can account for 37 per cent of the returns to speculators in all markets and 56 per cent in the three large markets.

Rockwell decomposed the returns, in Table 5.3, to the three groups. Rows 1a, 2a and 3a measure the extent to which the trader's return can be described by a naive strategy of being constantly are one side of the market. It is the return from being net long (short) on the average in markets where prices rise (decline) on average. Rockwell called this 'basic skill', and it is referred to as 'trend' in Table 5.3. 'Special forecasting skill' is defined as the residual between the total return R_i and the return to being, on average, on the correct side of the market. A comparison of rows 2b and 2c of Table 5.3 shows that large speculators have special skill to profit from varying their positions from period to period to profit from short-run price movements.

Conclusions, based upon Rockwell's data, are as follows.

1 Large speculators make substantial profits in both large and small markets.
2 In large markets, the gains are due both to backwardation and to their special forecasting ability.
3 In small markets, the returns are exclusively due to special forecasting ability.

4   Small speculators break even in all markets, gross of commissions. Their losses in small markets are offset by their gross gains in large markets. In the small markets, they lose to the professional speculators. In large markets, they gain at the expense of the hedgers. In no market do they exhibit special forecasting ability.

Hartzmark reclassified the data of reporting (i.e. large) traders in terms of type of firm. If the firm's hedge position tended to dominate, it was classified as a *commercial* firm. If its speculative position tended to dominate, it was classified as a *noncommercial firm*. This classification corresponds to the entities in Chapters Two and Three. Tables 5.5 to 5.7 summarize Hartzmark's results concerning daily profits of reporting (i.e. large) traders from 1 July 1977 to 31 December 1981 in nine markets. The main results are as follows.

1   The reporting (i.e. large) trading firms combined made profits on futures in each of the nine markets examined. This implies that small (i.e. nonreporting) traders lost in each of the nine markets.
2   Reporting commercial firms made profits in eight of the nine markets.
3   Their profits generally arose from their short positions.
4   Noncommercial reporting firms made profits in six of the nine markets.
5   Their profits generally arose from their short positions.

Table 5.5   Total dollar returns, all reporting traders

Commodity	Total ($ million)	Net long ($ million)	Net short ($ million)
Oats	10.28	−0.85	11.14
CBT wheat	59.14	−117.20	176.85
MGE wheat	19.01	15.43	3.58
KBT wheat	2.15	−36.45	38.72
Pork bellies	80.56	−51.65	132.20
Live cattle	66.85	250.25	−183.30
Feeder cattle	104.55	109.58	−5.04
T-bonds	390.02	−1012.68	1403.85
T-bills	120.44	−147.49	267.97

Source: Hartzmark, 1984, Table 3

Table 5.6   Total dollar returns, commercial traders

Commodity	Total ($ million)	Net long ($ million)	Net short ($ million)
Oats	9.63	−0.26	9.90
CBT wheat	42.94	−78.54	121.48
MGE wheat	21.17	19.03	2.14
KBT wheat	2.62	−30.96	33.69
Pork bellies	79.05	3.96	75.10
Live cattle	−130.27	24.47	−154.74
Feeder cattle	29.13	35.46	−6.31
T-bonds	559.09	−276.46	835.60
T-bills	114.96	−35.77	150.73

Source: Hartzmark, 1984, Table 3

Table 5.7   Total dollar returns, noncommercial traders

Commodity	Total returns ($ million)	Net long ($ million)	Net short ($ million)
Oats	0.64	−0.59	1.24
CBT wheat	16.19	−39.18	55.37
MGE wheat	−2.17	−3.60	1.44
KBT wheat	−0.47	−5.49	5.03
Pork bellies	1.48	−55.61	57.10
Live cattle	197.12	225.78	−28.56
Feeder cattle	75.42	74.12	1.27
T-bonds	−169.07	−736.22	568.25
T-bills	5.48	−111.72	117.24

Source: Hartzmark, 1984, Table 3

6   The profits of the four most successful commercial and non-commercial firms over the entire period were examined. Profits for the four most successful commercial firms were made on the contracts with less than 180 days to maturity, and small losses were made on the longer contracts. The major profits for the four most successful noncommercial firms were made on contracts with maturities 30–180 days. Smaller profits were made on the shorter and longer maturities.

Hartzmark's data refute the Backwardation MRE view that: (a) futures speculators and commercial firms both have MRE, i.e. have the same knowledge of the objective distribution of cash prices; (b) commercial firms pay a risk premium to equally knowledgeable futures speculators by selling a futures contract to them below the commonly shared MRE cash price; (c) commercial firms on average lose on their short positions in futures. It is seen in Table 5.6 that commercial firms profited on their short positions in seven of the nine markets, and made profits on their total futures operations in eight of the nine markets. This contradicts points (b) and (c) above. Thus the first term in equation (5.21), representing speculative profits from the 'bias' or net hedging pressure, is not a source of loss to the large commercial firms. The expected profits of the large commercial firms $E\pi_0 = -E\pi_s$ is the negative of the expected profits of the noncommercials. This is equation (5.26), the negative of equation (5.16):

$$E\pi_0 = w_s\gamma_0^2 \text{ var } y_s(\omega - Q) \tag{5.26}$$

In so far as the large commercials profit in the tables above,

$$Q = \frac{\text{var } y_0}{\text{var } y_s} < \frac{w_s}{w_0} = \omega$$

Ratio Q of the variance of the forecasting error of commercials to all futures speculators is less than the ratio of the weight of all futures speculators to producers in determining the futures price. The superior forecasting ability of large commercial firms relative to *all* futures speculators (large and small) accounts for the profits cited in Table 5.6. *Both the reporting commercials and their complement noncommercial futures speculators could not have MRE.*

In so far as all reporting traders, commercial and noncommercial combined, made profits, nonreporting (small) traders must have made losses. The latter are generally speculators. We can classify the reporting traders as the professionals ($i = 1$) and the nonreporting traders as the amateurs ($i = 2$). Equation (5.17a), repeated here, states that expected profits of the professionals $E\pi_1$ are

$$E\pi_1 = \frac{(1 - \gamma_1)^2}{\beta_1} \frac{\text{var } \epsilon_1}{\text{var } p} (Q - \omega) = -E\pi_2 \tag{5.17a}$$

$Q = \text{var } \epsilon_2/\text{var } \epsilon_1$; $\omega = \gamma_1/(1 - \gamma_1)$. Profits earned by the professionals arise from quantity $(Q - \omega)$, where Q is the variance of the forecasting error of the amateurs relative to that of the professionals.

Hartzmark's data concerning the losses of the small traders confirm the results of Stewart's earlier study. Stewart had data from one of the largest brokerage firms on the Chicago market. Trading was done on the Chicago Board of Trade during the nine years from 1 January 1924 to 31 December 1932 by 8922 different persons in the sample. These traders were mostly small speculators. Stewart's results are summarized as follows.

1   The great majority of small speculators lost money in the futures market. Their losses from trades were approximately six times their profits from trades.
2   The amateur speculator is more likely to be long than short in the futures market. In general, the chance for success in grain futures trading did not differ from one occupation to another.

Stewart noted the following.

... the losses of traders in the sample were much higher than their profits. If these results are representative of trading by small speculators generally, there must be other groups – large speculators, scalpers, spreaders or hedgers – which made very large profits. (Stewart, 1949, p. 9)

Professional and amateur traders cannot both have MRE. The professionals have superior forecasting ability. The Bayesian analysis in Chapter Three ascribes the superior forecasting ability of the large firms to their larger sample sizes. In terms of Figure 3.1, the ratio $Q = \text{var } y_i/\text{var } y_j$ is equal to n_j/n_i, the ratio of sample sizes. Using the urn analogy above, the one who draws the larger sample has the smaller Bayesian error. Reporting (large) traders are continually in the market, operate in large volume with geographically dispersed customers and receive many bits of information during an interval of time. This is formally equivalent to drawing many samples, and each is of a large size. Amateurs operate on a small scale, are not in the market continuously, do not devote their full time to this activity and experiment with different forecasting schemes. That is why they have a higher variance of forecast error than do the professionals. The Backwardation MRE hypothesis is not consistent with the data. The theory of diverse precisions is a better explanation.

5.2   Induced Structural Changes

Futures markets affect the supply of output equations in two ways. First, they provide opportunities to redistribute risk. In so far as the risks encountered by producers, processors and distributors of goods are negatively related, those who are at risk of a price decline can sell futures to those who are at risk of price rise. Figure 2.4 describes this situation, where the hedging is balanced among the commercials. Quite often there will be noncommercials (speculators) who add depth to the market and accept the balance of risk of the commercials. This is the situation described in Figure 2.5.

Secondly, the futures price embodies the information and misinformation of many participants in the market: commercial firms, professional speculators and amateur speculators. In the absence of futures markets, each commercial must rely upon its own resources to determine the true mean price. The evidence adduced in this part suggests that, in the absence of futures markets, firms make large Bayesian errors and that MRE does not prevail. The existence of futures markets pools the information of many participants and makes it available to all at negligible cost. By increasing the sample size of information available to each participant, the variance of the Bayesian error is reduced and the convergence to MRE is accelerated. This theme is the subject of this part of the chapter.

A distinction must be made in the theory of futures markets between the case where there are no inventories (Chapters Two and Three) and when there are continuous inventories (Chapter Five).

5.2.1 No Inventories Are Carried

In this part, I apply the theory developed in Chapters Two and Three, for a commodity where no inventories are carried to the empirical studies of the futures market in potatoes.

The late summer and autumn potatoes account for 80 per cent of total annual production. This crop must last until the next summer's potatoes become available; however, the old crop should not be carried into the summer when the fresher supplies are available. During the summer, the new crop which is approximately 6 per cent of the total annual production, is equal to consumption, and inventories are not carried from the summer to the autumn.

Potato prices are highly variable, both absolutely and relative to the prices of farm products. In the period 1920–60, excluding the years 1943–50 with government price supports, the year to year variation in prices received by farmers for potatoes *around the general farm price level* averaged 53 per cent.[5]

Futures trading in Maine potatoes became active since 1952, and are used in several different ways by different commercial firms.

1   A potato grower in the spring may sell potato futures for autumn delivery, or he may sell his crop forward to a dealer.
2   The dealer who has purchased the crop forward from the grower may sell potato futures to hedge his forward purchases. Combining 1 and 2, the growers and dealers tend to be short futures during the growing season.
3   Dealers may have sold potatoes forward to producers of potato chips and french fries. These forward sales are made in advance of the autumn crop. To hedge their subsequent purchases of potatoes, dealers may purchase potato futures at the time when they negotiate their forward sales to the producers of potato chips or french fries.

Commercial firms (1 and 2) tend to be short hedgers, and commercial firms (3) tend to be long hedgers. The balance of hedging by commercials, at any time, is ambiguous. For that reason, there is no presumption that bias or backwardation, δ, will be significantly different from zero.

5.2.1.1   Theoretical Considerations

The manner whereby the supply of production is affected by the use of futures markets is through a change in the relation between the subjective and objective expectations and the magnitude of the risk premium. If the MRE hypothesis were valid, the two expectations would always be equal. Then futures markets would have no effect upon the relation between the subjective and objective expectations. An alternative view advanced in this chapter is that futures markets speed the convergence of the market's subjective expectation to the objective expectation. Unless the underlying distribution has been stationary for a long time, the MRE hypothesis is unlikely to be correct without futures markets. The subsequent argument is based upon the analysis in Chapter Three.

Let the spring time be denoted by θ and the autumn by t. Production decisions are made at θ and output occurs at subsequent time t.

When there are no (N) futures markets, each producer must form his own subjective estimate of what will be the mean price at time t. Output produced will be such that, for each producer, marginal cost plus an endogenous risk premium equals the subjectively expected price.

If there were MRE, that is if there were no Bayesian error ($y_m = 0$), the supply curve for the industry is equation (5.27) graphed in Figure 5.3. It relates the objective mean price $Ep(t)$ to output $S(t)$. The first term $cS(t)$ is marginal cost and the second term $R_j S(t)$ is the risk premium. Term $R_j, j = $ N, F, is affected by the existence of futures markets.

$$Ep(t) = cS(t) + R_j S(t) \qquad\qquad (5.27)$$

$$R_j = \text{var } p/M_j \qquad j = \text{N, F} \qquad\qquad (5.27a)$$

Curve $ED(t)$ in Figure 5.3 is the objective expectation of the demand at time t:

$$Ep(t) = W - bS(t) \qquad\qquad (5.28)$$

The objective mean intercept is W, but the actual intercept has a positive variance, which is the source of the uncertainty.

The MRE hypothesis assumes that there are no Bayesian errors: the producers know the mean demand $ED(t)$. This hypothesis asserts that the expected price and output will be at point H_N. The

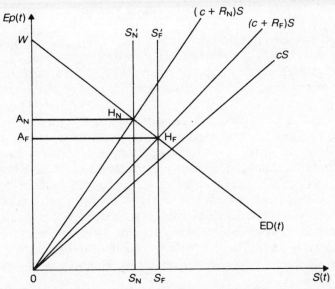

Figure 5.3 The MRE hypothesis implies that output S will be produced where marginal cost plus risk premium $(c + R_j)S$ is equal to the expected demand $ED(t)$. The risk premium is R_F with futures and R_N when there are no futures. Then output will be constant S_N or S_F as long as the expected demand is $ED(t)$, and will be independent of the previously realized price.

crucial implication of this analysis is that as long as the mean demand is constant at ED(t), output will be constant at S_N. Algebraically, this output is

$$S_j(t) = \frac{W}{b + c + R_j} \qquad (5.29)$$

This is the MRE supply, based upon equations (5.27) and (5.28). The realized price $p(t)$ will vary along $S_N S'_N$ as stochastic demand varied. On average, the price would be A_N.

When there are futures (F) markets, output is at the point where marginal cost is equal to the futures price. The latter is equal to the market subjectively expected price, adjusted for an endogenous risk premium. The sharing of risk among the non-commercials increases M_j and lowers the risk premium R_j. In this case the supply curve is $(c + R_F)S(t)$ when there are MRE and futures markets.

The rationally expected price and output would be at point H_F. As long as the mean demand is constant at ED(t), output will be constant S_F. On average, the realized price will be A_F but the realization at any time would be along the vertical supply curve $S_F S'_F$.

If MRE occurred whether or not there were futures markets, the sole advantage of futures markets would consist of risk sharing. The greater participation in the market by futures speculators reduces the risk premium and rotates the supply curve closer to the marginal cost curve.

The conclusion is that if there were MRE and expected demand is constant, then current output is independent of lagged prices. The MRE hypothesis is an arbitrary assumption which is not based upon economic theory. The diverse precisions hypothesis developed in Chapter Three, which was called asymptotically rational expectations (ARE), implies that MRE is the limit of a process. At any time, there will be Bayesian errors. In Section 5.1 it was shown that there is a systematic difference in Bayesian errors among market participants. This analysis is extended in this part to show how the existence of futures markets accelerate the converge to MRE.

Based upon the Bayesian analysis in Chapter Three, the subjective expectation of the ith group is equation (5.30), which is equation (3.4). It is a linear combination of the prior belief which should be the price in the previous autumn and the current sample of information whose value is $\bar{x}_i(\theta)$:

$$E_i p(t; \theta) = \frac{\tau(t-1)}{\tau(t-1) + n_i s} p(t-1) + \frac{n_i s}{\tau(t-1) + n_i s} \bar{x}_i(\theta) \quad (5.30)$$

The variance of the difference between the subjective and objective expectations is

$$\text{var } [E_i p(t; \theta) - Ep(t)] = \text{var } p/N_i \quad (5.31)$$

which is equation (3.10) where var p is the price variance and N_i is the product of the sample size and the number of samples taken by the ith agent. Variable N_i is the current information available to the ith agent.

An example of N_i is as follows. A dealer who is purchasing a potato crop forward from the growers contacts N_i commercials, measured by their volume, who process the potatoes into chips or frozen french fries. The dealer inquires about the quantity demanded at various prices by the processors. The estimated price, resulting from the direct contact by the dealer, is $\bar{x}_i(\theta)$. Dealers who trade in large volume, who are in regular contact with their customers, have higher N_i than do smaller dealers who are only in contact with a small segment of the market. In the extreme case, if each producer operates in isolation, his current sample size N_i of information in the spring is very small concerning the demand for the autumn crop. Then his posterior subjective expectation is very heavily weighted by his prior subjective expectation.

Several important implications of this theory are as follows. First, when there are no futures markets each producer must act exclusively upon his own information. Since his sample size of current information N_i is small, his subjective expectation is very close to his prior. In turn, his prior would be heavily weighted by the price of the previous autumn crop $p(t-1)$. Consequently, the supply of output would be approximated by

$$S_N(t) = \frac{p(t-1)}{R_N + c} \quad (5.32)$$

Secondly, when there is a futures market, the quantity supplied depends upon the futures price. The latter depends upon the subjectively expected price by the market as a whole $E_m p(t; \theta)$, which is a weighted average of the subjectively expected prices by both producers and futures speculators. This weighted expectation is based upon the sum of the samples of information drawn by all of the market participants. Since they are pooling their information, the futures price is a closer approximation to the objective expectation of the distribution. This is implied by equation (5.31) above that the variance of the difference between the subjective and objective distributions is inversely proportional to the sample size. Consequently, when there are many participants in the futures market, the supply of output would be

$$S_F(t) = \frac{W}{(b+c) + R_F}$$
(5.33)

based upon equation (5.29). It is primarily a function of the objective mean of the distribution $Ep(t)$ rather than of the prior. The futures price reflects more 'information', i.e. it is based upon a larger sample of current information, and less weight is placed upon the priors. Consequently, the *supply decision is more closely related to the sample mean and less upon the previous price.*

5.2.1.2 Empirical Evidence
During the period 1931–41, there was limited futures trading in Maine potatoes. Trading was inactive during World War II, and volume was light in the immediate post-war years. Activity increased substantially during 1952–60 on the New York Mercantile Exchange. Idaho potato producers made little use of the New York futures market in either of the two periods.

Will M. Simmons of the US Department of Agriculture estimated supply equations for Maine and Idaho potatoes during the periods 1931–41 and 1952–60. Table 5.8 contains regression equations for $A(t)$, the current year's planted acreage for late summer and autumn potatoes in the area under study on the

Table 5.8 Acreage estimating equations for Maine and Idaho potatoes: 1930–41, 1952–60

		a_0	a_1	a_2	R^2
Maine	1931–41	0.38	0.84	16.68	0.76
			(0.196)	(3.815)	
	1952–60	123.69	0.100	3.020	0.21
			(0.111)	(2.381)	
Idaho	1931–41	30.57	0.635	13.962	0.36
			(0.314)	(7.775)	
	1952–60	−54.77	1.14	23.692	0.96
			(0.1)	(5.317)	

Notes: $A(t) = a_0 + a_1 A(t-1) + a_2 p(t-1)$. Variable $A(t)$ is acreage planted and $p(t)$ is the price deflated by the index of farm prices. Standard errors are in parentheses.
Source: Simmons, 1962, p. 79, equations J–M

previous year's planted acreage, $A(t-1)$, the previous year's season average price $p(t-1)$ received by farmers for late summer and autumn potatoes in the area under study, deflated by the index of prices received by farmers for all farm products. The two areas are Maine and Idaho. During 1931–41, there was not much futures trading in either commodity but during 1952–60 there was substantial futures trading in Maine potatoes.[6]

The coefficient a_2 of the previous year's relative price $p(t-1)$ declines drastically when futures trading became active. Whereas $a_2 = 16.68$, with $t = 4.37$, in the 1931–41 period; it became $a_2 = 3.02$, with $t = 1.27$, in the 1952–60 period. With the development of futures trading in Maine potatoes, the lagged relative price was no longer a significant determinant of the acreage planted.

By contrast, in Idaho the coefficient of the lagged price increased between the two periods. In neither one was there significant use of futures by Idaho producers. The value $a_2 = 13.96$, with $t = 1.8$, in the 1931–41 period. During 1952–60, $a_2 = 23.69$ with $t = 4.46$.

The difference between the two regions is consistent with the hypotheses summarized in equations (5.32) and (5.33) above. A cobweb cycle continued in Idaho potatoes, where planned output in t depended upon the price in $t-1$. With the development of a future market in Maine potatoes, the cobweb cycle was eliminated.

The acreage planted tended to stabilize in Maine. Neither the coefficient a_1 of the previous year's acreage nor the coefficient a_2 of the previous year's price was significant during the period of futures trading. In Idaho, the planted acreage was growing (since $a_1 = 1.14$) and was responsive to the previous year's price.

5.2.2   Continuous Inventory Models

The theory for continuous inventories developed in Chapter Four is richer but more complicated than the case examined above. A simplified exposition based upon Chapter Four can nevertheless convey the essence of the argument.

Dealers are intermediaries between producers and consumers. The profits of the dealer consists of two parts: deterministic and stochastic. Dealers charge their customers commissions and fees, and there may be a spread between their bid and ask prices. From these sources of revenue the dealer must subtract the cost of inventory acquired, finance and storage costs. If the price were not expected to change, then the optimal inventory held is such that the marginal revenue from commissions and spreads is equal to the marginal cost of financing and storage, plus an endogenous risk premium.

There are also profits and losses resulting from changes in the value of inventory due to market price changes. This stochastic element has a high variance, which overwhelms the deterministic source of profits.

Combining the deterministic and stochastic elements the optimal inventory for a dealer $s(t)$ must satisfy equation (5.34) based upon equation (4.16). The subjectively expected price $E_m p(t + 1; t)$ plus the marginal revenue from commissions and spreads is equal to the acquisition price of the good plus financing costs, plus the marginal cost of storage plus endogenous risk premium:

$$E_m p(t + 1; t) = p(t) + gS(t) - v \tag{5.34}$$

The market subjectively expected price is equation (5.35), based upon equations (5.5a)–(5.5c) above, where y_m is the Bayesian error and η is the unavoidable error. Substitute

$$E_m p(t + 1; t) = p(t + 1) + y_m(t) + \eta \tag{5.35}$$

into equation (5.34) and derive

$$p(t + 1) = p(t) + gS(t) - v - y_m(t) - \eta \tag{5.36}$$

for the price $p(t + 1)$.

If there were no Bayesian errors between the subjective and objective expectations of the mean price in $t + 1$ (i.e. if there were MRE), then

$$p(t + 1) = a_0 + a_1 p(t) + bS(t) + \epsilon(t + 1); \qquad \epsilon = \text{noise} \tag{5.37}$$

should result. The price $p(t + 1)$ should be related to the lagged price $p(t)$ and the aggregate inventory $S(t) = \Sigma s(t)$, but $p(t + 1)$ should be independent of prices lagged by more than one period.

If, however, there were Bayesian errors so that MRE did not prevail, the Bayesian errors will be serially correlated. For example, if expectations were adaptive, the price $p(t + 1)$ would depend upon the immediately preceding price $p(t)$ and upon earlier prices. The general regression equation (5.38) for the price of storable commodities permits one to test the hypothesis that futures markets accelerate the convergence to MRE:

$$p(t + 1) = a_0 + a_1 p(t) + \sum_{t=1} c_i p(t - i) + bS(t) + \epsilon(t + 1) \tag{5.38}$$

If there were no Bayesian errors, then a_1 is positive and each c_i is not significantly different from zero.

My hypothesis is that the existence of futures markets accelerates the convergence to MRE. In the absence of futures markets, the contribution of

$$\sum_{i=1} c_i p(t-i)$$

to the explanation of $p(t+1)$ should be significant, whereas it should not be significant when there are developed futures markets.

Table 5.9 summarizes results found by Cox for six commodities: storable and nonstorable. There was no futures trading during the first period but there was futures trading during the second period. Prices are observed one day at weekly intervals. The F statistic reflects the contribution of

$$\sum_{i=1} c_i p(t-i)$$

to the explanation of price $p(t+1)$. The significance level is in parentheses following the F statistic.

Again the evidence supports the diverse precisions hypothesis. First, the F statistic is always significant at the 5 per cent level when there is no futures trading. Thereby, the MRE hypothesis is rejected in the absence of future markets. Secondly, the value of the F statistic is always reduced when futures trading is active. Third, except for cattle, the F statistic is not significant when there is futures trading. The MRE hypothesis, which is a special case of ARE, is consistent with the data only during the period with futures trading.

5.3 Conclusion

The enormous advantage of the MRE hypothesis is that it is a logically consistent and analytically feasible way of dealing with anticipations. Economists agree that MRE will exist in the steady state. Futures markets, however, develop when the underlying distributions of the stochastic variables are changing in the direction of more risk. If the distributions are stationary then asset diversification, ordinary insurance or options are sufficient to enable commercials to avoid risk. The question at issue is how to explain price anticipations when the distributions of the stochastic variables are changing, and the economy is not at the steady state.

Many authors realized that replication of the market process in a stationary environment is both necessary and sufficient for

Table 5.9   Contribution of prices lagged by more than one period to the cash price. F statistics and significance level

Commodity	No futures	Futures
Onions	10.67 (0.01)	0.60 (NS)
Potatoes	4.35 (0.01)	1.46 (NS)
Pork bellies	3.05 (0.05)	0.56 (NS)
Hogs	2.32 (0.05)	0.46 (NS)
Cattle	7.89 (0.01)	2.50 (0.05)
FCOJ	2.92 (0.01)	0.28 (NS)

Symbol: NS, not significant.
Source: Cox, 1976, Table 2

MRE.[7] Grossman (1976, 1977) and Grossman and Stiglitz (1976, 1980) disagree on theoretical grounds with Fama's (1970) MRE view that prices at any time fully reflect all available information.[8] Evidence from experimental games, conducted by Forsythe, Palfrey and Plott (1982, 1984), is inconsistent with the MRE view, but is consistent with the ARE hypothesis (based upon diverse precisions) developed here. These authors found that the market price converges asymptotically to the MRE price, but the deviation between the market price and the MRE price is serially correlated. When there is no futures market, the errors are always in one direction. The convergence is always from below (Forsythe, Palfrey and Plott, 1982, Figures 2–6). When a futures market is introduced, the convergence to MRE is greatly accelerated.

An alternative called ARE, based upon Bayesian analysis, was developed in Chapter Three. The Bayesian error y_i (for the ith group of agents) is defined as the difference between the subjective mean (the prior) and the objective mean of a distribution. It was proved that: (a) the variance of the Bayesian error var y_i is inversely proportional to the cumulative number of items sampled and directly proportional to the noisiness of the system; (b) the Bayesian errors are serially correlated but converge asymptotically to zero. MRE is the asymptotic solution to ARE as the cumulative number of items sampled from a stationary distribution grows very large.

The ARE hypothesis is applied in this chapter to two cases. First, it is used to explain profits made by large commercials and large speculators. It is shown that expected profits of group i relative to group j result from the difference

$(\text{var } y_j / \text{var } y_i) - (w_i / w_j),$

where w_i is the ratio of the number in group i divided by the average risk aversion. Hence, the variance of the Bayesian error will be smaller for large commercials and noncommercials who draw upon large sample sizes. These groups make large profits market to market and year by year.

Secondly, the ARE analysis is used to explain why MRE does not occur without futures markets, but the introduction of these markets speeds the convergence to MRE. For example, the cobweb cycle in acreage planted of Maine potatoes was eliminated with the introduction of futures markets. The reason is that in the absence of futures markets, the subjective expectations of firms tends to be the past price. When futures markets are introduced, information is pooled and the futures price is closer to the mean estimated by pooling the information of many market participants.

5.4   Appendix C
Expected Profits of Professional and Amateur Speculators

If there were only two groups of speculators, professional $(i = 1)$ and amateur $(i = 2)$, but no net hedging pressure from producers, then the gains of the former are the losses of the latter. A formula is derived for the expected profits of the professional speculators $E\pi_1$.

If there were no net hedging pressure, then the futures price is such that the sum of the positions Z_i is zero.

$$\sum_{i=1}^{2} Z_i = 0 \tag{C1}$$

where

$$Z_i(t) = \frac{E_i p(t+1; t) - q_{t+1}(t)}{\beta_i \text{ var } p} \qquad i = 1, 2 \tag{C2}$$

Then the futures price is equation (C3), a linear combination of the subjectively expected prices:

$$q_{t+1}(t) = \gamma_1 E_1 p(t+1; t) + (1 - \gamma_1) E_2 p(t+1; t) \tag{C3}$$

where $\gamma_1 = w_1 / (w_1 + w_2)$ and $w_i = \xi_i / \beta_i \text{ var } p$. Using definitions (5.5a)–(5.5c) in the text for the error, the market-clearing futures price is

$$q_{t+1}(t) = p(t + 1) + \gamma_1 \epsilon_1 + (1 - \gamma_1) \epsilon_2 \tag{C4}$$

Profits of the professional speculators are

$$\pi_1 = (p - q)(p + \epsilon_1 - q)/\beta_1 \text{ var } p \tag{C5}$$

Using equation (C4) in (C5) and taking expectations, derive

$$E\pi_1 = \frac{(1 - \gamma_1)^2 \text{ var } \epsilon_2 - \gamma_1(1 - \gamma_1) \text{ var } \epsilon_1}{\beta_1 \text{ var } p} \tag{C6}$$

Define the relative quality Q of professional to amateur speculators as the ratio of the variance of the error of amateurs to that of the professionals: $Q = \text{var } \epsilon_2/\text{var } \epsilon_1 > 1$. Define the relative weight of professional to amateurs as ω: $\omega = \gamma_1/(1 - \gamma_1)$. Using the definitions of these two parameters, equation (C6) can be written as

$$E\pi_1 = \frac{(1 - \gamma_1)^2}{\beta_1} \frac{\text{var } \epsilon_1}{\text{var } p} (Q - \omega) \tag{C7}$$

which is equation (5.17a) in the text.

Notes

1 See the excellent analysis by Figlewski (1982).
2 Kawai (1983) is a typical example.
3 See Draper (1985) for a description of the amateur speculators.
4 The controversy concerning the relative sources of profits to the non-commercials (futures speculators) between backwardation and special forecasting ability continues (see Carter, Rausser and Schmitz, 1983; Chang, 1985). The evidence adduced in Chapters 1 and 2 is that net hedging pressure is small and unlikely to be a significant source of profits to noncommercials. See also Cootner (1967) and Telser (1958).
5 See Simmons (1962). The next most variable crop was onions. Futures trading in onions was prohibited in 1958.
6 Maine producers became more specialized in the production of potatoes than were the Idaho producers, during the second period.
7 See the survey article by Bray (1985).
8 Van Horne and Heaton (1983) showed that government securities dealers have information superior to that of the market. This violates the strong form market efficiency test, i.e. rejects Fama's claim. The results of this chapter support the ARE hypothesis in Stein (1982).

6

Futures Markets, Speculation and Welfare

The social utility of futures markets has been evaluated by various authors in different ways. Some view futures markets as socially desirable if they reduce the price variance in the underlying cash market. Others ask if the futures markets are 'efficient', in the sense that the futures price is an unbiased estimate of, and contains all relevant information concerning, the subsequent cash price. A more general approach is taken here to evaluate the welfare effects of futures markets and the other approaches are shown to be components of the more general quantitative measure derived here.

Futures markets affect theintertemporal allocation of consumption and the economic welfare of a household depends upon its time profile of consumption. A direct measure of the effect of futures markets upon economic welfare is derived, where the welfare loss is shown to be proportional to the expectation of the square of deviation between the futures price and the subsequently realized price. The components of his social loss can then be identified.

6.1 Economic Welfare: General Considerations

A comparison is made between a pair of situations denoted by S and S^*. Situation S^* is said to Pareto dominate S_i if there exists a reallocation of goods among households in situation S^* which could make everyone better off (or some people better off and others no worse off) than they were in situation S_i. Economic welfare is then said to be raised by a change from situation S_i to S^*. A perfect foresight competitive equilibrium S^* cannot be Pareto dominated by any other situation.

A quantitative measure of welfare loss denoted by L_i is constructed between situation S_i and the perfect foresight competitive equilibrium S^*. Situation S_1 is said to yield a higher level of welfare than situation S_2 if welfare loss L_1 is less than welfare loss L_2. Situations 1 and 2 may be associated with different institutions: the presence or absence of futures markets, or two different futures markets. Associated with each institutional framework the expected welfare loss $E(L_i)$ is calculated, where the expectation is taken over the appropriate stochastic variables. Institution 1 is said to be preferable to institution 2 if the expected welfare loss $E(L_1)$ is less than $E(L_2)$.

Let there be n households in an economy, c be the vector of goods and services consumed by the household at present and s be the corresponding vector of goods and services consumed by the household at a later date. For the economy as a whole, the vectors of goods are $C = \Sigma c$ and $S = \Sigma s$ summed over the households. Goods C and S could be the same goods consumed at different times, or different goods consumed at different dates.

A household has a utility function described by

$$u = u(s, c); \qquad u_i > 0, u_{ii} < 0; \qquad u_{ij} = 0 \qquad \text{for } i \neq j \quad (6.1)$$

Utility functions differ by household, but the subscript for the household will not be written explicitly. The analysis is considerably simplified if it is assumed that the utility function is separable: $u_{sc} = 0$.

Compare two situations. In the initial situation, the aggregate vectors are (S_0, C_0) and a given household consumes vector (s_0, c_0). In the new situation the aggregate vectors are (S, C). The new situation Pareto dominates the old one if there exists a reallocation of the totals (S, C) among households such that each household is better off than it was initially.

Let the totals be reallocated in such a way that each household receives an equal share of the change. Then the new consumption of a given household is:

$$s = s_0 + (S - S_0)/n = s_0 + \Delta S/n$$
$$c = c_0 + (C - C_0)/n = c_0 + \Delta C/n$$

Equation (6.2) describes the change in utility of a given household. The derivatives are evaluated at (s_0, c_0), the initial consumption levels:

$$u(s, c) - u(s_0, c_0) = u_s \frac{\Delta S}{n} + u_c \frac{\Delta C}{n} + \frac{1}{2} u_{ss} \left(\frac{\Delta S}{n}\right)^2$$

$$+ \frac{1}{2} u_{cc} \left(\frac{\Delta C}{n}\right)^2 \tag{6.2}$$

since the utility function was assumed to be separable.

Since the household selects its optimal consumption, equations (6.3a) and (6.3b) are satisfied, where (p_s, p_c) are the prices and λ is the marginal utility of income:

$$u_s = \lambda p_s \tag{6.3a}$$

$$u_c = \lambda p_c \tag{6.3b}$$

The second derivatives are given by

$$u_{ss} = \lambda \frac{\partial p_s}{\partial s} + p_s \frac{\partial \lambda}{\partial s} \tag{6.4a}$$

and

$$u_{cc} = \lambda \frac{\partial p_c}{\partial c} + p_c \frac{\partial \lambda}{\partial c} \tag{6.4b}$$

Using equations (6.3) and (6.4) in (6.2), the change in utility of a given household is described by

$$\frac{\Delta u}{\lambda} \cdot n = \left(p_s \Delta S + \frac{1}{2} \Delta p_s \Delta S\right) + \left(p_c \Delta C + \frac{1}{2} \Delta p_c \Delta C\right) + 0(\Delta) \tag{6.5a}$$

and

$$0(\Delta) = \frac{1}{2}\left[p_s \frac{1}{\lambda} \frac{\partial \lambda}{\partial s} n(\Delta s)^2 + p_c \frac{1}{\lambda} \frac{\partial \lambda}{\partial c} n(\Delta c)^2\right] \tag{6.5b}$$

Term $\Delta u/\lambda$, measured in dollars, is the change in utility of a given household divided by its marginal utility of income and n is the number of households. Expression $0(\Delta)$ involves the percentage changes in the marginal utility of income and the square of changes in the household consumption. In general $0(\Delta)$ will be small. Then the dollar equivalent of the change in utility $L \equiv (\Delta u/\lambda)n$ is

$$L = \left(p_s \Delta S + \frac{1}{2} \Delta p_s \Delta S\right) + \left(p_c \Delta C + \frac{1}{2} \Delta p_c \Delta C\right) \tag{6.6}$$

This contains the aggregate quantities ΔC and ΔS. If L is positive, then everyone could be made better off in the new situation (S, C) than he was in the initial situation (s_0, c_0), and the change will have increased economic welfare. Quantity L is the underlying welfare measure. An operational measure of L, used in the evaluation of futures markets, is developed below.

The second term on the right-hand side of equation (6.6) is now shown to equal the negative of the marginal increment of cost of producing S. The change in the aggregate output of good $C = F(N_c, K_c)$ is

$$\Delta C = F_N \Delta N_c + F_K \Delta K_c \qquad (6.7)$$

where F_N is the marginal product of labour and F_K is the marginal product of capital. The given quantities of labour (N) and capital (K) are allocated between the two types of goods:

$$N = N_s + N_c \qquad (6.8a)$$

$$K = K_s + K_c \qquad (6.8b)$$

Assume that industry C is competitive so that the values of the marginal products are equal to the factor prices, and that both industries pay the same prices V_N and V_K for the inputs of labour and capital:

$$p_c F_N = V_N \qquad (6.9a)$$

$$p_c F_K = V_K \qquad (6.9b)$$

Then, using equations (6.8) and (6.9) in (6.7),

$$p_c \frac{\Delta C}{\Delta S} = -\left(V_N \frac{\Delta N_s}{\Delta S} + V_K \frac{\Delta K_s}{\Delta S} \right) = -M(S) \qquad (6.10)$$

is derived. The term in parentheses on the right-hand side of equation (6.10) is the marginal cost of producing S, denoted by $M(S)$. It is seen to be the value of output C that is sacrificed to produce an increment of S.

For discrete changes in C and S, equation (6.10) can be written as

$$p_c \Delta C + \frac{1}{2} \Delta p_c \Delta C = -\left[M(S) \Delta S + \frac{1}{2} \Delta M(S) \Delta S \right] \qquad (6.11)$$

Substitute equation (6.11) into (6.6) for the change in economic welfare and obtain

$$L = \left[p_s \Delta S + \frac{1}{2} \Delta p_s \Delta S \right] - \left[M(S) \Delta S + \frac{1}{2} \Delta M(S) \Delta S \right] \quad (6.12)$$

In this approach, no dichotomy is made between 'producers' and 'consumers' (as is done in Newbery and Stiglitz, 1982 and Turnovsky and Campbell, 1985). Everyone is a consumer. Instead, I ask if there exists an allocation of the totals (S, C) which could make everyone better off than he was in the initial situation (s_0, c_0). The monetary value of the change in aggregate welfare is precisely L in equation (6.12).

At time t firms could produce quantity $C(t)$ of present consumption or they can invest resources to produce consumption $S(t + 1)$ which will be available at time $t + 1$. It is convenient to think of S as storage at time t and the cost of this storage is the sacrifice of present consumption C. It makes no difference to the analysis whether the same good is consumed at two subsequent dates or two different goods are consumed at two different dates. At present time t, the firms know the marginal costs including interest of producing good $S(t + 1)$ which (by equation 6.11) is the value of present consumption that is sacrificed to produce future consumption. There is, however, demand uncertainty concerning the term $[p_s \Delta S + \frac{1}{2} \Delta p_s \Delta S]$ the value of the additional output that will be available at time $t + 1$.

An optimal intertemporal allocation of resources occurs when L, defined in equation (6.12), is zero. Associated with any institutional framework is the expected value $E(L_i)$ of the welfare loss. Institutions are to be compared in terms of the expected values of their associated welfare losses $E(L_i)$. Futures markets are deemed to have increased welfare in so far as their expected values of social loss are less than would prevail in their absence.

6.2 Analysis of Welfare Loss in Futures Markets

6.2.1 Determination of the Futures Price

A very brief recapitulation of the theory developed in Chapters Two and Four, which is graphically described in Figure 6.1, leads into the analysis of the welfare loss.

When commercial firms optimize, and the hedging instrument is perfect so that there is no basis risk, the quantity of output

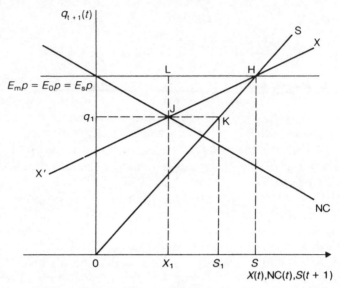

Figure 6.1   The supply of output $S(t + 1)$, curve OS, is positively related to the futures price $q_{t+1}(t)$. The net supply of futures by commercial firms (producers) is curve XX', which is positively related to the futures price. When the latter is equal to the subjectivity expected price $E_0p(t + 1; t)$, all of the output is hedged. This is point H. The net demand for futures by non-commercial firms (futures speculators) is curve NC. It depends upon the difference between the subjectively expected price $E_sp(t + 1; t)$ and the futures price. Market-clearing futures price is $q_1 = X_1J$; and the ratio of hedged to total output is OX_1/OS_1. The risk premium JL/X_1L depends upon the net hedging pressure and the 'adequacy of speculation'. As the risk premium declines, curve NC rotates to the horizontal line, and the futures price rises to the subjectively expected price $E_sp(t + 1; t)$. In this figure, the subjective expectations of the two groups are drawn to be the same.

$S(t + 1)$ produced for sale in the future $(t + 1)$ is such that current marginal cost $cS(t + 1)$ is equal to the futures price $q_{t+1}(t)$. Supply curve OS in Figure 6.1 describes this condition, which is

$$q_{t+1}(t) = cS(t + 1)$$

futures price = marginal cost.   (6.13)

The net supply of futures by commercial firms is curve XX' in Figure 6.1. If the futures price $q_{t+1}(t)$ were equal to their subjectively expected price $E_0p(t + 1; t)$, then their sale of futures $X(t)$ would equal planned output $S(t + 1)$ at point H. The subjective expectation E, taken at time t, of the price $p(t + 1)$ that will prevail at time $t + 1$ is denoted by $E_i p(t + 1; t)$, where $i = 0$ refers to commercial firms and $i = s$ refers to 'futures speculators'.

In so far as the futures price is below (above) the subjectively expected price by the commercial firms, their supply of futures is less (greater) than planned production. Depending upon the relation between the futures price and their subjectively expected price, commercial firms can be short $(X > 0)$ or long $(X < 0)$ futures.

The net demand for futures by noncommercial firms (i.e. futures speculators) is curve NC. It depends upon the difference between their subjectively expected price $E_s p(t + 1; t)$ and the futures price $q_{t+1}(t)$. For geometric simplicity, Figure 6.1 is drawn so that the commercial and noncommercial firms have the same subjectively expected price. It was shown in Chapter Five that the large commercial firms have more accurate forecasts than do the smaller noncommercial firms.

The market-clearing futures price is $q_1 = X_1 J$ in Figure 6.1. This price is a discounted for risk value of a weighted average of the subjectively expected prices by the market participants $E_m p(t + 1; t)$. Discount factor $\delta = \text{JL}/X_1 \text{L} = (h/w)/E_m p(t + 1; t)$. Term h, defined in equation (2.44), is the excess supply of futures by commercials that would occur if the futures price were equal to the expected price. It is referred to as net hedging pressure, distance OS, which can be positive, zero or negative (see Figure 2.4). Term $1/w$, defined in equations (2.47), (2.40) and (2.34a), represents the risk premium required to induce speculative positions by the sum of commercials and noncommercials. Term δ reflects net hedging pressure and the adequacy of speculation:

$$q_{t+1}(t) = (1 - \delta) E_m p(t + 1; t), \qquad \delta \gtreqless 0 \qquad (6.14)$$

When $\delta = 0$, then the equilibrium is at point H. Producers then hedge all of their output, and the futures price is equal to $E_s p$.

There is no presumption here that the subjectively expected price by noncommercial firms $E_s p(t + 1; t)$ is the objective (i.e. true) mean price. This issue, discussed in Chapter Three, is of crucial importance and is an important element in the analysis below. This is a recapitulation of the determination of the futures price.

6.2.2   The Ex-Post Welfare Loss

At time $t + 1$, the demand for output by consumers is negatively related to the cash price $p(t + 1)$ and depends positively upon a stochastic parameter of demand $u(t+1)$. At time $t+1$ it has a mean value of $Eu(t+1)$ and a variance var u. Quite likely, the mean value of the distribution $Eu(t+1)$ varies over time. Equation (6.15) describes the demand curve in period $t+1$:

$$p(t+1) = u(t+1) - bS(t+1) \qquad (6.15)$$

Figure 6.2 is the essence of the subsequent analysis. Curve Q_1 is the same as marginal cost curve $0S$ in Figure 6.1, where marginal cost $cS(t+1)$ is equal to the futures price $q_{t+1}(t)$. Curve ED is the objectively expected demand for the output in period $t+1$. It is demand curve equation (6.15) when the stochastic term $u(t+1)$ is at its objectively expected value $Eu(t+1)$. Curve D in Figure 6.2 is the realized demand at time $t+1$, when $u(t+1)$ exceeds its mean value.

A perfect foresight competitive equilibrium with no risk premium (δ is zero) is a situation where the futures price $q_{t+1}(t)$ at time t for delivery at $t+1$ is equal to the subsequently realized cash price $p(t+1)$. In Figure 6.2, suppose that the realized demand were curve D. Then point C, where the futures price is S_1C, would be a perfect foresignt competitive equilibrium. At that futures price, production would be S_1 where marginal cost $cS_1 = S_1C$ is equal to the futures price. When output S_1 is sold at time $t+1$, the realized price would indeed be S_1C. This situation corresponds exactly to a value of $L = 0$ in equation (6.12). This is a competitive equilibrium which is a Pareto optimum and it occurs because the futures price is equal to the subsequently realized price.

Continue to assume that $\delta = 0$ and the realized demand is curve D in Figure 6.2. If the futures price were S_3G then realized output would be S_3. At time $t+1$, this output would sell for price S_3K. Price exceeds marginal cost by GK.

Ex-post welfare loss L in Figure 6.2 is the area under the realized demand curve D and above marginal cost curve Q_1, between the actual output and the perfect foresight competitive equilibrium output. When the futures price is S_3G, output S_3 sells for price S_3K in the next period. The loss in utility (divided by the marginal utility of income of the consumers of the product), resulting from output S_3 instead of perfect foresight competitive equilibrium output S_1 is area GCK. Too little future consumption is produced relative to current consumption.

In general, the ex-post welfare loss $L(t+1)$ is the triangular area between the realized linearized demand curve and the linearized marginal cost curve, between the actual output $S(t+1)$ and the

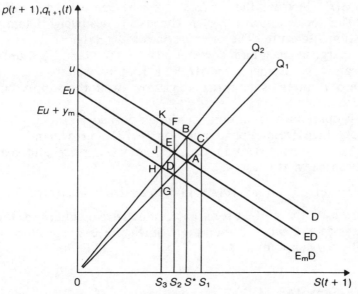

Figure 6.2 Mean demand is ED and its realized value is D. Output is produced along curve Q_1 where the futures price $q_{t+1}(t)$ is equal to marginal cost
$cS(t + 1)$. When there is a risk premium δ, due to net hedging pressure and
insufficient speculation, curve Q_2 is the relation between the subjectively
expected price and output. When there is a Bayesian error $y_m = HJ < 0$
between the subjectively expected price and objectively expected price, the
objectively expected price exceeds the subjectively expected price by HJ.

Let demand be D, which exceeds its mean value ED. When there are MRE
and no risk premium, the futures price is S^*A, where expected demand is
equal to marginal cost, the social loss is triangle ABC which is unavoidable.
When there is also an endogenous risk premium, the futures price is S_2D
where expected demand exceeds marginal cost by endogenous risk premium
DE. Social loss is triangle DFC.

When there is a Bayesian error JH < 0 as well as an endogenous risk
premium, the futures price is S_3G. The objectively expected price S_3J exceeds
the subjectively expected price S_3H by HJ. The subjectively expected price
S_3H exceeds the futures price by risk premium GH. The realized price S_3K
exceeds the marginal cost S_3G. Social loss is triangle GCK.

perfect foresight competitive equilibrium output, denoted S_1. It is

$$L(t + 1) = \frac{1}{2} [p(t + 1) - q_{t+1}(t)][S_1 - S(t + 1)] \qquad (6.16)$$

This positive sum is the product of: (a) the price deviation or
'forecast error' $p(t + 1) - q_{t+1}(t)$ and (b) the deviation of produc-

tion $S(t+1)$ from the perfect foresight competitive equilibrium S_1. The social loss $L(t+1)$ is the usual 'deadweight' loss in the taxation literature. The price deviation $p(t+1) - q_{t+1}(t)$ is price less marginal cost and corresponds to the 'tax'. Resource misallocation is distance $S_1 - S(t+1)$. Ex-post welfare loss $L(t+1)$ is zero if there is no price deviation or if the supply curve is vertical.

An operational equation for the ex-post social loss $L(t+1)$ can be obtained from supply equation (6.13) and demand equation (6.15). Distance $p(t+1) - q_{t+1}(t)$ between price and marginal cost can be written as

$$p(t+1) - q_{t+1}(t) \equiv [p(t+1) - p_1] + [p_1 - q_{t+1}(t)] \qquad (6.17)$$

where p_1 is the perfect foresight competitive equilibrium. It corresponds to $S_1 C$ when demand is D in Figure 6.2. The slope of the supply curve is c in

$$c = \frac{p_1 - q_{t+1}(t)}{S_1 - S(t+1)} \qquad (6.18)$$

The slope of the demand curve is b in

$$b = \frac{p(t+1) - p_1}{S_1 - S(t+1)} \qquad (6.19)$$

Sum these two equations and obtain

$$\frac{p(t+1) - q_{t+1}(t)}{S_1 - S(t+1)} = (b+c) \qquad (6.20)$$

Therefore, the deviation between the actual and perfect foresight competitive equilibrium output is

$$S_1 - S(t+1) = \frac{[p(t+1) - q_{t+1}(t)]}{(b+c)} \qquad (6.21)$$

Geometrically it is

$$S_3 S_1 = \frac{GK}{(b+c)} \qquad (6.21a)$$

Substitute output deviation (6.21) into the ex-post welfare loss equation (6.16) to obtain

$$L(t+1) = \frac{[p(t+1) - q_{t+1}(t)]^2}{2(b+c)} \qquad (6.22)$$

abbreviated as

$$L(t + 1) = K[p(t + 1) - q_{t+1}(t)]^2 \qquad (6.22a)$$

where K is defined in

$$K = \frac{1}{2(b + c)} \qquad (6.22b)$$

Ex-post social loss L(t + 1) *is a multiple* K *of the square of the price deviation between the subsequently realized cash price* p(t + 1) *and the futures price.* The futures price measures the marginal cost of producing output $S(t + 1)$. In the case of a nonstorable good it reflects the value of other goods that could be produced at time t. If the good is storable it reflects the price of the good at time t plus the marginal storage, interest and insurance costs. Thus the analysis applies to both storable and nonstorable goods.

6.2.3   Determinants of the Deviation Between the Futures Price and Subsequently Realized Cash Price

Price deviation between the subsequently realized price and the futures price can be written as

$$p(t + 1) - q_{t+1}(t) = [p(t + 1) - Ep(t + 1)]$$
$$+ [Ep(t + 1) - E_m p(t + 1; t)]$$
$$+ [E_m p(t + 1; t) - q_{t+1}(t)] \qquad (6.23)$$

For example, it is distance GK in Figure 6.2 whose components are described in

$$\text{GK} \qquad = \qquad \text{JK} \qquad + \qquad \text{HJ}$$

price deviation = unavoidable error + Bayesian error

$$\text{GH}$$

$$+ \text{ risk premium} \qquad (6.23a)$$

Each component is discussed in turn. First, the futures price (equation 6.14) is a discounted for risk value of the subjectively expected price by the market. Risk premium $E_m p(t + 1; t) - q_{t+1}(t)$ is distance GH in Figure 6.2, which is equal to distance JL in Figure 6.1. Algebraically, the risk premium GH is

$$E_m p(t + 1; t) - q_{t+1}(t) = \delta E_m p(t + 1; t) \qquad (6.24a)$$

$$\delta = \frac{JL}{X_1 L} \tag{6.24b}$$

in Figure 6.1. The magnitude of the risk premium δ depends upon net hedging pressure and the 'adequacy of speculation'.

Secondly, the difference between the realized price $p(t + 1)$ and $Ep(t + 1)$, the objective mean price in $t + 1$, is distance JK in Figure 6.2. It represents unpredictable shifts of the demand parameter $u(t + 1)$ around its mean value $Eu(t + 1)$:

$$p(t + 1) - Ep(t + 1) = u(t + 1) - Eu(t + 1) \tag{6.25a}$$

$$\text{unavoidable error} \quad = \quad \text{JK}$$

Thirdly, deviation $E_m p(t + 1; t) - Ep(t + 1) = \text{JH} = y_m$ is the Bayesian error, analysed in Chapter Three and given empirical content in Chapter Five. A brief recapitulation of the salient features of that analysis is as follows.

When the distribution of demand changes, market participants attempt to learn the new mean $Ep(T)$ of the price that will prevail at time T. At time τ, an agent has a subjective distribution, with a subjective mean $E_m p(T; \tau)$. He then takes a sample of size n from the demand. For example, he contacts potential customers to establish what will be the demands in the subsequent periods. Large firms have larger samples to draw upon than do smaller firms. On the basis of the sample, the agent revises his subjective estimate and obtains a posterior subjective estimate of the mean $E_m p(T; \tau + 1)$. The market estimate is a weighted average of the estimates of the market participants.

Bayesian error y_m is the difference between the subjective and objective expectations:

$$y_m(\tau) \equiv E_m p(T; \tau) - Ep(T) \tag{6.25b}$$

Two theorems were proved in Chapter Three concerning the Bayesian error. The variance of the Bayesian error var y is inversely related to the total number of elements sampled. At any time, large agents have more precise estimates of the true mean $Ep(T)$ than do small agents. Over time, the total number of items sampled by an agent grows. If the new distribution of demand is stationary, each agent will have a more precise estimate of the objective mean. The convergence of var y to zero, which is the convergence of the subjective expectation to the objective mean, is called (Chapter Three) asymptotically rational expectations (ARE). By contrast, the MRE assumption is that $y_m = 0$. There is no Bayesian error, because agents always know the true expectation.

On average, the Bayesian errors converge to zero. However, they will be serially correlated. On average, when the new mean demand has changed, the subjective expectation will lag behind the objective expectation.

Using equation (6.23) in (6.22), the ex-post welfare loss can be written as

$$L(t+1) = K\{[p(t+1) - Ep(t+1)] - y_m(t)$$
$$+ \delta E_m p(t+1;t)\}^2 \qquad (6.26a)$$

$$L(t+1) = K\{[p(t+1) - Ep(t+1)] - (1-\delta)y_m(t)$$
$$+ \delta Ep(t+1)\}^2 \qquad (6.26b)$$

ex-post welfare loss $= K$ [unavoidable error

$+$ Bayesian error $+$ risk premium]^2

6.2.4 *Graphic Analysis of the Welfare Loss*

Figure 6.2 and Table 6.1 describe the composition of the ex-post welfare loss based upon equation (6.22). Three cases are distinguished: (a) MRE, no risk premium; (b) MRE and an endogenous risk premium; (c) ARE and an endogenous risk premium.

Curve Q_1 is the marginal cost curve, described by equation (6.13). Given the futures price, curve Q_1 determines the output $S(t+1)$. Equation (6.14) relates the futures price to the subjectively expected price $E_m p(t+1;t)$. Combining equations (6.13)

Table 6.1 Analysis of expected social loss

$p(t+1) - q_{t+1}(t)$	MRE $y_m = 0$ $\delta = 0$	MRE $y_m = 0$ $\delta > 0$	ARE var $y_m > 0$ $\delta > 0$
Unavoidable	AB	EF = AB	JK = AB
Risk premium		DE	GH
Bayesian error			HJ
Total area	ABC	CDF = ABC + ADFB	CGK = ABC + ADFB + GDKF
Output produced	S^*	S_2	S_3
SL	1	$1 + \dfrac{\delta^2 (Ep)^2}{\text{var } u}$	$1 + \dfrac{\delta^2 (Ep)^2}{\text{var } u} + (1-\delta)^2 \dfrac{\text{var } y_m}{\text{var } u}$

and (6.14), curve Q_2 is derived. It relates the subjectively expected price to the output that will be produced. This is

$$E_m p(t + 1; t) = \frac{c}{1 - \delta} S(t + 1) \qquad Q_2 \text{ curve} \qquad (6.27)$$

This is the supply curve which coincides with the marginal cost curve Q_1 when there is no risk premium ($\delta = 0$).

The actual demand curve is

D curve

$$p(t + 1) = u(t + 1) - bS(t + 1) \qquad (6.15)$$

in Figure 6.2 when $u > Eu$. The objectively expected demand curve is

ED curve

$$Ep(t + 1) = Eu(t + 1) - bS(t + 1) \qquad (6.28)$$

in Figure 6.2.

There may be a Bayesian error $y_m(t) = E_m p(t + 1; t) - Ep(t + 1)$ between the subjective and objective means. Then the subjective expected demand is

$$E_m p(t + 1; t) = Eu(t + 1) + y_m(t) - bS(t + 1)$$

$$E_m D \text{ curve} \qquad (6.29)$$

in Figure 6.2 when $y_m < 0$.

Output occurs where equations (6.27) and (6.29) are satisfied, i.e. where curves Q_2 and $E_m D$ intersect. This yields output $S(t + 1)$ and the subjectively expected price $E_m p(t + 1; t)$. Using equation (6.14) the futures price is determined and using equation (6.15) the market-clearing price $p(t + 1)$ is determined.

The relation between the futures price and subsequently realized price is expressed as

$$p(t + 1) = \frac{q_{t+1}(t)}{1 - \delta} + \epsilon(t + 1) - y_m(t) \qquad (6.30a)$$

or

$$q_{t+1}(t) = (1 - \delta)[p(t + 1) - \epsilon(t + 1) + y_m(t)] \qquad (6.30b)$$

6.2.4.1   MRE, No Risk Premium

When there are MRE ($y_m = 0$) and no risk premium ($\delta = 0$), the futures price is equal to the objective expected price. Production occurs where the objectively expected price is equal to marginal cost. Curve Q_1 in Figure 6.2 is the supply curve, relating the objectively expected price to output, that would exist if the futures price were equal to the objectively expected price.

Firms expect the price to be determined by the intersection of the expected demand ED [where $Ep(t+1) = Eu(t+1) - bS(t+1)$] and the supply curve Q_1 [where $Ep(t+1) = cS(t+1)$]. This intersection is a point A in Figure 6.2. Output $S(t+1) = S^*$ is produced and the rationally expected price is S^*A.

At time $t+1$, the realized demand may be D rather than ED, because the parameter of demand is $u(t+1)$ rather than its mean value $Eu(t+1)$. When that occurs, output S^* sells for S^*B rather than at its expected price S^*A. Price exceeds marginal cost by AB $= u(t+1) - Eu(t+1)$, due to the inherent variance of demand. Ex-post welfare loss is triangle ABC, which is unavoidable. Column 1 of Table 6.1 describes this situation of MRE with no risk premium.

Alternatively, the difference between the objectively expected price and the realized price is the unanticipated variation in demand around its mean:

$$u(t) - Eu(t+1) = AB = JK \equiv \epsilon(t+1)$$

which is unpredictable. In this case, the ex-post social loss is

$$L(t+1) = K\epsilon(t+1)^2 \qquad (6.31)$$

which is triangle ABC.

6.2.4.2 *MRE and an Endogenous Risk Premium*
When there are MRE but an endogenous risk premium $(\delta > 0)$, the futures price is a discounted value of the objectively expected price. The supply curve relating the objectively expected price Ep and output $S(t+1)$ is curve Q_2, when there is an endogenous risk premium. Market participants, in this MRE framework, expect market clearing to be at point E (Figure 6.2) where the expected demand ED intersects supply curve Q_2. The expected price is S_2E and the futures price is S_2D $= (1 - \delta)S_2$E, since the endogenous risk premium is DE. Output S_2 is produced at the point where marginal cost is equal to the futures price. This output is expected to sell for price S_2E in the next period.

If demand is described by curve D instead of ED, the realized price will be S_2F, which exceeds the expected price S_2E by deviation EF $= u(t+1) - Eu(t+1) \equiv \epsilon(t+1)$. Deviation DF between the realized price $p(t+1)$ and the futures price $q_{t+1}(t)$ is the sum of two parts. First is an unavoidable error EF = $\epsilon(t + 1)$ resulting from the unpredictable movement in demand (row 1, column 2 in Table 6.1). Second is an endogenous risk premium DE (row 2, column 2 in Table 6.1). Ex-post welfare loss is triangle CDF = ABC + ADFB, (row 4, column 2 in Table 6.1). It is the sum of the unavoidable loss triangle ABC plus the social loss resulting from the endogenous risk premium, trapezoid ADFB. The resulting ex-post welfare loss is

$$L(t + 1) = K[p(t + 1) - q_{t+1}(t)]^2$$

$$= K\left[\frac{\delta}{1 - \delta} q_{t+1}(t) + \epsilon(t + 1)\right]^2 \qquad (6.32)$$

which is triangle CDF.

6.2.4.3   Asymptotically Rational Expectations
When the objective distribution of demand parameter u has changed, there is a Bayesian error y_m (equation 6.25b) between the market's subjective expectation $E_m p(t + 1; t)$ and the objective mean $Ep(t + 1)$. If the distribution of u is stationary, the variance of y_m (var y_m) will converge to zero as repeated samples of information are drawn by market participants.

When there is a Bayesian error JH = $y_m < 0$, the subjective expectation is less than the new objective mean. The subjective expected demand is $E_m D$ in Figure 6.2. The subjectively expected price is JH dollars below the objectively expected price.

If the objectively expected price were $S_3 J$, the subjectively expected price would be $S_3 H$. Difference HJ = $y_m < 0$ is a transitory Bayesian error (row 3, column 3 in Table 6.1). A risk premium of GH (row 2 of column 3 of Table 6.1) is then applied to the subjectively expected price so that the futures price is $S_3 G$.

At futures price $S_3 G$, producers generate an output whose marginal cost of production is $S_3 G$. If demand were at its expected value ED, the realized price would be $S_3 J$. When demand is D instead of at its mean value, output S_3 sells for $S_3 K$. Deviation JK (row 1, column 3 in Table 6.1) is an unavoidable error, due to the unexpected level of demand.

If demand D could have been predicted, the optimal output is S_1. In fact output S_3 is produced. Ex-post welfare loss is triangle CGK, the sum of three elements in row 4, column 3 in Table 6.1. Triangle ABC results from the unavoidable error of predicting demand movements around its objective expectation. As a result of the unavoidable error, output S^* was produced instead of output S_1. Trapezoid ADFB results from the risk premium, whereby output S_2 is produced instead of S^*. Trapezoid DGKF results from the Bayesian error HJ, whereby output S_3 rather than S_2 is produced.

The relation between the futures price and the subsequently realized price is equation (6.30). Social loss is

$$L(t+1) = K[\epsilon(t+1) - (1-\delta)y_m(t) + \delta Ep(t+1)]^2 \qquad (6.33)$$

which is triangle CGK.

6.2.4.4   A Serendipity from Covariances

It is possible that, during an interval of time, the Bayesian error y_m is positively correlated with the unavoidable error ϵ. This is a serendipity illustrated in Figure 6.3. The objectively expected demand is ED. The market mistakenly thinks that the expected demand is $E_m D$. By luck, the realized demand $D(t+1)$ coincides with the subjective expected demand. Output S^* is produced where supply curve $0Q_2$ intersects the subjective expected demand $E_m D$. Realized loss L is $\triangle ABC$.

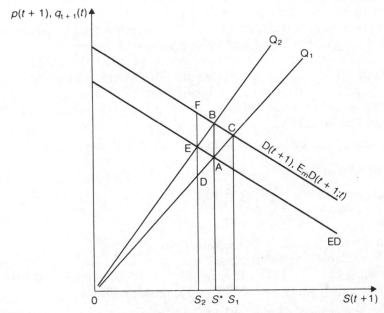

Figure 6.3   By luck, the realized demand $D(t+1)$ coincides with the incorrect subjectively expected demand $E_m D(t+1; t)$. Output is S^* and loss is $\triangle ABC$. The corresponding MRE solution is output S_2 with loss $\triangle DFC$.

The MRE solution with a risk premium leads to a rate of output S_2 where supply Q_2 intersects the objective expected demand ED. In that case, the loss L is $\triangle$ DFC.

This serendipity produces a situation where the loss is less than the unavoidable loss $K \operatorname{var} u$ (see Section 6.3). In general, $\operatorname{cov}(y, u)$ should be zero. There should be no relation between the Bayesian error y and the random disturbance $\epsilon = u - Eu$. Over a long period of time, the minimal loss should be $K \operatorname{var} u$, the unavoidable loss.

6.3   A Theoretical Measure of Welfare Loss

My welfare measure of social loss is the ratio SL of the expected social loss to the expected unavoidable social loss. Graphically, the welfare measure of social loss denoted by SL is the expectation of triangle CGK divided by the expectation of triangle ABC in Figure 6.2. The expectations are taken over stochastic variables $u(t + 1)$ and $y(t)$:

$$SL = E(\triangle CGK)/E(\triangle ABC)$$

Algebraically, the expected loss $E(L) = E(\triangle CGK)$ is derived by taking the expectation of $L(t + 1)$ in equation (6.33). Since the three components ϵ, y_m and Ep are independent, equation (6.34) results. The Bayesian error y_m is independent of the variation of demand around its objective mean. The former results from the inability of the market to locate the objective mean. The variance of the price around its objective mean is the variance of the demand parameter u:

$$E[p(t + 1) - Ep(t + 1)]^2 = E[u(t + 1) - Eu(t + 1)]^2 = \operatorname{var} u$$

Expected loss is

$$E(L) = K [\operatorname{var} u + \delta^2(Ep)^2 + (1 - \delta)^2 \operatorname{var} y_m] = E(\triangle CGK)$$

$$(6.34)$$

when $u - Eu$, y and Ep are independent.

Unavoidable expected social loss, denoted $E(L_0)$, is $K \operatorname{var} u$. This is the expectation of triangle ABC. It is the expected loss that would occur if there were MRE and no risk premium:

$$E(L_0) = K \operatorname{var} u = E(\triangle ABC) \qquad (6.35)$$

Divide expected total loss $E(L) = E(\triangle CGK)$ in equation (6.34) by the expected unavoidable loss $E(L_0) = E(\triangle ABC)$ and derive the social welfare loss SL ratio:

$$SL = \frac{E(L)}{E(L_0)} = 1 + \frac{\delta^2(Ep)^2 + (1-\delta)^2 \text{ var } y_m}{\text{var } u} = \frac{E(\Delta CGK)}{E(\Delta ABC)}$$

(6.36)

With MRE and no risk premium, the social welfare loss SL is unity. This is its minimal value (when the covariances are zero) and indicates that the futures market is functioning perfectly. All social losses are unavoidable (row 6, column 1 of Table 6.1).

When there are MRE but a risk premium resulting from net hedging pressure and inadequate speculation, then the welfare loss SL ratio is the sum of the first two elements in equation (6.36) (row 6, column 2 of Table 6.1).

With ARE, there is a Bayesian error whereby the market participants have not tracked the objective mean of the distribution of demand. This is the var y_m in equation (6.36). It contributes an additional term to the welfare loss SL ratio (row 6, column 3 of Table 6.1). This component goes asymptotically to zero, if the distribution of demand parameter $u(t + 1)$ is stationary.

6.4 Empirical Measures of Social Welfare Loss

6.4.1 Decomposition of the Social Loss

In this section, I derive empirical approximations of the welfare loss SL statistic of the ratio of expected total loss to expected unavoidable loss and relate the SL statistic to the 'Efficient Market Hypothesis'. The resulting approximations are utilized in the next section to evaluate how well various futures markets are functioning.

The expected social loss $E(L)$ was decomposed theoretically in equation (6.34) to isolate the sources of the loss. Here, I am restricted to empirically observed magnitudes. I then attempt to relate the empirical to the theoretical.

Equation (6.34), which is K times the mean square error (MSE), can be decomposed into three empirical terms, as described by equations (6.37) and (6.38a)–(6.38c):

$$\frac{E(L)}{K} = \text{MSE} = E[(p - \bar{p}) + (\bar{p} - \bar{q}) - (q - \bar{q})]^2 = E(p - q)^2$$

(6.37)

where $p = p(t + k)$ is the realized cash price at time $t + k$, $\bar{p}$ is the mean of the above cash prices over the sample period, $q = q_{t+k}(t)$ are the futures prices at time t of a $t + k$ contract and $\bar{q}$ is the mean of the above futures prices over the sample period.

$$E(L)/K = (\bar{p} - \bar{q})^2 + [\sigma_q(1 - b)]^2 + (1 - r^2)\sigma_p^2 \qquad (6.38a)$$

$$E(L)/K = (\bar{p} - \bar{q})^2 + (\sigma_q - r\sigma_p)^2 + (1 - r^2)\sigma_p^2 \qquad (6.38b)$$

and

$$E(L)/K = (U_M + U_R + U_D)\text{MSE} \qquad (6.38c)$$

where σ_p is the standard deviation of $p(t + k)$, σ_q is the standard deviation of $q_{t+k}(t)$, r is the correlation between $p(t + k)$ and $q_{t+k}(t)$, and b is the cov $(p, q)/\text{var } q$. This decomposition of a forecast error, used by Theil (1971) and Maddala (1977), corresponds to components of a welfare measure of loss. There are three components of the social loss. The first $U_m = (\bar{p} - \bar{q})^2/\text{MSE}$ is the fraction of MSE due to the difference between the two mean prices $\bar{p}$ and $\bar{q}$. Note that $Ep(t + k)$ in the theoretical equations is not necessarily the same as $\bar{p}$ in the empirical equations. The former is the mean of the distribution of prices at specific time $t + k$. The latter is the mean of cash prices observed over the sample period. If the distribution of prices changes during the sample period, the two concepts are quite different.

The second $U_R = \sigma_q^2(1 - b)^2/\text{MSE}$ is the fraction of the MSE due to a risk premium which produces a deviation between b and unity. If the regression coefficient b of $p(t + k)$ on $q_{t+k}(t)$ were unity, then U_R would be zero. See equation (6.30a).

The third $U_D = (1 - r^2)\sigma_p^2/\text{MSE}$ is a combination of two disturbances, and is the variance of $\epsilon(t + k) - y_m(t)$ in equation (6.30a) as a fraction of the MSE. When ϵ and y are independent, component $U_D = (\text{var } u + \text{var } y_m)/\text{MSE}$, where var u is the variance of the unavoidable error and var y_m is the variance of the Bayesian error.

It is not sufficient to ask if the mean futures price $\bar{q}$ is equal to the mean subsequently realized cash price $\bar{p}$, in evaluating the social losses in futures markets. It will be seen that term U_m is generally small but significant social losses result from $U_R + U_D$, the inability of the futures price to track variations in the cash price relative to its mean for the period. Consider Figure 6.2. Future price G is below the cash price K, and social loss triangle CGK is generated. Consider another case where the futures price exceeds the cash price by distance GK, because there is a large

Bayesian forecast error. The average social loss is still triangle CGK, even though on average the futures price is equal to the subsequent cash price.

6.4.2 The Efficient Market Hypothesis

The traditional way of evaluating the functioning of speculative markets has been to test the 'Efficient Market Hypothesis' (EMH). This concept is originally due to Samuelson (1965) and Working (1949a). I show how the EMH tests relate to the SL statistic for social loss.

In an ideal market there is no risk premium ($\delta = 0$) or Bayesian error ($y = 0$). Hence, there is no avoidable social loss (SL $= 1$). The cash and futures price are related by equation (6.39) which is a special case of equation (6.30a). This equation,

$$p(t + k) = q_{t+k}(t) + [u(t + k) - Eu(t + k)] \tag{6.39}$$

satisfies the EMH which consists of four assumptions.

(A1) The price of an asset is the discounted expectation by the market of future cash flows, $q_T(t) = E_m p(T; t)$.

(A2) Market anticipations are unbiased estimates of subsequently realized prices, $E_m p(T; t) = Ep(T; t)$.

(A3) New information about cash flows is reflected immediately, without any lagged response, in the price of the asset. The market uses the new information correctly in setting asset prices.

(A4) New information arrives randomly.

Combining (A1) and (A2), we obtain $q_T(t) = Ep(T; t)$, where $Ep(T; t)$ is the objective expectation of price $p(T)$, conditional upon all available information at earlier time t. Assumption (A4) is described by the following:

$$Ep(T; t) - Ep(T; t - 1) = \eta(t)$$

$$E\eta(t) = 0; \qquad E\eta(s)\eta(t) = 0, \qquad s \neq t$$

New information $\eta(t)$ is not predictable, has no structure and has a zero expectation.

Assumptions (A1)–(A4) imply several relations. First, the difference between the futures price and subsequently realized price is a pure stochastic term with no structure. Secondly, changes in the futures price are completely unpredictable:

$$q_T(t + 1) - q_T(t) = \eta(t + 1); \qquad E\eta = 0 \tag{6.40}$$

That is, the change in the futures price is a 'fair game'. Thirdly, the futures price is a martingale:

$$Eq_T(t + 1; t) = q_T(t) \qquad (6.41)$$

The expectation of the price $q_T(t + 1)$ conditional upon information at time t, denoted by $Eq_T(t + 1; t)$ is equal to its current value $q_T(t)$. Fourthly, there is no continually used system whereby a speculator can be expected to make profits on futures contracts. Let variable $W(t)$ represent accumulated wealth resulting from a strategy $[Z(t)]$ or filter rule. When Z is 1 the agent buys and when Z is -1, the agent sells. Then wealth at time t is

$$W(t) = W(t - 1) + [q_T(t) - q_T(t - 1)] Z(t - 1) \qquad (6.42)$$

It is initial wealth $W(t - 1)$ plus the profit or loss on a futures contract, the second term, resulting from the marking to market process. Using the martingale property, the expected value of wealth $EW(t)$ is

$$EW(t; t - 1) = W(t - 1) \qquad (6.43)$$

If the EMH were valid, no continually used strategy can be expected to be profitable. This is known as the 'Impossibility of Systems' (Feller 1966, pp. 210 ff.). Fifthly, the relation between the cash price $p(t + k)$ and the futures price $q_{t+k}(t)$ is

$$p(t + k) = q_{t+k}(t) + \sum_{i=1}^{k} \eta(t) \qquad (6.44)$$

The entire literature concerned with testing the EMH is based upon the above five points. There are three main statistical tests of the EMH.

The first set of tests (T1) concerns the nature of the deviation $e(k)$ between the price realized at time $t + k$ and the price at time t of a futures contract: $e(k) \equiv p(t + k) - q_{t+k}(t)$.

(T1)   Deviation $e(t + k) \equiv p(t + k) - q_{t+k}(t)$ is just 'noise'. It has a zero expectation and is without structure.

(T2)   The second set of tests concern equations (6.45a) and (6.45b). If the EMH were correct, they are the same equation,

$$p(t + k) = a(k) + b(k)q_{t+k}(t) + \epsilon(k) \qquad (6.45a)$$

$$[p(t + k) - p(t)] = a(k) + b(k)[q_{t+k}(t) - p(t)] + \epsilon(k) \qquad (6.45b)$$

In the regression above, $b(k)$ is unity and $a(k)$ is zero. These are referred to as 'bias' tests.

(T3)   The third set of tests investigates whether there are variables $X_i(t)$, known at time t, in addition to the futures price $q_{t+k}(t)$, which can be used to predict the subsequently realized price $p(t + k)$. Tests (T3), referred to as 'efficiency' tests, concern

$$p(t + k) = a(k) + b(k)q_{t+k}(t) + \sum_{i=1}^{m} c_i X_i(t) + e \qquad (6.46)$$

In equation (6.46), coefficient $b(k)$ is unity, and coefficients $a(k)$ and c_i are zero. No filter rule can be profitable. Arbitrage profits cannot exist over any significant period of time.

There are several limitations to the tests (T1)–(T3). The *social loss (SL) depends upon the expectation of the square of the difference* p(t + k) − q$_{t+k}$(t) *whereas the EMH focuses exclusively upon the expectation of the difference.* When tests (T1)–(T3) are passed, then all losses are unavoidable and SL is minimal. Test (T2) alone does not imply that all losses are unavoidable.

It is quite possible for $a = 0$ and $b = 1$ although there are large social losses, SL exceeds unity, as is now shown. Figure 6.4 describes the ideal market where SL $= 1$. If the expectation $Ep(t + k)$ is constant at Ep_1 (which would correspond to S^*A in Figure 6.2), then the futures price is equal to Ep_1. The actual price $p(t + k) = Ep_1 + [u(t + k) − Eu(t + k)]$ will vary randomly around Ep_1 in so far as $u(t + k)$ varies around its constant mean $Eu(t + k)$. There would be no variance to the futures price in this case but the variance of $p(t + k)$ would equal the variance of $u(t + k)$. In this case, the regression coefficient $b = \text{cov}\,(p, q)/\text{var}\,q$ would not be defined because var $q = 0$. The only way that b would be defined is if there was a variation in $Eu(t + k)$, i.e. the distribution of demand changed over time.

If the expectation $Ep(t + k)$ varied over time from Ep_1 to Ep_2 to Ep_3, because $Eu(t + k)$ varied over time, then the futures price would vary to equal the corresponding expected prices (Figure 6.4). The actual distribution of spot prices would be contained in the vertical segments.

When there is a change in the distribution of demand [i.e. $Eu(t + k)$ changes] there may be Bayesian errors. In general, a regression of $p(t + k)$ on $q_{t+k}(t)$ would yield a regression coeffi-

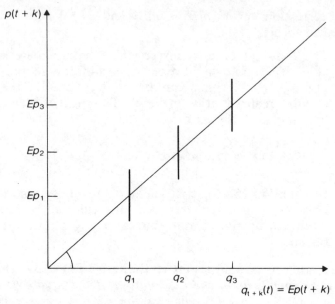

Figure 6.4   In an ideal market, where SL = 1, the futures price is fixed at the expectation of the cash price (*Ep*) but the actual price fluctuates around the given expectation. This is described by the vertical lines.

cient b given by equation (6.47), based upon equation (6.30a).

$$b = \text{cov } (p, q)/\text{var } q$$

$$= \text{cov} \left(\frac{1}{1 - \delta} q - y + \epsilon, q \right) \bigg/ \text{var } q$$

$$b = \frac{1}{1 - \delta} + \frac{\text{cov } (\epsilon, q)}{\text{var } q} - \frac{\text{cov } (y, q)}{\text{var } q} \qquad (6.47)$$

This general equation for b indicates that it may take on a large range of values, when the covariances are not zero.

It is quite possible that SL exceeds unity in equation (6.36) even though $b = 1$. Suppose that there is no risk premium ($\delta = 0$) and all covariances are zero: $\text{cov } (\epsilon, q) = 0$, $\text{cov } (\epsilon, y) = 0$ and $\text{cov } (y, q) = 0$, then $b = 1$. However, the social loss in this case is

$$\text{SL} = \frac{E(L)}{E(L_0)} = 1 + \frac{\text{var } y}{\text{var } u} > 1 \qquad (6.48)$$

based upon equation (6.36), since

$$p(t + k) = q_{t+k}(t) + \epsilon(t + k) - y(t).$$

Hence, the mere existence of $a = 0$ and $b = 1$ does not imply that there are no significant social losses.

Tests (T1)–(T3) cannot convey an order of magnitude. They are incapable of evaluating *quantitatively* how well the futures markets are functioning. If some of the tests fail to support the EMH, what is to be concluded? Does this mean that the market is functioning badly? If the EMH is not rejected, because the standard errors are large, does this mean that the market is functioning well?

Tests (T1)–(T3) have very little to say about the causes of the deviation of the futures price from the subsequently realized price. Several authors (Fama, 1984; Hodrick and Srivastara, 1984) refer to this deviation as a 'time varying risk premium'. Such an approach is inadmissible because it is tautological and devoid of economic content. A risk premium must be related to the economic structure. In equation (6.14), the risk premium is δ and it affects the coefficient of the futures price, not the residual, in equation (6.30a) or (6.39) above. In foreign exchange, the deviation $e(k)$ cannot be called a time varying risk premium until economic theory determines which of the pair of currencies carries the risk premium. Even if the capital asset pricing model is used to determine a risk premium, the latter would be determined by the historical variance–covariance matrix. It cannot be a tautological 'time varying error term'.

The EMH tests, however, do have a direct relation to the welfare losses resulting from a misallocation of resources. The magnitude of the social losses are the triangles in Figure 6.3 or Table 6.1, and are second moments of distributions because

$$E[L(k)] = KE[p(t + k) - q_{t+k}(t)]^2.$$

The EMH tests concern the first moments but can be viewed as useful complements to social loss measures.

The usefulness of the SL statistic, equation (6.36) and empirical measures related to equation (6.38), in evaluating the performance of speculative markets is as follows. First, it measures welfare losses in terms of the sum of producer and consumer surplus relative to the inherent noisiness of the system. Secondly, since it is a pure number, it can be used to compare different markets. It provides a *quantitative* measure of the relative performance of different markets. Thirdly, by combining the SL statistic with the EMH it permits a decomposition of the losses in terms of the ability to locate the mean and the ability to track changes in the distribution of the cash price. The former is related to the existence of risk premium δ; the latter is related to var y_m, the lag of changes in the subjective expectation behind changes in the objective expectation.

6.5   Welfare Losses: Empirical Analysis

6.5.1   Limitations of the Efficient Market Hypothesis

The limitations of the EMH tests discussed above clearly emerge from an analysis of Tables 6.2 and 6.3. Tests (T2) and (T3) have been the most widely used means of evaluating the performance of speculative markets. In test (T2), regression equation (6.49) is used:

$$\log p(t + k) - \log p(t) = a(k) + b(k)[\log q_{t+k}(t) - \log p(t)]$$

$$(6.49)$$

The EMH states that $b(k) = 1$ and $a(k) = 0$, where parameter k represents time to maturity.

Alternatively, equation (6.50) is used to implement test (T3):

$$\log p(t + k) = a(k) + b(k) \log q_{t+k}(t) + c \log p(t) \qquad (6.50)$$

The hypothesis is $b(k) = 1$ and $a(k) = 0$, $c = 0$.

Table 6.2 contains the estimates of equation (6.50) for the Canadian dollar relative to the US dollar, during the period June 1970 to December 1981, for maturities ranging from 1 to 12 months. Table 6.3 does the same for the US dollar relative to the pound sterling, for the same period. The numbers in parentheses are standard errors of the regression coefficients.

Consider the foreign exchange evidence. Several results are immediately apparent and they apply to other currencies as well. The value of $b(k)$, the coefficient of the forward price, is consistently negative for the pound (Table 6.3) and significantly so for the one- and three-month maturities. Coefficient $b(k)$ is significantly negative for the Canadian dollar (Table 6.2) with a one-month maturity; and it is significantly below unity for a two-month maturity. *These results reject the EMH.* In both Tables 6.2 and 6.3, the standard errors of $b(k)$ are very large. The hypothesis that $b(k) = 0$ can never be rejected, whereas the EMH claims that $b(k) = 1$. Alternatively, in view of the large standard errors, the test of the hypothesis that $b(k)$ equals unity has almost no power. In both Tables 6.2 and 6.3, we can reject the hypothesis that coefficient c is zero for nearby maturities. For other maturities, the standard errors are so large that the test has no power. The confidence intervals for c span too wide a range. In the case of the pound sterling, we can always reject the joint EMH hypothesis that $b = 1$ and $c = 0$, as shown by the chi-square statistics.

The other currencies exhibit the same results (Longworth, Boothe and Clinton, 1983, Table D:1, p. 71). What are we to conclude from Tables 6.2 and 6.3 concerning the functioning of the foreign exchange market? Is the Canadian dollar market functioning better or worse than the British pound? Is either market functioning well? What understanding of the market is provided by the EMH? The high standard errors of the coefficients imply that the tests of the EMH have little power. Consider the pound sterling in Table 6.3. Those who reject the EMH would point to the consistently negative values of $b(k)$ for the pound, and say that the futures price has no predictive value since regression coefficient $b(k)$ is not significantly different from *zero*. Those who believe in the EMH would point to the large standard errors and say that, only in two cases ($k = 1, 3$), can they reject the hypothesis that $b(k)$ is unity, even though the estimates are always negative.

Table 6.2 Estimate of $\log p(t + k) = a(k) + b(k) \log q_{t+k}(t) + c \log p(t)$ for the US–Canadian dollar exchange rate 1970–81 by months to maturity

k	$a(k)$	$b(k)$	c	SEE
1	0.002	−0.431**	1.412**	0.01061
	(0.001)	(0.547)	(0.546)	
2	0.003	0.037*	0.947	0.01557
	(0.002)	(0.572)	(0.571)	
3	0.004	0.163	0.821	0.01815
	(0.004)	(0.602)	(0.599)	
6	0.007	1.008	−0.009	0.02653
	(0.007)	(0.784)	(0.722)	
12	0.025	1.491	−0.555	0.03723
	(0.018)	(0.965)	(0.893)	

Symbols: * (**) indicates that coefficient is significantly different from its hypothesized value ($b = 1$, $c = 0$, $a = 0$) at the 10 per cent (5 per cent) level. k, distance in months from maturity at time $t + k$; $q_{t+k}(t)$, forward rate at time t; $p(t + k)$, realized price at time $t + k$. Standard errors in parentheses are adjusted by the Hansen–Hodrick procedure.
Source: Longworth, Boothe and Clinton, 1983, Table 4.2

Table 6.3　Estimate of $\log p(t + k) = a(k) + b(k) \log q_{t+k}(t) + c \log p(t)$ for the US dollar–pound sterling exchange rate 1970–81 by months to maturity

k	a(k)	b(k)	c	SEE	chi-square (2)
1	−0.0220	−1.4159**	2.3778**	0.02894	12.19**
	(0.0174)	(0.8393)	(0.84162)		
3	0.0735	−0.8389*	1.7179*	0.05438	6.7**
	(0.0577)	(0.9723)	(0.9284)		
6	0.1572	−0.5152	1.2757	0.07715	5.0*
	(0.1176)	(1.0689)	(1.0924)		
12	0.4229	−0.0486	0.4259	0.11021	5.78*
	(0.2325)	(1.1270)	(1.2048)		

Symbols: See Table 6.2.
Source: Longworth, Boothe and Clinton, 1983, Table D:1

A similar situation exists for the Canadian dollar. The EMH is clearly rejected for nearby maturities. However, the high standard errors imply that the tests have negligible power. For maturities of three or more months, coefficient $b(k)$ could be hypothesized to be either zero or unity. All that everyone can agree about is that the futures price is a worthless forecast.

The tests of the efficient market hypothesis are not useful in understanding and evaluating the functioning of futures markets.

6.5.2　Measures of Social Loss

The social loss SL (equation 6.36) is the ratio of expected loss $E(L) = E(\Delta CGK)$ in Figure 6.3, to the expected unavoidable loss $E(L_0) = E(\Delta ABC)$. Each expected loss is K times the mean square error (MSE) between the futures price and the subsequently realized price (equations 6.37, 6.38 above). Two different measures of expected unavoidable loss are used.

The expected unavoidable loss $E(L_0)$ is K times the MSE on the nearest contract to maturity. The rationale is as follows. The expected social loss (see Table 6.1) is the sum of the unavoidable error K var u, the loss due to the risk premium $K\delta^2(Ep)^2$ and the loss due to the Bayesian error $K(1 - \delta)^2$ var y_m, when the covariances are zero.

On the nearest contract to maturity, the Bayesian error is assumed to be the smallest. Market participants know more about the true mean of the distribution of price $p(t + k)$ on the closest to maturity contract than on the more distant contracts. In addition, since the length of time that the market will be holding the nearby contract is less than that for more distant contracts, the risk premium is assumed to be the smallest. Hence, the major part of the MSE on the nearby contract is assumed to be K var u or unavoidable error. The first measure of social loss SL is

$$SL(k) = \frac{MSE\ (k)}{MSE\ (1)} \approx 1 + \frac{\delta^2 (Ep)^2 + (1 - \delta)^2 \text{ var } y_m}{\text{var } u} \qquad (6.51)$$

where MSE (1) is the MSE on the nearest contract.

The expected unavoidable loss K var u may be positively related to the variance of the cash price var $p(t + k)$. Therefore, the second estimate of the social loss is the ratio of the MSE to the variance of the cash price SL*:

$$SL^*(k) = \frac{MSE\ (k)}{\text{var } p} \qquad (6.52)$$

These two measures allow us to compare the welfare losses in two different markets. They are the empirical estimates of SL in equation (6.36) for the ratio of $E(\Delta CGK)/E(\Delta ABC)$.

Table 6.4 (derived from Agmon and Amihud, 1981) analyses three currencies relative to the dollar: the pound sterling, the D-Mark and the Swiss franc, during the period mid-1973 to mid-1977. The authors also consider the subperiods mid-1973 to mid-1975, and mid-1975 to mid-1977. The mean square error is calculated as

$$MSE(k) = \frac{1}{n} \sum_{t=1}^{n} \left[\ln \frac{p(t + k)}{p(t)} - \ln \frac{q_{t+k}(t)}{p(t)} \right]^2 \qquad (6.53)$$

Column 1 contains social loss SL*(k) and column 2 contains social loss SL(k). On every maturity, the pound sterling fares the worst and the D-Mark fares the best. The orders of magnitude are quite high on contracts with maturities 3–6 months. Quantity SL*(3) = 1.22 for the pound and SL*(3) = 1.05 for the D-Mark.

Another measure of social loss is SL(k) (equation 6.51) and is contained in column 2. The assumption here is that on the nearby one-month contract most losses are unavoidable. Bayesian error var y_m is minimal, as is risk premium δ, in equation (6.51).

The same results are observed for the two social loss measures. Consider SL(6). For the pound sterling SL(6) = 1.177, for the

Table 6.4   Measures of social loss: pound sterling, D-mark and Swiss franc relative to US dollar, mid-1973 to mid-1977 for maturities

	1 SL*(k)	2 SL(k)
Pound		
$k = 1$	1.13	1
$k = 3$	1.22	1.08
$k = 6$	1.33	1.177
D-Mark		
$k = 1$	1	1
$k = 3$	1.05	1.05
$k = 6$	1.04	1.04
Swiss franc		
$k = 1$	1.02	1
$k = 3$	1.09	1.069
$k = 6$	1.12	1.0980

Notes: Column 1 is $\bar{U}^2$. Column 2 is column 1 divided by SL*(1). k is 1, 3, 6 months.
Source: Agmon and Amihud, 1981, Tables 1 and 2.

Swiss franc SL(6) = 1.098 and for the D-Mark SL(6) = 1.04. The conclusion is that, in terms of welfare measures, the D-Mark functions the best, the Swiss franc is next and the pound sterling fares the worst. Compare these welfare results with the vacuous results of the EMH described above.

Welfare losses for traditional commodities are most revealing, when the analysis in this chapter is applied to the study by Tomek and Gray (1970). Corn and soybeans are produced seasonally and carried continuously during the year. Potatoes are quite different. They are produced seasonally, but most of the stocks from the autumn potato crop are sold by the beginning of June. Potatoes conform to the model in Chapters 2 and 3, whereas corn and soybeans are a combination of the models in Chapters 2–4.

For all three commodities, production decisions are made in the spring and the harvest occurs in the autumn. Inventories are seasonally large just after the harvest. The December future is the first new crop future for corn, whereas the November contract is the first new future for Maine potatoes and soybeans. Social loss SL* is equation (6.52), the ratio of the mean square error to the variance of the cash price (in November or December).

Table 6.5 analyses the social loss for the three commodities. Row 1 indicates that the social loss SL* is almost identical for

Table 6.5   Welfare losses in corn, soybeans and potatoes, 1952-68

	Corn	Soybeans	Potatoes
SL* = MSE/var p	0.44	0.43	0.79
U_M	0.18	0.23	0.06
U_R	0.04	0.02	0.39
U_D	0.78	0.76	0.55
var p/var q	1.20	1.68	26.09

Source: Derived from Tomek and Gray, 1970, Tables 1 and 2

corn (SL* = 0.44) and soybeans (SL* = 0.43), but almost twice as large for potatoes (SL* = 0.79).

Rows 2–4 decompose the sources of the MSE according to equation (6.38) above. Again, corn and soybeans are similar in terms of the fraction U_M of the MSE due to differences in the mean prices and U_D the fraction due to $(1 - r^2)$ var p, which is the variance of the unavoidable plus Bayesian errors. Potatoes are quite different; the social loss is more evenly divided between component U_D and component U_R which is the fraction of the MSE due to a slope less than unity.

Row 5 indicates that the ratio of variances of the cash and futures prices is 1.2 for corn and 1.68 for soybeans but 26.09 for potatoes. This is consistent with the much larger ratio U_R for potatoes.

The reason for the differences in social loss SL* seems to be that there are no continuous inventories in potatoes but that they exist for corn and soybeans. Say that the price in December $p(12)$ can be forecasted fairly well from the information available in April concerning developments from April to December, denoted by

$$\sum_{t=4}^{12} I(t; 4)$$

Let different groups have the different pieces of information $I(t; 4)$. If there are no continuous inventories, then the futures price $q_{12}(4)$ will be based upon $I(12; 4)$, the information available to those who only use the December contract. Hence, $q_{12}(4)$ is based upon a small sample of information $I(12; 4)$. When there are continuous inventories, then the prices of two successive futures $q_T(4)$ and $q_{T+1}(4)$ are linked by the cost of carry (less any marginal convenience yield). But each futures $q_T(4)$ is based upon

$I(T; 4)$, a specific piece of information available in April concerning developments in month T. Hence, the April price of a December future contains

$$\sum_{t=4}^{12} I(t; 4)$$

all of the information, available in April, concerning future developments. Since the futures price is based upon a larger set of information, it is a more accurate forecast. That is why social loss SL is lower with continuous inventories.

6.5.3 Conclusion

The functioning of futures markets has been evaluated by different authors in different ways. Some have focused upon the resulting changes in the variance of the cash price. Others have asked whether the futures market is efficient in the sense that the futures price is an unbiased estimate of the subsequent cash price and that no trading rule can generate net profits. Others have looked at the effect of the futures market upon the expected utility of consumers plus the expected utility of profits of producers. A more general and traditional approach is taken in this chapter. I ask whether there exists a reallocation of the new intertemporal pattern of consumption produced by futures markets which can make everyone better off than he was in the initial situation. No distinction is made between producers and consumers: everyone is viewed as a consumer.

A resulting measure of welfare loss is derived for each market, which is proportional to the mean square deviation between the futures price and the subsequently realized price. This loss is decomposed into an unavoidable loss due to the inherent uncertainty of demand the the avoidable loss due to risk premiums and Bayesian errors. The resulting social loss statistic SL is the ratio of the mean square error to the variance of the cash price.

The efficient market hypothesis is a component of the SL statistic but the efficient market tests are incapable of providing quantitative estimates of how well a given futures market is functioning in terms of welfare, relative to another market.

Social loss statistics are derived for three foreign currencies and three traditional commodities. For foreign exchange, the SL statistic is smallest for the D-Mark, slightly higher for the Swiss franc and highest for the pound. In the case of traditional commodities, the SL statistic concerns the optimality of planned production, where the production decision is taken in the spring, and output is available in the autumn. The SL statistic is similar for corn and soybeans but almost twice as large for potatoes. The reason for the high SL statistic in potatoes is that there are continuous inventories for corn and soybeans but there are no inventories of potatoes from June to the autumn. When there are continuous inventories, the prices of successive futures are linked by the cost of carry. Each futures price contains some information. Hence, when there are continuous inventories, there is a larger information set that is reflected in the price of the December future than occurs when no inventories are carried.

The theory developed in the first part of the chapter is applied in the second part to the evaluation of different futures markets.

7

The Effects of Interest Rate and Stock Index Futures upon the Rate of Capital Formation

The United States Congress, the Federal Reserve Board, the Commodity Futures Trading Commission (CFTC) and the Securities and Exchange Commission (SEC) were concerned, in 1982 and 1983, about the effects of trading in interest rate and stock index futures upon the rate of capital formation. This chapter applies the theory developed in the previous chapters to the markets in interest rate futures and stock index futures. Considerable attention is given to the institutional arrangements, so that the theory corresponds to reality. This chapter ties together the theory developed in the previous chapters by applying it to an extremely important policy issue.

7.1   The Framework of Analysis

The effects of futures markets upon the rate of capital formation can be viewed within the context of the supply of and demand for risky assets (or demand for and supply of loanable funds) during a period of time (Table 7.1). The major users of the new futures markets are subsumed under items (1), (3) and (5). The level of security prices or rate of interest adjusts to equate the two sides of the table. The resulting cost of capital or rate of interest determines the rate of capital formation.

Item (1) is the rate of planned investment, or sale of risky assets by firms, during a time interval. This rate is positively related to the level of security prices relative to the cost of production of new capital goods.

Table 7.1 Supply of and demand for risky securities, during a time interval

---

Supplies of securities

(1) Planned investment by firms
(2) Government budget deficit

Demand for securities

(3) Savings less the change in demand for money
(4) Change in the supply of money
(5) Dealers' investment in inventories of securities

Keynes described the crucial role of the relative level of security prices in the secondary market upon planned capital formation. The main determinant of the rate of planned investment by firms is the ratio of the market value of equity plus debt to the reproduction cost of the firms.

... the daily revaluations of the Stock Exchange, though they are primarily made to facilitate transfers of old investments between one individual and another, inevitably exert a decisive influence on the rate of investment. For there is no sense in building up a new enterprise at a cost greater than that which a similar enterprise can be purchased; whilst there is an inducement to spend on a new project what may seem an extravagant sum, if it can be floated off on the Stock Exchange at an immediate profit. (Keynes, 1936, p. 151)

Tobin formalized Keynes's analysis and denoted by q the ratio of the market value of the equity plus debt of the firm to its reproduction cost. If q exceeds unity, it is profitable to purchase newly produced output and use it as a capital good. This constitutes a demand for investment. If q is less than unity, it is cheaper to purchase an existing asset than a newly produced investment good and capital formation is discouraged. Whatever raises the market value of equity plus debt of a firm relative to its reproduction cost, raises the rate of planned capital formation.

Little distinction need be made between the primary and secondary markets for securities in analysing the capital formation process. First is the argument of Keynes quoted above. Secondly, the securities offered in the primary market are substitutes for comparable securities in the secondary market. If the value of the latter rises, investors will demand securities in the primary market. The latter raises the q ratio and capital formation is stimulated. Third is an argument made in a later section that the liquidity and stability of prices in the secondary market affect the rate of savings and the fraction of savings invested in risky assets.

Investment in residential housing is a large fraction of net fixed capital formation. I explain below how the use of futures markets by the FNMA reduces the risk premium that it charges to mortgage bankers and savings and loan associations. As a result of the lower risk premium, mortgage interest rates are reduced and planned investment in housing is increased.

Item (2) is the supply of risky assets generated by the government budget deficit. Futures markets have no direct effect upon this item. The sum of items (1) and (2) constitutes the supplies of risky assets by firms and the government, which is a demand for loanable funds.

Item (3) is savings less the change in the demand for money. This item constitutes the savings directed towards risky assets during a time interval. A large part of the public's savings is managed by institutional investors: pension funds and insurance companies, which are subsumed under this category. In a later section I show how the use of futures markets by institutional investors improves the trade-off between expected return and risk on their investment. This improvement leads to an increase in the flow of savings directed towards risky assets and raises the market value of corporate equity plus debt. Capital formation is thereby stimulated. If no futures markets existed in Treasury securities and stock market indices, the expected return for a given level of risk available to institutional investors would be lower. A greater proportion of current savings would then be directed towards holding money or near money. The lower flow demand for securities would tend to raise interest rates (i.e. lower the level of security prices) which would adversely affect the rate of capital formation.

Item (4) is the change in the supply of money, which corresponds to a demand for risky assets by banks or the Federal Reserve System. Futures markets have no significant effect upon Federal Reserve behaviour.

In the standard macroeconomic literature, the interest rate (or price of securities) adjusts to equate the sum of items (1) and (2), the supplies of risky assets, with that of items (3) and (4), the demand for risky assets. On average over a period of a year that view is correct. Over shorter periods of time, item (5) must also be considered.

If there were no securities dealers, then intra-month or intra-year variations in the government budget deficit or planned investment by firms would have to be absorbed by savings less the change in demand for money. The latter is not highly responsive to changes in the interest rates. Therefore, intra-month variations in the supplies of risky assets, item (1) plus item (2), would be associated with very large variations in security prices. Such a phenomenon would increase the risks of holding equities and fixed income securities, and would decrease the savings directed towards risky assets, item (3). In this manner, an increase in the variability of interest rates would raise the average level of interest rates. Capital formation would be reduced.

Dealers in fixed income securities in both the primary and secondary market, and in equities only in the secondary market, are major users of futures markets. The economic function of dealers is to provide an inventory investment in securities. Short-period variations in the excess supply of securities (items 1 plus 2) less the sum of items 3 plus 4 in Table 7.1) lead to price variations. As the price declines below (rises above) the present value of the price expected to prevail later, dealers purchase (sell) the securities for (from) temporary inventory. In this manner, dealers mitigate the magnitude of the price fluctuations. In so far as their anticipations are correct, they are able to dispose of (replenish) their inventories at higher (lower) prices. The greater the elasticity of demand by dealers for investment in inventories of securities, the smaller will be the price (interest rate) variation associated with short period variations in items (1)–(4). Since the rate of planned investment by firms (item 1) and savings directed towards risky assets (item 4) are negatively related to the risks in holding securities, the existence of dealers tends to stimulate the rate of capital formation.

Two components of risk are involved in the dealers' purchases or sales of securities for inventory investment or disinvestment. One part is the *market risk* resulting from changes in the market index. For fixed income securities, it is the height of the yield curve on Treasuries. For equities, it is the S&P 500 index. The second part is the *portfolio specific risk* which concerns the prices of the particular securities purchased or sold *relative* to the level of the index.

Later, I explain how dealers use futures markets to diversify away the market risks. This diversification leads to a reduction in the risk premium they must charge their customers via commissions and spreads. The net effect of the dealers' use of futures markets is to lower the variance of interest rates and raise the q ratio. In this manner, futures markets are conducive to a higher rate of capital formation.

7.2   Dealers, Futures Markets and the Cost of Capital

Dealers in government bonds, corporate fixed income securities and equities are financial intermediaries between savers and investors, just as grain dealers are intermediaries between producers and consumers. Inventory management is the essence of their business because they stand ready to sell securities to customers at their ask prices and purchase from them at their bid prices. Dealers intend to offset the transactions relatively quickly, generally within five minutes, rather than acquire a long-term investment portfolio. They are often unable to even out their positions quickly without suffering large losses. Consequently, they face risks in managing their temporary portfolio of inventory. This risk management is the subject of this section. These professional risk bearers are *transactions* and *customer oriented*, rather than *investment oriented* as are institutional investors.

Securities dealers have separate divisions for government and corporate fixed income securities, equity underwriting and stock block trading. These divisions operate independently of each other. The profit equations and optimization calculus for all division or type of dealer are similar, although the institutional details and quantitative values of parameters are different. In this part I explain how futures markets in Treasury securities and stock market indexes enable dealers to manage risk more effectively, reduce the cost of capital to firms and raise their q ratios and thereby reduce the price variance of securities. The longer-run net effect is to raise the investment demand schedules of firms, and supply of savings directed to risky assets.

First, I show how the greater risks of doing business have increased substantially since 1979 and forced firms to use futures markets to manage risk. Secondly, I explain how the optimal use of futures by dealers changes their demand curves for temporary inventory. The latter consists of securities purchased but not as yet sold to customers.

7.2.1   The Change in the Sources of Risk

The profit equation of dealers equation (7.1) abbreviated as (7.1a) is the focal point of the analysis. Let $p(t)$ be the price and $s(t)$ be the portfolio of securities purchased $(+)$ or sold $(-)$ at time t. The dealer will sell this portfolio at price $p(t + 1)$ or, if he does not sell it, the price of his unsold inventory will be $p(t + 1)$ at time $t + 1$.

The financing costs of the inventory are at rate $r(t)$, which is either the Treasury bill or broker loan rate from time t to $t + 1$.

The dealer has several additional sources of revenue. Commissions and bid-ask spreads contribute to the profits, and he may receive interest and dividends on the portfolio. These two sources of revenue less total operating costs can be subsumed under the term $V[s(t)]$:

$$\pi(t + 1) = \{p(t + 1) - [1 + r(t)]p(t)\}s(t)$$

$$+ V[s(t)] - [q_T(t + 1) - q_T(t)]x(t) - T[x(t)] \quad (7.1)$$

$$\pi = s\Delta p + V(s) - x\Delta q - T(x) \quad (7.1a)$$

$$\pi = \pi_N \qquad - x\Delta q - T(x) \quad (7.1b)$$

where Δp is the $p(t + 1) - [1 + r(t)]p(t)$, $p(t)$ is the price of portfolio, Δq is the $q_T(t + 1) - q_T(t)$, $s(t)$ is the purchase $(+)$ and sale $(-)$ of securities, $q_T(t)$ is the price at time t of a futures contract maturing at T, $r(t)$ is the net interest rate, $V(s)$ are the commissions and spreads less direct operating costs, $T(x)$ are the transactions costs on futures, $x(t)$ are the sales $(+)$ and purchases $(-)$ of futures and, $\pi_N = s\Delta p + V(s)$ are the profits if futures are not used.

Profits from these transactions in the cash market π_N derive from the change in price less financing costs

$$s\Delta p = [p(t + 1) - p(t)(1 + r(t))]s(t)$$

plus interest and dividends plus revenues from commissions less total operating costs $V[s(t)]$. Profits from transactions in the futures market are based upon the last two terms and are discussed later.

Dealers operate with very high leverage. A ratio of position at risk to capital of 50 is not uncommon for nonbank dealers. Since 1979, several elements of risk, which have substantially altered the ways dealers operate, have emerged. They stem from regulatory changes, greater interest rate volatility and an increase in the size of transactions.

Formerly, a corporate treasurer would discuss with a dealer the prospects of issuing new corporate fixed income securities. A price 'talkout' would ensue, whereby the dealer would conduct a roll call of institutional investors to get an indication of interest in purchasing the issue. After the relatively slow process of consulting with the distribution network of institutional investors, the dealer could quote a price $p(t)$ to the corporate treasurer. A firm price could be given to the corporate treasurer, and a fixed price to the public could be established in a bona fide offering. The dealer would expect to profit from the commissions or spread $V[s(t)]$ in excess of any financing costs. The dealer had very little price risk because the price talkout established the price and quantity that the institutional investors were willing to accept. In effect, the dealer bought the issue forward from the corporate treasurer and sold a large part of it forward to institutional investors.

Large dealers had advantages in this set of arrangements because they have a considerable and widespread clientele distributed over the country and know what their clients' preferences for securities are. When the corporate treasurer discussed a new issue with the dealer, the latter would call the potential customers to determine the quantities demanded at various possible prices. In this manner, the large dealer would sample the demand curve before he made a bid for the new corporate issue. Small dealers do not have this wide distribution network and have much less information about the state of demand.

Recent regulatory changes have fundamentally altered this process. SEC rule 415 introduced in March 1982 created a shelf registration process for new issues. Under this rule, large corporations can register the full amount of debt or equity they reasonably expect to sell over a two-year period. After the initial registration, firms can sell securities in variable amounts without further delay whenever conditions seem favourable. This technique is attractive to corporate treasurers. It offers the corporate treasurer flexibility to react quickly to market conditions and it reduces the costs of issuing securities by saving legal, accounting and printing expenses.

At the same time, the shelf registration rule increases the risks to the dealers. Corporate treasurers could act quickly without circulating a prospectus for a particular issue. Instead of the slow talkout process whereby the dealer had the luxury and leisure of putting together a book of the customers for the issues, the corporate treasurers can now bring the issues off the shelf quickly. The dealer is asked for an immediate firm bid $p(t)$ for a particular issue. Some dealers have exclusive relations with particular corporations, and are expected to offer the corporate treasurers the best price in the market. In other cases, if there is no special relation, the dealers bid for the issues.

Corporate treasurers tend to bring more issues off the shelf when interest rates on long-term government bonds decline, that is, the prices of government bonds rise.

A significant negative relation, equation (7.2), exists between the index of the value of new corporate debt issued during the month $IY(t)$ relative to its mean value during the period and the *change* in the interest rate on ten-year Treasury bonds

$$i(t) - i(t-1)$$

from the previous month. When long-term government bond interest rates decline from month $t-1$ to month t, the value of new corporate debt brought off the shelf in month t is relatively high compared to its average over the sample period January 1982 to September 1983. Regression equation (7.2) is the speculative supply of securities offered by corporate treasurers per month during the period January 1982 to September 1983.

$$IY(t) = 93.6 - 69.15[i(t) - i(t-1)];$$

$$(t =) \qquad (-5.99) \qquad R^2 = 0.67; \qquad n = 20 \qquad (7.2)$$

When government bond prices rise [that is, $i(t) - i(t-1)$ is negative], corporate treasurers quickly bring debt issues off the shelf. They want to take advantage of the temporary rise in bond prices. Dealers are asked to quote prices for the issue immediately. There is no time to have a price talkout and no book can be put together before bidding on an issue.

Dealers in the primary market face two asymmetrical risks. First, corporate treasurers are offering their debt as a result of the current rise in bond prices. If the treasurers thought that bond prices would rise further, they would wait longer before taking the issue off the shelf. When they offer their debt to dealers, the corporate treasurers think that it is more likely that prices will decline rather than rise.

Secondly, dealers fix an offering price to the public in a bona fide offering. This is a ceiling price. They cannot raise the price to the public, even if bond prices in the market rise. If bond prices should fall and dealers are unable to market the issue, the offering price to the public is reduced. Dealers face a downside price risk but cannot benefit from a rise in the market price.

Another element of risk in both the primary and secondary market is that interest rate volatility has increased, particularly since October 1979. Before that date, the Federal Reserve tended to stabilize the federal funds rate and indirectly short-term market rates of interest. As a consequence, the Federal Reserve was unable to control the growth of monetary aggregates. In October 1979 the Federal Reserve adopted a new operating procedure whereby the federal funds rate was allowed to fluctuate within wider limits, and began to focus the conduct of monetary policy upon the growth of monetary aggregates. This new policy implied that short-term interest rates would be more volatile as a result of changes in the banks' demands for total reserves. The mean and standard deviation of monthly three-month Treasury bills in the pre- and post-1979 period reflect the greater volatility (Table 7.2).

The increased yield or price volatility in interest rates on treasuries created more difficulty for both dealers and their customers in knowing what the price of the securities during the next period would be. Dealers are especially at risk as a result of the asymmetry of pricing of new issues.

The price risks were serious because the size of the typical transaction increased for all dealers: stock block traders, corporate fixed income traders and government bond dealers. Before 1976, one million dollars was considered a large bond transaction in the secondary market. By 1983, it was ten million dollars. A major reason for the increase in the size of dealers' transactions is that money management is now institutionalized. Because of the 1974 federal pension fund reform law and the higher inflation, pension fund assets have more than tripled since 1971. It is estimated that in 1984 approximately $1500 billion is managed by professional money market managers, two-thirds of which is pension money. There is keen competition among money managers who are trying to outperform the market. They are much more trading oriented than their predecessors who invested their money in the large corporations and had long investment horizons. As a result, purchases and sales are more volatile and are substantially larger.

Table 7.2   Mean and standard deviation of Treasury bill rates 1976–78 and 1980–83

	Mean (% p.a.)	Standard deviation (% p.a.)
1976	5.00	0.28
1977	5.27	0.64
1978	7.22	1.00
1980	11.61	2.88
1981	14.08	1.60
1982	10.72	2.29
1983	8.62	0.48

The scale of the operations of government bond dealers increased as a result of the growth in the size and variability of the deficit in the national accounts budget. From the first quarter of 1977 to the last quarter of 1979 the mean quarterly deficit seasonally adjusted at annual rates was $30 billion. From the first quarter of 1980 to the third quarter of 1983 the corresponding mean quarterly deficit was $108 billion. The net effect of these three developments was to increase the price risk reflected in the variance of profits in equation (7.1) above.

7.2.2 Market Risk and Portfolio Specific Risk

The portfolio of securities $s(t)$ purchased by dealers during a day consists of heterogeneous elements. Dealers in fixed income securities manage many issues, stock block traders are constantly offered a broad spectrum of securities and government bond dealers transact business all along the yield curve of government securities. Each day the portfolio $s(t)$ of securities purchased or sold differs. The price risk concerns the change in price net of financing costs $\{p(t+1) - p(t)[1 + r(t)]\}$ denoted by Δp on the portfolio of securities purchased or sold during the day.

The change in the net price $\Delta p = p(t+1) - p(t)[1 + r(t)]$ can be decomposed into two independent parts. The first term in equation (7.3), $\beta\{I(t+1) - I(t)[1 + r(t)]\}$, denoted by $\beta\Delta I$, describes how the price of the portfolio (net of finance costs) varies with changes in the market index (net of finance costs). The market index $I(t)$ refers to a broad set of securities of which portfolio $s(t)$ is a subset. If $s(t)$ consists of a specific portfolio of equities, then $I(t)$ is the S&P 500 price index. For fixed income securities, the yield would be based upon the yield curve of Treasury securities times a risk premium. Coefficient β describes the variation in the price of the securities relative to the movement in the relevant overall market index. The change $\beta\Delta I$ is the market risk which can result from changes in monetary and fiscal policy which produce sudden and substantial rises in interest rates.

The second element of the net price change is $\epsilon_1(t+1)$, the portfolio specific risk. It is the change in the relative price of the portfolio *not* associated with changes in the market index. If the earnings of a particular firm are significantly lower than usual, then ϵ_1 will be negative and its price will decline relative to its historical relation to the market index. In the case of fixed income securities, the dealer may believe that the current risk premium relative to the Treasury securities yield curve is too high and that it will decline. This means that the relative price of the bond will rise, which is a subjective ϵ_1 which is positive. The dealer hopes that a combination of the relative price change ϵ_1 plus commissions and spreads $V(s)$ will lead to a profitable transaction. The ϵ_1 embodies the security specific risk and return. His vaunted expertise lies in evaluating *relative* prices: Which issues are currently overvalued or undervalued relative to the market. There is evidence that government securities dealers do have better forecasting abilities than does the market. Van Horn and Heaton (1983) examined dealers' net inventories during the period January 1966 to December 1980. They concluded that for securities with less than one-year maturity, which represented 70–90 per cent of the dealers' net inventories, dealers showed significant forecasting skills in all but the 1971–75 period. Their results are consistent with the analysis in Chapter Five.

Separating the overall price risk (Δp) into its market risk ($\beta \Delta I$) and specific (ϵ_1) risk gives

$$p(t+1) - p(t)[1 + r(t)] = \beta\{I(t+1) - I(t)[1 + r(t)]\}$$

$$+ \epsilon_1(t+1) \qquad (7.3)$$

abbreviated as

$$\Delta p = \beta \Delta I + \epsilon_1 \qquad (7.3a)$$

The overall risk, measured by the variance, is

$$\text{var } \Delta p = \beta^2 \text{ var } \Delta I + \text{var } \epsilon_1 \qquad (7.4)$$

assuming that the two risks are independent.

For a high grade *fixed income* security in either the primary or secondary market, the market risk ($\beta^2 \text{ var } \Delta I$) dominates the relative price risk (var ϵ_1), because the risk premium relative to Treasury securities is relatively constant. Therefore, the price of a high grade corporate *fixed income* security varies almost proportionately with the price of a comparable Treasury issue. For lower grade corporate fixed income securities, the risk premium relative to Treasuries is not relatively constant but depends upon the likelihood that full debt servicing will be made, which varies with the fortunes of the corporation. Hence, var ϵ_1/var Δp is higher for low grade than for high grade fixed income securities.

In the equity market, a distinction exists between the underwriting of corporate equities and the secondary market for equities from the viewpoint of the stock block trader. The earnings of a particular corporation have a high variance: they are very difficult to predict. Earnings are affected by the quality of management of the corporation, the fortunes of the industry and the course of the economy. The third factor would be reflected in the movements of the S&P 500 index. Variable ϵ_1 reflects the first two factors. Changes in the stock price, for that reason, are poorly correlated with changes in the net price of the index. Variance ϵ_1 is high relative to the variance of ΔI.

A different situation prevails in the secondary market for equities from the viewpoint of the stock block trader. He purchases and sells many different issues in the secondary market during the course of a day and $s(t)$ should be interpreted as a vector of securities. On a particular issue, the relative price risk, is high compared with the market risk. When one considers the entire portfolio of purchases, one sees significant negative covariances between the relative price risks. Consequently, the major risk that a stock block trader faces is the market risk.

A specific example can be given. There are estimates of equation (7.4) for portfolio of n securities from the New York Stock Exchange (Fama, 1981, Table 7-5, p. 160). In Table 7.3 the left column lists the number (n) of securities, and the right column is $R^2 = \beta^2$ var ΔI/var Δp, the proportion of total risk due to the market. This situation corresponds exactly to the theoretical analysis in Chapter Two where I explain why dealers are the main users of futures. I showed that R^2 is described by equation (2.49) repeated here as

$$R^2 = \frac{1}{1 + (1/n)[(N-n)/(N-1)]} \qquad (7.5)$$

where n is the number of securities handled by the dealer and N is the total number of securities in the index I.

Thus the ratio of market risk to total risk is at least 90 per cent for a stock block trader handling at least 20 issues, but only 30 per cent for an underwriter of a single issue of equity. It is the market

Table 7.3   The ratio of market to total risk related to the number of securities in the portfolio

Number n of securities	$R^2 = \beta^2$ var ΔI/var Δp
1	0.30
2	0.46
10	0.81
20	0.90

risk that increased substantially since 1979. The use of futures markets is designed to eliminate the market risk while the dealer wants to profit from the portfolio specific risk.

Even before the development of futures markets in government bonds and stock indexes, dealers were able to hedge the downside risk of declines in the market index upon the values of their temporary portfolios. Large dealers engaged in 'homemade hedging'. Dealers created a portfolio of securities that approximated the market index, either of corporate fixed income securities or equities. The hedging portfolio was constructed to have a β of unity, although to reduce transactions costs it contained fewer securities than are in the index. This *surrogate portfolio* was sold or purchased as a means of hedging away the market risk and just keeping the portfolio specific risks.

Dealers would sell part of the surrogate portfolio in anticipation of a decline in the market index. At time $t + 1$ when the portfolio of securities $s(t)$ is sold at price $p(t + 1)$, the dealer repurchases the surrogate portfolio. In so far as the change in the value of the surrogate portfolio is close to the change in the value of market index, the homemade hedging has reduced the riskiness of the dealer's position resulting from movements in the market index.

This homemade hedging procedure has several problems, which account for its limited use. First, only large dealers could assemble and maintain a hedging portfolio which is a good approximation to the market index. Secondly, transactions costs of selling the many different securities composing the homemade hedging portfolio severely reduces the profit margin derived from the commissions, spreads and returns $V[s(t)]$ earned on the portfolio of transactions. Suppose that $10 million of equities $p(t)s(t)$ are hedged by selling the homemade hedging portfolio. The average share price for the S&P 500 index is $41 so that 243 902 shares are involved in the homemade hedging. Under the realistic assumption of 10 cents a share commission, the round trip transactions costs would be $24 390. Such large transactions costs are at the expense of the commissions $V[s(t)]$ earned by the dealers. Thirdly, for government bond dealers, the interest rate on long-term government bonds exceeds the yield on the shorter maturities that are purchased with the proceeds of the short sale. Moreover, a fee which may range as high as 1/2 per cent must be paid to borrow securities. Short sales are often quite expensive. Fourthly, in so far as a hedging portfolio of equities in the secondary market is used, selling equities is difficult in a declining market because the stock exchange restricts the ability of specialists to sell when the price is declining.

7.2.3 Dealer Uses of Futures

Futures markets in Treasury securities and stock indexes fundamentally changed the *modus operandi* of dealers and facilitated
risk management.

To hedge against the market risk var (ΔI) on a portfolio of
securities $s(t)$ purchased (+) or sold (−), quantity $x(t)$ units of a
homogeneous futures contract are sold (+) or purchased (−).
Futures contracts that mature at time $T \geq t + 1$ are sold at price
$q_T(t)$. At time $t + 1$, when the portfolio $s(t)$ is sold at price
$p(t + 1)$, the futures contracts are repurchased at price $q_T(t + 1)$.
Transactions costs on the futures contracts are $T[x(t)]$. The profit
equations with futures $\pi(t + 1)$ is equation (7.1) abbreviated as
(7.1a).

The advantage of futures over homemade hedging are considerable, because of very low transactions costs. First, considerable
transactions costs are saved since the homogeneous futures contract is in a large denomination. Suppose that the $10 million
portfolio of equities mentioned above is hedged by selling futures
contracts on the S&P 500 index. If the S&P futures index were
trading (in 1983) at 140 then each futures contract would have a
value of $70 000 ($500 × 140). The dealer could sell 143 contracts against the $10 million portfolio. The transactions cost is
$15 per futures contract. On a round trip, the commissions would
be $4290 ($15 × 2 × 143). This is only 17 per cent of the commissions involved in the homemade hedging described above.

Secondly, there is considerable leverage in dealing with futures.
For a hedger, a 3 per cent margin is required, and for a speculator
in the futures contracts on the S&P 500 an 8 per cent margin is
required. Collateral on the initial margin can be posted in the form
of Treasury bills with no loss of interest. A dealer has no need to
tie up scarce capital in a surrogate portfolio to the market index,
as he does with homemade hedging.

Thirdly, the futures market in the broad based instrument has
'depth, breadth and resiliency' which very few cash markets pos-
sess. Dealers need not worry about affecting the market prices
with their purchases and sales. In selling the surrogate portfolio,
since some of the securities are infrequently traded or have thin
markets, the dealer may be affecting the market price to his dis-
advantage. This market power vitiates the usefulness of homemade
hedging. By contrast, the homogeneous futures contract is used by
many different market participants who are hedging different
portfolios. Some hedgers may be long and others short (see Tables
1.6–1.8). Therefore, the futures markets in the homogeneous con-

tract is extremely broad, and no single party can exert much of an effect upon the market price. In so far as the futures in the stock index is concerned, there are no restrictions about selling in a declining market. Dealers use futures markets to eliminate *market risk* by utilizing the relations described by equations (7.3) and (7.7).

Selling a stock index future is like selling the entire S&P 500 index with very low transactions costs and without affecting the market prices of the underlying securities. Selling a Treasury bond future is like selling a high grade corporate bond with a constant risk premium relative to the Treasury, with very low transactions costs and without affecting bond prices. A relation exists between the change in the price of the futures $\Delta q_T = q_T(t+1) - q_T(t)$ and the change in the market index ΔI, derived from equation (7.6). This arbitrage equation concerns the relation between the futures price $q_T(t)$ and the underlying index $I(t)$ on which the futures is based. The differential between the futures price and the cash price is equal to the expected net carrying cost $E_t r(t, T)$ from time t to maturity date T. The latter consists of the known one period net carrying cost $r(t)$ from t to $t+1$ plus the expected net carrying costs $E_t r(t+1, T)$ from $t+1$ to maturity at T. Equation (7.6) is the 'no arbitrage' relation:

$$q_T(t) = I(t)[1 + E_t r(t, T)] = I(t)[1 + r(t) + E_t r(t+1, T)] \quad (7.6)$$

The simplest version of equation (7.6) is the case where $I(t)$ is the cash price of a Treasury bond and $q_T(t)$ is the price of a Treasury bond future. The cash bonds can be purchased for $I(t)$ and the net financing costs from to t to T is $r(t, T)$. If financing can be arranged at time t over the interval to T, then arbitrage between the cash and futures market would ensure that the difference $q_T(t) - I(t)$ is equal to the net financing costs $r(t, T)I(t)$, the direct financing cost that is based upon the Treasury bill rate or repurchase agreement REPO rate over the period less the interest received on the Treasury bonds.

Another example concerns the index $I(t)$ of stock prices and $q_T(t)$ the price at time t of a futures contract on that index which matures at time T. At maturity, the futures price $q_T(T)$ is set equal to the index $I(T)$. The expected net financing costs $E_t r(t, T)$ from t to T are equal to the interest rate on Treasury bills less the forecast dividend flows from the securities constituting the index. These dividend flows are not known with certainty at initial date t.

Professional arbitrageurs, dealers and funds hold the index funds or approximations to the index. These institutions can either buy the index fund for $I(t)$ or the future for $q_T(t)$. If they buy the index fund, they expect the cost to be $I(t)[1 + Er(t, T)]$. To buy the futures costs them $q_T(t)$. In each case, at time T, their position is worth the same amount $q_T(T) = I(T)$. By arbitraging between these two alternatives, they tend to produce an approximation to equation (7.6).

The relation between the change in the futures price

$$\Delta q_T = q_T(t + 1) - q_T(t)$$

and the net change in the market index

$$\Delta I = I(t + 1) - I(t)[1 + r(t)]$$

is derived by taking first differences of equation (7.6) and is

$$q_T(t + 1) - q_T(t) = \{I(t + 1) - I(t)[1 + r(t)]\}$$
$$+ [I(t + 1)E_{t+1}r(t + 1, T) - I(t)E_t r(t + 1, T)]$$

$$(7.7)$$

abbreviated as

$$\Delta q = \Delta I + \epsilon_2 \tag{7.7a}$$

The variance of ϵ_2 is called the 'basis risk'.

There are several components to deviation ϵ_2 between the change in the futures price Δq and the return on the index ΔI. First are the effects of unexpected changes in the shape of the yield curve upon the more distant future. An unexpected rise in the yield curve at time $t + 1$ reflected by $r(t + 1, T)$ will raise the price of the future $q_T(t + 1)$ relative to the value of the index. When the maturity date T coincides with $t + 1$, this component will be zero and there is no basis risk. Secondly, when I is the index of corporate fixed income securities and q is the price of a Treasury bond future, the variations in risk premium between the Treasury bond and corporate bond index are also contained in the ϵ_2 term. The variance of the change in the future is

$$\text{var } \Delta q = \text{var } \Delta I + \text{var } \epsilon_2 \tag{7.8}$$

when the covariance $\text{cov } (\Delta I, \epsilon_2)$ can be disregarded. The first term is the market risk and the second term is basis risk.

Substitute equations (7.3a) and (7.7a) into profit equation (7.1) to obtain

$$\pi(t + 1) = [s(t)\beta - x(t)]\Delta I + \epsilon_1 s(t) - \epsilon_2 x(t)$$
$$+ V[s(t)] - T[x(t)] \tag{7.9}$$

for the profits of a dealer who just purchased portfolio $s(t)$. *This is the crucial equation for an understanding of dealer behaviour.* Expected profits $E\pi$ are

$$E\pi = (s\beta - x)E\Delta I + sE\epsilon_1 - xE\epsilon_2 + V(s) - T(x) \qquad (7.10)$$

and the variance of profits is

$$\text{var } \pi \quad = (s\beta - x)^2 \text{ var } \Delta I + \qquad s^2 \text{ var } \epsilon_1 \qquad + x^2 \text{ var } \epsilon_2$$

total risk =   market risk   + portfolio specific risk + basis risk

$$(7.11)$$

when ΔI, ϵ_1 and ϵ_2 are independent and time subscripts are to be understood.

The dealer who has acquired portfolio $s(t)$, which he plans to sell to other customers as soon as possible faces three risks. First, there is the market risk generated by var ΔI, changes in the market index of securities. Dealers who purchased portfolios of corporate bonds just prior to the change in Federal Reserve policy in October 1979 would have suffered losses from the fall in corporate bond prices, regardless of how astutely they estimated the *relative* prices of the issues they purchased. Secondly, a portfolio specific risk var ϵ_1 which concerns the price of the portfolio is relative to its historic relation to the market. The dealer's judgment involves purchasing underpriced securities and selling overpriced securities. The dealers specialize in taking this type of risk and they hope that, combined with the commissioners and spreads $\epsilon_1 s(t) + V[s(t)]$, will be positive. As was indicated above, there is evidence that dealers do succeed in that task. In periods of high interest rate volatility the portfolio specific risk var ϵ_1 is overwhelmed by the market risk var ΔI in the case of high grade corporate bonds in either the primary or secondary market or in a portfolio of many equities temporarily acquired for a short time by the stock block trader in the secondary market. This is not generally the case in the underwriting of a new stock issue. Thirdly, when the dealer uses the futures market, he faces basis risks var ϵ_2 concerning changes in the futures price relative to net changes in the market index. These risks are primarily due to unexpected changes in the yield curve. To facilitate the exposition, the three risks are assumed to be independent. That is, the sum of the covariances is assumed to be relatively small compared to the sum of the variances.

7.2.4 Optimizing Decisions

The aim of the dealer is to select the optimal temporary inventory $s(t)$ and amount of futures $x(t)$ sold (+) or purchased (−). These quantities change from day to day, if not sooner. Dealers have great aversion to risk, despite the fact that they are professional risk bearers. Penalties for large losses, which may lead to bankruptcy, weigh more heavily than do rewards for large gains. Dealer firms are often partnerships. Their behaviour can be understood by modelling their decisions as if they were maximizing the expectation of a concave utility function of profits from their current transactions. Equation (7.12) describes a general class of expected utility $EU(\pi)$ functions, where α is the coefficient of risk aversion of the dealer:

$$\underset{s,\,x}{\text{Max }} EU(\pi) = E\pi - \frac{\alpha}{2}\,\text{var }\pi \tag{7.12}$$

where expected profits $E\pi$ are equation (7.10) and the variance of profits var π are equation (7.11). The control variables are the inventory $s(t)$ and amount of futures $x(t)$.

The *optimal* futures position $x = x^*$ is

$$x^*(t) = \beta s(t)\,\frac{1}{1 + \gamma_2} - \frac{1}{\alpha}\,\frac{E(\Delta q_T) - T'(x)}{(1 + \gamma_2)\,\text{var }\Delta I} \tag{7.13}$$

where

$$\gamma_2 = \text{var }\epsilon_2/\text{var }\Delta I$$

is the basis risk/market risk and

$$\text{var }\Delta q_T = (1 + \gamma_2)\,\text{var }\Delta I.$$

Equation (7.13) indicates the 'hedging' and 'speculative' aspects of the use of futures. The first term in the equation is the optimal hedging that would be done if the futures price were not expected to change by more than the transactions costs. Under these conditions, fraction $\beta/1 + \gamma_2$ of the cash position $s(t)$ is hedged in the futures market. The greater the ratio γ_2 of the basis risk to market risk, the smaller will be the fraction hedged. The greater the β, the responsiveness of the price of the portfolio to changes in the market index, the greater the fraction hedged.

The second term in equation (7.13) is the speculative term. It is the optimal position in the futures market that would be taken, if the dealer had no position in the cash market. Position $x^*(t)$ would be long (short) if the futures price were expected to rise (decline) by more than the transactions costs. The risk on a pure futures transaction var (Δq_T) is the denominator of the second term.

The optimum inventory investment during the period of time by the dealer can now be derived. The exposition is facilitated by assuming that: (a) the basis risk is a negligible fraction of the market risk $\gamma_2 = \text{var } \epsilon_2/\text{var } \Delta I$ is small; (b) neither the futures price nor the index is expected to change, $E(\Delta I)$ and $E(\Delta q_T)$ are approximately zero. Assumption (b) implies that the expected return on the portfolio $E(\Delta p)$ is just that specific to the portfolio $E(\epsilon_1)$. These assumptions imply

$$E(\Delta p) = \beta E(\Delta I) + E(\epsilon_1) = E(\epsilon_1) \tag{7.14}$$

where $E(\Delta p) \equiv Ep(t+1;t) - [1 + r(t)]p(t)$. Under these assumptions, the optimal cash position $s(t)$ occurs when equation (7.15) is satisfied. The marginal expected profits (the left-hand side of equation (7.15) are equal to the marginal risk premium (the right-hand side of equation (7.15)), when the optimal position x^* is taken in the futures market:

$$E(\epsilon_1) + V'(s) = \alpha (\text{var } \epsilon_1 + \beta^2 \text{ var } \epsilon_2)s \tag{7.15}$$

The marginal expected profits from inventory investment consist of two parts: (a) the relative net price of the portfolio is expected to appreciate by $E(\epsilon_1)$, relative to its systematic relation to the market; (b) the income earned from commissions and spreads $V(s)$ less costs is positively related to the portfolio of transactions.

The nonspeculative profit function $V[s(t)]$ is described by equation (7.16a) and marginal profits $V'[s(t)]$ by equation (7.16b). The latter is negatively sloped, for two reasons: (a) total revenue rises at a slower rate than the volume of business because the dealer competes for business by offering more favourable commissions or spreads and because the dealer's purchases and sales affect market prices; (b) marginal costs of operation are positively related to the volume of business.

$$V(s) = \left(v_0 - \frac{v_1}{2}s\right)s \tag{7.16a}$$

$$V'(s) = v_0 - v_1 s \tag{7.16b}$$

Term v_0 is marginal profit when $s = 0$. It reflects the state of demand for dealer services and the cost of providing them and v_1 reflects how the spread or commission must decline to increase the volume of business and the corresponding rise in marginal cost. The optimal temporary inventory of the dealer $s_F(t)$ is

$$s_F(t) = \frac{Ep(t+1;t) - [1 + r(t)]p(t) + v_0}{v_1 + \alpha \, (\text{var } \epsilon_1 + \beta^2 \text{ var } \epsilon_2)} \tag{7.17}$$

when the futures market is used optimally.

The dealer's inventory investment at the end of a day depends: (a) positively upon the expected change in the relative price of the portfolio net of finance cost plus the marginal profit v_0; (b) negatively upon the risk when the optimal hedge ratio is used, times the coefficient of risk aversion; and (c) negatively upon the reduction in commissions and spreads required to increase business.

Write equation (7.17), the dealers' investment in inventories, in inverse form as

$$p(t) = \frac{Ep(t+1;t) + v_0}{1 + r(t)} - \frac{[v_1 + \alpha \, (\text{var } \epsilon_1 + \beta^2 \text{ var } \epsilon_2)]}{1 + r(t)} s_F(t)$$

$$\tag{7.18}$$

abbreviated as

$$p(t) = A(t) - B_F s(t) \tag{7.18a}$$

this is graphed as curve FF′ in Figure 7.1.

When there is *no* futures market, the optimal inventory investment $s_N(t)$ satisfies equation (7.19). It is derived by maximizing equation (7.12) with respect to s, using equations (7.10) and (7.11), and setting the futures position x equal to zero. Write

$$s_N(t) = \frac{Ep(t+1;t) - [1 + r(t)]p(t) + v_0}{v_1 + \alpha(\beta^2 \text{ var } \Delta I + \text{var } \epsilon_1)} \tag{7.19}$$

in inverse form as

$$p(t) = \frac{Ep(t+1;t) + v_0}{1 + r(t)} - \frac{[v_1 + \alpha \, (\text{var } \epsilon_1 + \beta^2 \text{ var } \Delta I)]}{1 + r(t)} s_N(t)$$

$$\tag{7.20}$$

abbreviated as

$$p(t) = A(t) - B_N s(t) \tag{7.21}$$

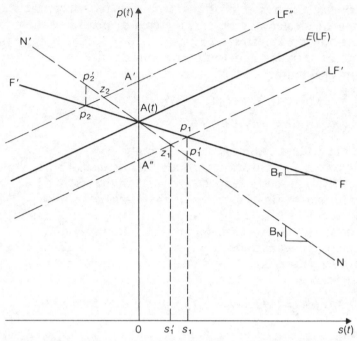

Figure 7.1 The excess supply of securities (excess demand for loanable funds) by nondealers is curve E(LF), LF' or LF". The inventory investment demand by dealers is NN' when there are no futures markets and FF' when the futures markets are used optimally. Transitory variations in the LF' curve, around its mean value $E(LF)$, produce smaller price variations when dealers use futures markets optimally.

This is graphed as curve NN' in Figure 7.1.

The optimum temporary inventory $s_N(t)$ that will be absorbed by the dealer when there are no futures markets depends upon the following factors: (a) it depends positively upon the expected capital gain on the inventory net of financing costs $E\Delta p$, and upon the level v_0 of commissions and spreads; (b) it depends negatively upon v_1, the degree of market power that the dealer has in affecting price; (c) the position depends negatively upon the product of risk aversion α and total risk $\beta^2 \operatorname{var} \Delta I + \operatorname{var} \epsilon_1$.

7.2.5 The Effects of Futures

Using the above analysis of the dealer demand for inventory investment, the effects of futures markets upon the price variance of the portfolio can now be explained.

The vertical intercept $A(t)$ of the inverse demand curve is the present value of the expected price of the portfolio plus the marginal profit on the first unit acquired. This is the primary source of uncertainty since $p(t + 1)$ is unknown at time t. Graphically, the intercept term keeps shifting around its mean value. The absolute value of the slope of the inventory investment demand curve B_F or B_N depends on whether futures markets are used optimally by dealers. If no hedging were possible, the dealer faces the entire risk on the portfolio var $\Delta p =$ var $\epsilon_1 + \beta^2$ var ΔI. If futures are used optimally, the dealer diversifies away the market risk β^2 var ΔI and substitutes a much smaller basis risk β^2 var ϵ_2. Since slope B_F is much smaller in absolute value than slope B_N, curve FF′ is much flatter than curve NN′. Both the intercept and slope depend upon the particular securities acquired by the dealer.

Let s_1 of securities be offered to dealers during an interval of time. It could be a new issue of corporate fixed incomes, blocks of equity or an issue of government bonds. The aim of the dealer is to dispose of these securities to the customers as soon as possible. According to Figure 7.1, the dealer will bid price p_1 when he uses the futures market optimally. Risk premium $A(t) - p_1$ reflects the risks of acquiring the particular portfolio plus the basis risk involved in hedging away the market risk. Contrast this with the situation where there are no futures markets in the broad based index. The inverse inventory function is equation (7.20), the curve NN′ in Figure 7.1.

Since the market risk β^2 var ΔI exceeds the basis risk β^2 var ϵ_1, the price that dealers offer when there is no futures p_1' is less than the price p_1 that they offer when they can use futures markets optimally. The effects of the dealers' uses of futures markets upon the macroeconomy can now be explained. Price $p(t)$ at which dealers purchase or sell securities is positively related to the q ratio and is negatively related to 'the interest rate'. Suppose that the face value of a bond is \$1 and the dealer is willing to purchase it for p dollars. If it were a zero coupon bond maturing in T years, the interest rate is $i = (1/T) \ln (1/p)$.

Consider the demand for and supply of loanable funds by nondealers, items (1)–(4) in Table 7.1. The demand for loanable funds is the supply of securities offered during a time interval. The supply of loanable funds is the demand for securities during a time interval.

The excess supply of securities $y(t)$, items (1) + (2) − (3) − (4), is negatively related to 'the interest rate', or positively related to the level $p(t)$ of security prices. It is drawn as the LF (loanable funds or excess supply of securities schedule) in Figure 7.1 and is equation (7.21) written in inverse form. Parameter $u(t)$ reflects the shifts in the LF schedule due to variations in income, the productivity of capital, thrift, liquidity preference or the government deficit. A transitory rise in the government deficit shifts the excess supply of securities curve from $E(\text{LF})$ to LF'. A transitory rise in the money supply increases the demand for securities and shifts the excess supply of securities curve from $E(\text{LF})$ to LF''.

$$p(t) = u(t) + ay(t) \qquad (7.21)$$

$y(t) =$ items (1) + (2) − (3) − (4) in Table 7.1.

The average value of the excess supply of securities curve is $E(\text{LF})$ associated with an average value of u denoted by $Eu = 0A(t)$ in Figure 7.1. At this price (100 − the interest rate) $0A(t)$, the demand for and supply of loanable funds are equal, on average during the period. Dealers, on average, are neither investing in or disinvesting in securities. This means that the average value of u, denoted Eu, is the intercept term

$$A = \frac{Ep(t+1;t) + v_0}{1+r}$$

of the dealers' inventory investment function.

$$Eu = \frac{Ep(t+1;t) + v_0}{1+r} = A \qquad (7.22)$$

as is obvious from Figure 7.1. Figure 7.1 shows how the use of futures by dealers adds depth, breadth and resiliency to the markets. Variations in portfolios offered or demanded do not lead to large price fluctuations.

Dealers provide an inventory investment or disinvestment cushion for fluctuations in the excess supply of securities variable $y(t)$. Suppose that the government deficit that is being financed through securities exceeds its average value for the period, and produces a *transitory* rise in the excess supply of securities curve to LF'. As the price declines below $A(t)$, the present value of the subsequently expected price, dealers would increase their inventories of securities.

If there were no dealers, the price would decline to A''. If dealers cannot use futures markets, their inventory investment function is NN'. The price would temporarily decline to z_1 and dealers' inventory investment would be s_1'. Risk premium $A(t) - z_1$ is the expected return over the financing costs.

When dealers use futures markets optimally, the inventory investment function is FF$'$. The *transitory* rise in the excess supply of securities to LF$'$ leads to a price of p_1; and dealers' inventory investment is s_1. Risk premium $A(t) - p_1$ is the expected excess return over financing costs. The distance between the FF$'$ and NN$'$ curves (e.g. $p_1 p_1'$ or $p_2 p_2'$) is the decrease in risk premium resulting from the optimal use of futures markets.

Graphically, the *average* price $Ep = A(t)$ is *not directly* affected by the dealers' use of futures, or even by their existence. At this average price, the average demand for and supply of loanable funds are equal. The variance of the price of securities, however, is profoundly affected by the role of the dealers. If there were no dealers, the range of price variation is from A$''$ to A$'$. If dealers cannot use futures markets, the range is from z_1 to z_2. If dealers use futures markets optimally, the range is reduced from p_1 to p_2.

Formally the expected price Ep is given by

$$Ep = A \tag{7.23}$$

and the variance of the price var p is given by

$$\text{var } p = \frac{\text{var } u}{[1 + (a/B_i)]^2} \qquad i = N, F \tag{7.24}$$

Since slope B_F is less than slope B_N (in Figure 7.1), the price (interest rate) variance is reduced by the dealer use of futures markets.

The percentage reduction in the (absolute value of) slope B of the inventory investment demand of dealers can be immediately derived from equations (7.18) and (7.20):

$$\frac{B_N - B_F}{B_N} = \frac{\alpha \beta^2 (\text{var } \Delta I - \text{var } \epsilon_2)}{v_1 + \alpha (\text{var } \epsilon_1 + \beta^2 \text{ var } \Delta I)}$$

$$= f\left(\frac{\text{market risk} - \text{basis risk}}{\text{price risk}}\right) \tag{7.25}$$

The greater the difference between the market risk (var ΔI) and the basis risk (var ϵ_2) as a percentage of the price risk (var Δp), the greater will be the depth, breadth and resiliency of the market. Fluctuations in the excess supply of securities from nondealers will be associated with smaller price fluctuations around the mean price (interest rate).

In Sections 7.3 and 7.4 I show that futures markets also affect the nondealer excess supply of securities or the expected net demand for loanable funds curve $E(LF)$. Thereby, the average price (interest rate) is affected. In particular, investment demand item (1) in Table 7.1 is increased, and the savings directed towards risky assets item (3) in Table 7.1 are also increased, as a result of the development of futures markets. These longer-run effects raise the rate of capital formation.

7.3   Financial Futures and the Mortgage Market

7.3.1   *The Need for Risk Management*

Investment in residential housing (in 1983) accounted for 55 per cent of net fixed capital formation. Home mortgage borrowing accounted for 37 per cent of the total borrowing by the private nonfinancial sector. For these reasons, the interest rates charged by mortgage bankers and savings and loan associations for home mortgages profoundly affect the aggregate rate of capital formation.

Intermediate between the savings and loan associations and mortgage bankers, which lend directly to home buyers, and the capital market, where private savings are offered, are the Federal National Mortgage Association (FNMA) and the Government National Mortgage Association (GNMA). The subject of this part is how the use of futures markets in Treasuries by the FNMA has lowered the interest rates on home mortgages in relation to what they would have been if there were no facilities for hedging. Since a similar analysis applies to the effects of futures markets on the operations of the GNMA, the effects of futures markets on investment in residential housing are qualitatively similar to the effects described in this chapter but quantitatively larger.

The FNMA is a federally chartered, privately owned, corporation. Its principal activity consists of the purchase of mortgages, primarily on residential properties. The FNMA is the nation's largest supplier of mortgage funds. These mortgages are held as investments. As of 31 December 1983 the FNMA owned a portfolio of $75.7 billion of mortgage loans. Substantially all mortgage purchases are made pursuant to *forward* purchase commitments, which totalled $18.607 billion in 1983.

The FNMA has two sources of revenue: (a) the seller of a mortgage generally pays a fee ranging from 1 to 3 per cent of the commitment on a fixed rate mortgage; (b) the acquired portfolio earns a rate of return.

The FNMA acquires funds to purchase a variety of home mortgages by selling its own securities in the capital market. These obligations are treated as US agency debt in the market, and are eligible for investment by supervised financial institutions without regard to legal limits imposed on investment securities. In this way the FNMA borrows in the capital market from institutions which would not otherwise invest in mortgages. It is correct to conceive of the FNMA as a huge savings and loan association which borrows in a national and international capital market and purchases heterogeneous mortgages from local mortgage originators.

Net income is related to the mortgage fees and the difference between a weighted average yield on its portfolio and a weighted average of its borrowing costs.

Savings and loan associations and mortgage bankers generate a relatively steady flow of new mortgage loans which are then offered to the FNMA. There are also large (for example, one billion dollar) sales of portfolios by the savings and loan associations of long-term mortgage loans which were financed at low interest rates. The savings and loan associations are trying to shorten the average duration of their portfolios. These large batches of old mortgages are offered to the FNMA at substantial discounts. Forward commitments to purchase these mortgages are usually on a three-month basis. Due to the required documentation process, there is a lag between the forward commitment to purchase mortgages and their subsequent delivery. 'Immediate' delivery in this market is 30 days. A distinction is made between the steady, predictable, flow of new mortgages and the nonpredictable, large, discrete sales of seasoned mortgages by these institutions. The latter require more careful risk management by the FNMA than does the former, for reasons discussed below.

The FNMA must obtain the approval of the Treasury for the issuance of its own obligations to finance its purchases of mortgages. The Treasury determines *when* the FNMA can enter the capital market *once a month* with its debentures. The rationale for this procedure is that the monthly borrowing by the FNMA, approximately one to one and a half billion dollars, should not adversely affect the Treasury's ability to borrow in the capital market. The Treasury is also concerned with avoiding congestion in the capital market of security sales among the several agencies. Borrowings by the Treasury or the agencies are so large that they affect market rates of interest. The FNMA can seek authority to sell public issues more frequently than one day in the month, if the calendar is free. This normally happens once or twice a year.

The basic point, however, is that the FNMA is uncertain when it will be allowed to go to market and what interest rates (yield curve) will exist on that one particular day.

There is a lag between the forward commitment to purchase mortgages and the subsequent sale of FNMA securities. For example, on 20 October 1983 the FNMA was asked to bid on a pool of approximately $750 million in seasoned mortgages offered by a single thrift institution seeking to restructure its balance sheet. This sale was not part of the regular flow of mortgages offered to the FNMA. The securities would not be delivered for several months. Given that the FNMA does not know when it will be allowed to enter the capital market and what its borrowing costs will be, what bid should it make on this batch of $750 million of mortgages? Too low a bid will be unsuccessful in obtaining the mortgages. Too high a bid will be unprofitable. This phenomenon generates the need for risk management.

If a regular flow of securities were offered to the FNMA, but its borrowing costs were cyclical around a given mean, the risks would be manageable. The FNMA could bid at a rate equal to its mean borrowing costs plus a mark-up. Movements in actual borrowing costs would average out and the net spread between its lending and borrowing rates could be expected to be profitable.

When there are discrete, 'lumpy', batches of mortgages offered, the FNMA cannot price the batch at the mean borrowing cost plus a mark-up. If borrowing costs exceeded the mean when the FNMA goes to market, it has no reason to believe that there will be an equally large subsequent offer which would be financed at a borrowing cost below the mean. Risk management techniques are essential to cope with the large, discrete, nonpredictable offers of seasoned mortgages.

7.3.2   The Profit and Behavioural Equations when there Is No (N) Futures Market

In this section the optimization of the FNMA is described when there is no futures market. The effects upon the mortgage market of this decision are contrasted with the effects of the optimization that results when the FNMA is able to use futures markets in Treasuries.

Equation (7.26), discussed below, describes the profits $\pi_N(\theta)$ where there is no (N) futures market:

$$\pi_N^*(\theta) = [P^*(\theta) - (1 - g)p(t)]s(t) \tag{7.26}$$

where $\pi_N^*(\theta)$ is the profit at time θ when there is no (N) futures market, $p(t)$ is the forward bid price by the FNMA for mortgages, $P^*(\theta)$ is the sales price at time θ of FNMA debentures of the same maturity as the mortgages, $s(t)$ is the face value of mortgages purchased at time t, $gp(t)s(t)$ are the fees charged by the FNMA on the value $p(t)s(t)$ of purchases, $EP(\theta; t)$ is the expectation, taken at time t, of the price of FNMA debentures marketed at subsequent date θ, * is the stochastic variable and var P is the variance of price P of FNMA debentures.

At time $t - 1$, the FNMA agrees to purchase face value $s(t)$ of mortgages at forward price $p(t)$ for delivery at time t. Some time later, on a day in the month assigned to it by the Treasury, call it θ, the FNMA goes to the capital market to sell its securities to finance the purchase. Assume that the maturity of the FNMA issue corresponds to the maturity of the mortgages purchased forward. Let the price of an FNMA debenture at time θ be $P^*(\theta)$. Although the FNMA holds the mortgages as investments, in effect in this case it is equivalent to selling the mortgages for $P^*(\theta)s(t)$. *Both the date θ of the borrowing and the price* $P^*(\theta)$ *received for the debenture are unknown at the time the forward commitment to purchase the mortgages is made.*

The FNMA will receive fees of $100g$ per cent of the mortgage from the seller. When there is no hedging, the profits are equation (7.26). Risks are that the price $P^*(\theta)$ of FNMA debentures may fall below $p(t)$, the forward commitment price. All of the risk is focused upon what will happen on one single day of the month when the Treasury permits the FNMA to borrow. During the period when interest rates were stable, this risk was not great. The FNMA could expect to profit from the fees $gp(t)s(t)$ plus the spread $[P^*(\theta) - p(t)]s(t)$ between the sale price of FNMA debentures and the forward purchase price of the mortgage, when the durations are similar.

The amount of mortgages that the FNMA can successfully purchase $s(t)$ depends upon the price $p(t)$ that it is willing to bid. The FNMA competes against dealers and investors all over the world for the purchase of mortgages. It must trade off volume $s(t)$ against spread $P^*(\theta) - p(t)$ between the selling price $P^*(\theta)$ of its debentures and the forward price $p(t)$ offered to sellers. Equation (7.27) describes the supply of mortgages to the FNMA at time t. Quantity $s(t)$ of both the regular flow of new, and irregular 'lumpy' sales of seasoned, mortgages depends upon the forward bid price $p(t)$ and other variables. Expository complexity is greatly reduced by writing the supply at time t as

$$s(t) = cp(t) \tag{7.27}$$

The profit function for the FNMA is derived by substituting equation (7.27) into (7.26), is

$$\pi_N^*(\theta) = P^*(\theta)cp(t) - (1-g)cp(t)^2 \tag{7.28}$$

Expected profits $E\pi_N(\theta)$ are

$$E\pi_N(\theta) = EP(\theta;t)cp(t) - (1-g)cp(t)^2 \tag{7.29}$$

and the variance of profits var π_N is

$$\text{var } \pi_N = [cp(t)]^2 \text{ var } P \tag{7.30}$$

Risks, measured by the variance of profits, depend upon the size of the forward commitment to purchase mortgages $s(t) = cp(t)$ and the variability of the price of FNMA debentures var P which are used to finance the purchases.

The FNMA's problem is to ⌐elect a forward bid price $p(t)$ for mortgages offered, in order to maximize expected utility described by equation (7.12) above. It has an expectation $EP(\theta;t)$ of what will be the market price of its debentures when it is allowed to go to market. The variance of that price var P is the risk the FNMA faces.

The solution of the problem is described in the equations below and is graphically described in Figure 7.2. Along the horizontal axis the forward bid price $p(t)$ is plotted. The vertical axis plots the expected price of FNMA debentures $EP(\theta;t)$ or marginal revenue, marginal cost MC and endogenous marginal risk premium RP.

The net price that the FNMA expects to receive from the sale of its debt in the capital market is $EP(\theta;t)$. It is the horizontal line denoted MR (marginal revenue) and it is the left-hand side of equation (7.31). The marginal cost of acquiring the mortgages from the mortgage bankers or savings and loan institutions is the line labelled MC. If there were no fees charged by the FNMA ($g = 0$), then the average cost of a mortgage acquired is p dollars (per dollar of face value). Because FNMA purchases affect the market price of mortgages, the marginal cost is $2p$ dollars. When fees are taken into account, then the marginal cost is $2(1-g)p(t)$ dollars per dollar face value of mortgages purchased. This is the first term on the right-hand side of equation (7.31) and the line labelled MC in Figure 7.2.

The FNMA must charge an endogenous risk premium $\alpha cp(t)$ var P because of the risk that it faces in marketing its debentures. The risks are that the FNMA does not know when it will be permitted to enter the market to finance its securities, or the price that its securities will sell for at the uncertain date. When the FNMA cannot hedge, the risk premium RPN is the second term on the right-hand side of equation (7.31). By adding the risk premium RPN to the marginal cost MC, line MC + RPN is the effective marginal cost to the FNMA for mortgages:

$$EP(\theta; t) = 2(1 - g)p(t) + \alpha cp(t) \text{ var } P \tag{7.31}$$

$$\text{MR} \quad = \quad \text{MC} \quad + \quad \text{RPN}$$

The optimal bid price $p_N(t)$ in Figure 7.2 is described by equation (7.32). It satisfies the condition that marginal revenue is equal to marginal cost plus an endogenous risk premium:

$$p_N(t) = \frac{EP(\theta; t)}{2(1 - g) + \alpha c \text{ var } P}, \tag{7.32}$$

By bidding price p_N, the FNMA is able to acquire s_N mortgages during the time period. Thus the market interest rate on mortgages (on a discount basis) is $100 - p_N$. This rate determines the rate of residential construction, the major part of net private fixed investment. A similar situation exists in the GNMA market.

When interest rates became more volatile, the FNMA had two ways to cope with the uncertainty. First, the FNMA could pre-borrow the funds at the earliest possible date after $t - 1$ when the forward purchase commitment was made. There were two difficulties with this procedure: (a) the FNMA could still only come to market once a month at a date determined by the Treasury and in the interim, bond prices could fall; (b) pre-borrowing precludes the opportunity to take advantage of favourable market changes from commitment time $t - 1$ to time t when the mortgages are actually delivered. Pre-borrowing removes timing flexibility in borrowing in order to avoid some interest rate uncertainty.

Secondly, the FNMA could engage in 'homemade hedging'. At the time the forward purchase commitment is made, it could sell short Treasury bonds at price $I(t)$. It would invest the funds at the Treasury bill rate but it must pay interest at the Treasury bond rate to the owners of the bonds. The magnitude of this differential depends upon the shape of the Treasury yield curve. At uncertain time θ when the FNMA enters the capital market, the debentures are sold for $P^*(\theta)$ and the Treasury bonds are purchased at $I^*(\theta)$. Since the price of FNMA debentures is highly correlated with the price of Treasury bonds, this homemade hedging reduces risk. This is a feasible strategy to reduce risk but it has some deficiencies:

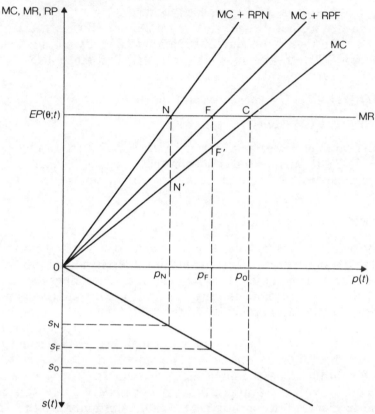

Figure 7.2   The FNMA selects a forward bid price for mortgages p at the point where the expected price of an FNMA debenture, marketed at uncertain time θ, denoted $EP(\theta;t)$ is equal to marginal cost of purchasing the mortgages forward MC plus a risk premium RP. When there are no facilities for hedging, the risk premium is RPN. The forward bid price is p_N and the FNMA purchases s_N of mortgages forward. When the FNMA uses the futures market optimally, the forward bid price is p_F and s_F of mortgages are purchased forward. If there were no risk premium, the forward bid price would be p_0 and s_0 of mortgages would be purchased forward. Ratio p_N to p_0 is $1/(1 + \delta_N)$. Ratio p_F to p_N is $(1 + \delta_N)/(1 + \delta_F)$.

(a) FNMA sales or purchases of large quantities of Treasury bonds in this over-the-counter market are quite noticeable to the other market participants. The identity of the seller is quickly revealed and there is often a perceptible effect on the market price and also the FNMA loses its anonymity which it values and has some power over the market price; (b) a fee is usually charged to borrow securities which are sold short, whose magnitude depends upon the availability of the coupon to borrow. The fee may range as high as half of 1 per cent of the coupon borrowed.

7.3.3 Risk Management with Futures Markets (F)

A superior risk management strategy was implemented in 1982, when the FNMA began taking positions in the futures market to hedge against interest rate increases between time $t - 1$ when the forward commitment was made to purchase mortgages and the specific time θ when it is allowed to enter the capital market to borrow to finance its purchases.

At any time between time $t - 1$ when the forward commitment is made to purchase the mortgages and the uncertain time θ when the Treasury permits the FNMA to enter the capital market, the FNMA sells $x(t)$ of futures contracts on either T-bonds, T-notes, T-bills, Certificates of Deposit or Euro-dollar futures, depending upon the maturity of the subsequent financing that the FNMA has in mind. Let the price of the future be $q_T(t)$ where T is the maturity of the contract. Assume that the FNMA sells the T-bond future in the nearby maturity. When the Treasury permits the FNMA to borrow on day θ, the hedge is lifted at price $q_T^*(\theta)$. For simplicity of exposition transactions costs on the debentures and on the futures are ignored. Profits $\pi(\theta)$ are described by

$$\pi^*(\theta) = [P^*(\theta) - (1 - g)p(t)]s(t) - x(t)[q_T^*(\theta) - q_T(t)] \quad (7.33)$$

Two elements of risk must be taken into account, which correspond to equations (7.3) and (7.7) above. First, there is a differential $\epsilon_1(t)$ between price $I(t)$ of a Treasury bond and price $P(t)$ of an FNMA debenture of comparable maturity. This differential is positive but not constant. The average value of the differential is m and the variance of the differential is var ϵ_1:

$$P(\theta) = I(\theta) - \epsilon_1(\theta) \quad (7.34)$$

where $P(\theta)$ is the price of an FNMA debenture, $I(\theta)$ is the price of a comparable Treasury security, $\epsilon_1(\theta)$ is the price differential $= I(\theta) - P(\theta)$ and $E\epsilon_1(\theta) = m$. The Treasury borrows at a lower rate than the FNMA but the differential is not constant.

Secondly, the change in the futures price of a Treasury bond contract is related to the change in the cash price of the Treasury bond by equation (7.7) or (7.7a) above, repeated here:

$$q_T(t + 1) - q_T(t) = \{I(t + 1) - I(t)[1 + r(t)]\} + \epsilon_2 \quad (7.7)$$

$$\Delta q_T \quad = \quad \Delta I \quad + \epsilon_2 \quad (7.7a)$$

The variance of ϵ_2 is the 'basis risk', which arises primarily from unexpected changes in the yield curve. The latter changes the relation between the cash price $I(t)$ and the futures price $q_T(t)$.

In so far as the return ΔI on the T-bond is independent of the basis risk, the variance of the change in the futures price can be written as equation (7.8) repeated here:

$$\text{var } \Delta q_T = \text{var } \Delta I + \text{var } \epsilon_2 \tag{7.8}$$

The relevant profit equation is equation (7.33) subject to three constraints: (a) the supply of mortgages offered during the period depends upon the forward price bid by the FNMA (equation 7.27), which varies by period; (b) the price of an FNMA debenture is equal to the price of a Treasury bond of comparable maturity less a variable differential (equation 7.34); (c) the change in the nearby futures price of a Treasury bond is equal to the change in the cash price of the underlying bond less a positive or negative cost of carry, depending upon the shape of the yield curve (equation 7.7 or 7.7a). The exact specifications of these equations are made to bring out the main results simply and clearly, whereas the more complex actual relations do not change the qualitative results.

Substitute equations (7.27), (7.34) and (7.7) into profit equation (7.33) to derive the crucial equation for the FNMA:

deterministic

$$\pi_F^*(\theta) = x(t)I(t) - [m + (1 - g)p(t)]s(t)$$

diversifiable risk

$$+ [s(t) - x(t)]I^*(\theta)$$

differential risk

$$- s(t)(\epsilon_1^*(\theta) - m)$$

basis risk

$$- x(t)\epsilon_2^*(\theta) \tag{7.35}$$

supply of mortgages

$$s(t) = cp(t) \tag{7.27}$$

There are four components to the profits of the FNMA, when it can use the futures market. The first component is deterministic, i.e. nonstochastic. This term reflects the profits of the FNMA if: (a) it hedged its forward purchases completely; (b) the differential between Treasury and FNMA debentures were constant at its average value m; and (c) there were no basis risk. In so far as hedging is not complete $x(t)$ differs from $s(t)$.

The second term is the value of the unhedged position $s(t) - x(t)$ times the uncertain price $I^*(\theta)$ of the Treasury debenture at uncertain time θ when the FNMA is permitted to go to market. This risk is diversifiable, since the FNMA can select its optimal unhedged position.

The third term is the risk related to $\epsilon_1^*(\theta)$, the price differential $I(\theta) - P(\theta)$ between Treasury and FNMA debentures, when it goes to market at uncertain time θ.

The fourth term is the basis risk $\epsilon_2^*(\theta)$ from hedging, whereby the futures price on Treasuries changes by a different amount than the cash price of Treasuries. Basis risk results primarily from changes in the yield curve on Treasuries.

Expected profits $E\pi_F(\theta)$ and the variance of profits var π_F, when the FNMA can use the futures (F) market in Treasuries optimally, are equations (7.36) and (7.37) respectively:

$$E\pi_F(\theta) = x(t)I(t) - [m + (1 - g)p(t)]s(t)$$
$$+ [s(t) - x(t)]EI(\theta; t) \tag{7.36}$$

$$\text{var } \pi_F = [s(t) - x(t)]^2 \text{ var } I + \quad s(t)^2 \text{ var } \epsilon_1 \quad + x(t)^2 \text{ var } \epsilon_2$$

$$\text{risk} \quad = \quad \text{diversifiable risk} \; + \text{differential risk} + \text{basis risk}$$

$$\tag{7.37}$$

The FNMA simultaneously selects a forward price $p(t)$ to bid for mortgages and a quantity $x(t)$ of Treasury bond futures to be sold (+), to maximize expected utility.

7.3.4 The Effects of the Optimal Use of Futures upon the Rate of Capital Formation in Housing

When the FNMA cannot hedge, the situation is described by equation (7.32) and curve MC + RPN in Figure 7.2. Risk premium RPN is added to the marginal cost to obtain the effective cost curve. The FNMA bids price p_N for the forward purchase of mortgages. This is the effective price of the mortgage to the seller or $100 - p_N$ is the mortgage rate (on a discount basis) to the borrower. At this price s_N of mortgages are offered to the FNMA.

When the FNMA uses the futures market optimally, the situation is described by equation (7.38) which can be compared to equation (7.31):

$$EP(\theta; t) = 2(1-g)p_F(t) + \alpha c(\gamma_1 + \gamma_2) \operatorname{var} I \cdot p_F(t) \qquad (7.38)$$

$$\text{MR} \quad = \quad \text{MC} \quad + \quad \text{RPF}$$

$$\gamma_1 \equiv \operatorname{var} \epsilon_1 / \operatorname{var} I \qquad \gamma_2 \equiv \operatorname{var} \epsilon_2 / \operatorname{var} I$$

The right-hand side of equation (7.38) is the middle curve in Figure 7.2.

Risk premium RPF, when the futures market is used optimally, depends upon the risks of variations in the differential between the prices of FNMA debentures and Treasury securities $\gamma_1 \operatorname{var} I$ and the basis risk $\gamma_2 \operatorname{var} I$ concerning movements of cash and future Treasury securities. By contrast, the risk premium RPN when the FNMA cannot hedge depends upon the variance (var P) of the price of FNMA debentures. Since the sum of the two *differential* risks $(\gamma_1 + \gamma_2) \operatorname{var} I$ is much less than the *absolute* risk var P, the risk premium with futures RPF is much less than RPN, the risk premium when hedging is not used. That is why curve MC + RPF is below MP + RPN in Figure 7.2.

With futures, the equilibrium point is F in Figure 7.2. The FNMA bids price p_F for the forward purchases of mortgages. Risk premium RPF is distance F'F, and marginal cost is p_FF'. At forward bid price p_F, the mortgage bankers and savings and loan institutions offer the FNMA quantity s_F of mortgages during the time period. The interest rate to the borrower (on a discount basis) has been reduced from $100 - p_N$ to $100 - p_F$, as a result of the use of futures markets. Thereby, the rate of capital formation in housing increases.

Quantitative estimates can be given for the reduction in the risk premium or rise in the forward bid price by the FNMA for mortgages. Equation (7.32) repeated here is the forward bid price if no hedging is possible:

$$p_N(t) = \frac{EP(\theta; t)}{2(1-g) + \alpha c \operatorname{var} P} \qquad (7.32)$$

If there were no risk aversion ($\alpha \operatorname{var} P = 0$), the forward bid price is $p_0(t)$ in

$$p_0(t) = \frac{EP(\theta; t)}{2(1-g)} \qquad (7.39)$$

In Figure 7.2, it is the point where the marginal cost is equal to the marginal revenue. Using equation (7.39) in (7.32), the forward bid price when there are no facilities to hedge can be expressed as

$$p_N(t) = \frac{p_0(t)}{1 + [\alpha c \operatorname{var} P/2(1-g)]} = \frac{p_0(t)}{1 + \delta_N} \qquad (7.40)$$

and

$$\delta_N = \frac{\alpha c \operatorname{var} P}{2(1-g)} \qquad (7.41)$$

Discount factor δ_N is applied to the no risk bid price $p_0(t)$ to obtain the forward bid price $p_N(t)$ when the FNMA cannot hedge.

When the futures market is used optimally, the forward bid price $p_F(t)$ is

$$p_F(t) = \frac{p_0(t)}{1 + [\alpha c(\gamma_1 + \gamma_2) \operatorname{var} I/2(1-g)]} = \frac{p_0(t)}{1 + \delta_F} \qquad (7.42)$$

and

$$\delta_F = \frac{\alpha c(\gamma_1 + \gamma_2) \operatorname{var} I}{2(1-g)} \qquad (7.43)$$

Discount factor δ_F is now applied to the no risk forward bid price $p_0(t)$ to obtain the price that the FNMA bids forward for mortgages.

A comparison of the two discount factors provides a quantitative estimate of the effect of the use of futures by the FNMA upon mortgage interest rates. Ratio δ_F/δ_N is

$$\frac{\delta_F}{\delta_N} = \frac{\gamma_1 + \gamma_2}{1 + \gamma_1} \qquad (7.44)$$

Quantity $\gamma_1 = \operatorname{var} \epsilon_1/\operatorname{var} I$ is the variance of the differential between FNMA and Treasury prices divided by the variance of the price of Treasuries. Quantity $\gamma_2 = \operatorname{var} \epsilon_2/\operatorname{var} I$ is the basis risk in hedging divided by the variance of the price of Treasuries.

An estimate of

$$\gamma_1 = \operatorname{var} \epsilon_1/\operatorname{var} I = 0.053$$

and

$$\gamma_2 = \operatorname{var} \epsilon_2/\operatorname{var} I = 0.515$$

(Stein, 1985, p. 180). Using these estimates:

$$\frac{\delta_F}{\delta_N} = \frac{0.515 + 0.053}{1.053} = 0.539 \qquad (7.45)$$

Hence, the discount factor used by the FNMA when it can hedge on the futures market is only 54 per cent of what it would use if it could not hedge.

On the basis of the previous analysis, the ratio of the price that the FNMA can bid forward for mortgages when it uses the futures market optimally $p_F(t)$ to what it can bid if no hedging were possible is

$$\frac{p_F(t)}{p_N(t)} = \frac{1 + \delta_N}{1 + \delta_F} \tag{7.46}$$

Using the estimates in equation (7.45), the price ratio is

$$\frac{p_F(t)}{p_N(t)} = \frac{1 + \delta_N}{1 + 0.5393\,\delta_N} \tag{7.47}$$

Table 7.4 contains estimates of this price ratio for several risk premiums δ_N that the FNMA might use of it could not hedge. If the risk premium δ_N used by the FNMA were 20 per cent (row 2) when it has no facilities to hedge, then it would bid 83.3 per cent of the no risk price for the face value of the mortgage. If the FNMA could use the futures market optimally, it could increase its bid price by 8.3 per cent (column 3) to 90.2 per cent of the no risk price for the face value of the mortgage (column 4). In this way, mortgage rates to the builder are lowered and capital formation in housing is increased.

The distinction between these two cases is extreme. Homemade hedging was used by the FNMA prior to the development of a futures market. Hedging can be homemade, by selling Treasury bonds short, or it can be done by selling Treasury bond futures. The futures market is more liquid than the cash market. A quantity of $100 million to $200 million can be traded 'more quietly' in the futures market than in the cash Treasury bond market. There is little effect upon the market price and anonymity is preserved in the futures market, which is an auction market. This is less true in the over-the-counter Treasury bond market. When the FNMA comes to market on its day of the month, it sells from 500 million to two billion of debentures. Due to its size, it prefers the futures market to homemade hedging. The net effect is that the forward price that the FNMA can offer to savings and loan associations is $p_F(t)$ when it hedges in the futures market, point $p_N(t)$ if it is unable to hedge (Figure 7.2). With homemade hedging, the forward bid price would be between $p_N(t)$ and $p_F(t)$. In this manner hedging in general, and futures markets in particular,

Table 7.4 Forward bid prices for mortgages associated with the optimal use of futures markets by the FNMA

δ_N	p_N/p_0	p_F/p_N	p_F/p_0
0.1	0.909	1.044	0.949
0.2	0.833	1.083	0.902
0.3	0.769	1.119	0.861

Symbols: δ_N, discount rate for risk when the FNMA cannot hedge; p_N, forward bid price when no hedging is possible; p_0, bid price in the forward market for \$1 face value of mortgages when there is no risk; p_F, forward bid price when the futures market is used optimally.

stimulate capital formation in residential housing. Planned investment by firms, item 1 in Table 7.1, is increased as a result of the optimal use of futures markets.

7.4 The Uses of Financial and Stock Index Futures by Institutional Investors

An important development in the last decade is that the financial assets of the private sector are controlled by institutional investors and managed by professional money market managers. As a result of the 1974 pension fund reform law and inflation, pension fund assets have more than tripled since 1971. There is been a keen competition among money managers to achieve the maximum return for a pre-determined amount of exposure. In fulfilling the role of fiduciary or trustee, the director of the investment programme is obligated to manage risk prudently. This part describes why and how institutional investors have been using futures markets in stock market indexes and financial instruments and analyses their optimization decisions. My conclusions can be summarized as follows.

1 Fund managers purchase or sell portfolios of securities based upon their expected relative price changes.
2 The principal sponsor and fund managers purchase or sell futures on a broad-based index to benefit from or to avoid expected market changes.
3 Rapid and transitory changes in desired total risk for a trust or a fund are achieved by selling or purchasing futures, not by transactions in the underlying securities.

This strategy is feasible because the sale (purchase) of futures on a broad-based index is equivalent to the sale (purchase) of the securities in the index but does not affect the market prices of the securities. Futures transactions involve low costs and do not interfere with the difficult and arduous process of security selection.

Through the use of financial and stock index futures by institutional investors, the trust or fund achieves a higher expected return on transactions for a given risk. Secondary markets in equities and fixed income securities thereby become more 'liquid', a dimension not captured not captured by the portfolio models in the literature.

In so far as savings in risky assets per unit of time of the private sector are affected by the liquidity of the secondary market, the new futures markets in equities and Treasury securities tend to increase savings and investment in risky assets (Table 7.1, item 3).

The institutional investor is most easily understood by considering two agents: a trustee/fiduciary who is the principal sponsor of pension funds and the fund manager. The principal sponsor may manage one part of the fund himself and assign the rest to several different fund managers. Each manager claims to have special expertise in security selection. One may have particular expertise in selecting the securities of new corporations, another in 'junk' bonds of firms in financial difficulties whose securities are believed to be undervalued by the market, another in the stocks of corporations engaged in innovation. The principal sponsor hopes to benefit from these special talents. Each fund manager selects a portfolio of securities and actively manages it in what he believes is an optimal manner. The trustee or principal sponsor distributes the assets among funds.

The process of institutional investment has two aspects: each fund must be managed optimally and the principal sponsor wants to achieve an optimal combination of expected return and risk for the entire trust or pension fund. The optimum risk–return point may fluctuate considerably from month to month or even week to week. The aim of this part is to show how these tasks are facilitated considerably by the use of futures markets.

7.4.1   *Risk Management Choices of Dynamic Adjustment*

I use two examples to explain the dynamic adjustment aspects of risk management. Although the cases are symmetrical, I explain them separately and in slightly different ways.

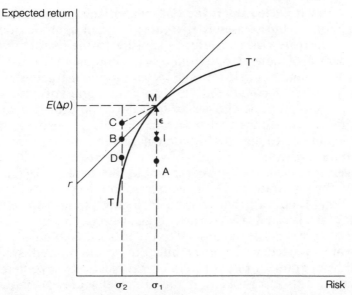

Figure 7.3   If there were no adjustment costs, the fund could move from point M to point B. With adjustment costs, the sale described above would move the fund to point D. The faster the attempt to reduce risk, the greater the distance between points D and B. By selling futures on the index, but keeping portfolio M, the fund moves to point C. The difference between points C and B results from lower transactions costs on futures. The portfolio M is expected to appreciate by ϵ more than the index, point I.

Figure 7.3 describes the risk–return possibilities facing either the fund manager or principal sponsor. The vertical axis represents expected returns to the entire fund or trust and the horizontal axis measures the corresponding risk reflected by the standard deviation. Curve TT' is the subjective transformation curve of the trust or fund which can be achieved from different combinations of portfolios. Let r be the Treasury bill rate, which is risk free in nominal terms. The subjective risk-return on the index (S&P 500 or bond index) is point I.

Suppose that a principal sponsor decides to change a fund manager whose performance at point A has been disappointing. This requires that the fund portfolio be sold, a new manager be found who must acquire a portfolio. Alternatively, as pension money continues to flow into a trust, the principal sponsor must decide how to distribute the funds among the existing funds or whether to hire another fund manager. In either case, the fund manager must decide upon the optimal portfolio to acquire. What is common to both cases is that the principal sponsor does not want to decrease risk and return exposure to the market during a given period of time as one fund is being liquidated for cash or he wants to maintain a risk–return exposure to the market as pension funds are being accumulated during a given period of time. In the first case several basic choices are possible. The principal sponsor can allocate the funds realized from the sale of portfolio that is being liquidated to different fund managers in various proportions. He would like time to decide how to allocate the funds among managers and each fund manager would like time to decide upon his investment strategy. Until the portfolio selection decisions are taken, the funds will be invested in highly liquid, safe but low yielding assets such as Treasury bills. During this interval, the principal sponsor loses exposure to the market. Graphically, if the funds are invested in Treasury bills during the interim, the fund would be at point *r* while the market is subjectively expected to be at point I. This is a problem if the principal sponsor believes that the market will appreciate in excess of the Treasury bill rate.

If, to obtain market exposure quickly, the principal sponsor or fund manager fails to take the time and effort in stock selection, then it is unlikely that the hastily chosen investment will earn the market rate of return. He believes that, with a carefully formulated investment strategy, he can achieve point M which is better than the market performance point I.

A symmetrical situation exists when the principal sponsor or fund manager wants to reduce total risk exposure for a short period of time. In the situation described in Figure 7.3, the fund managers have selected what they consider to be optimal portfolios at point M. These portfolios are expected to appreciate relative to the market and the fund managers may have investment horizons of several years. A manager may have invested, for example, in stocks of firms engaged in innovative processes.

The principal sponsor is generally concerned with quarterly results as well as longer-term performance. Suppose that he thinks that there is greater uncertainty concerning Federal Reserve policy, but it is more likely that interest rates will rise than decline in the near future. He expects these declines to be of a relatively short duration but he wants to avoid the situation that occurred in October 1979 when large portfolio losses occurred. There are several strategies available to reduce the total risk from σ_1 to σ_2 for a short period of time.

The principal sponsor could direct the fund managers to sell off some of their risky assets, or reduce the portfolio by a given percentage within a day or two, and invest the proceeds in safe assets during the period of uncertainty. This would be a temporary movement from point M to point B. When the uncertainty is resolved within a few weeks or months, the principal sponsor would move back to point M, which represents a long-term investment strategy. The risk reduction strategy, moving from σ_1 to σ_2, is transitory.

This would be a costly and disruptive strategy. Each fund manager has carefully assembled a portfolio on the basis of capital asset pricing model (CAPM) reasoning, where the subjective covariance matrix of the returns has been used to determine the optimum proportions of the securities. The portfolio includes many securities that the manager wants to keep because he believes that they are grossly undervalued by the market. To then be directed to sell off 'risky' assets undermines this strategy. No longer would the assets be held in optimal proportions and the fund manager would no longer be on his subjective opportunity locus between expected return and risk.

Transactions costs involved in the sale and subsequent repurchase of equity are considerable. If the value of the portfolio temporarily sold to reduce risk were $80 million, round trip transactions costs would be $200 000. This is a very high price to pay to reduce risk just for a short period of time. A formal analysis of these problems focuses upon equation (7.48).

Let $s(t)$ be *the transactions* [purchases (+) or sales (−)] *per unit of time* in acquiring or disposing of a portfolio. The sum of $s(t)$ is the total number of shares acquired or sold but $s(t)$ is the rate of change of a portfolio.

In capital theory, a distinction is made between the marginal efficiency of capital and the marginal efficiency of investment (Lerner, 1947, pp. 331–45). A similar distinction is of crucial importance in financial investment. The marginal efficiency of investment is described by

$$\Delta p$$

marginal efficiency of investment

$$= \qquad \beta \Delta I + \epsilon \qquad - \qquad (\gamma/2)s$$

= marginal efficiency of capital − adjustments costs (7.48)

The first two terms are the marginal efficiency of capital. The third term concerns the *rate* at which the portfolio has been acquired or sold *per unit of time*, which is a dynamic adjustment cost. Term Δp is the capital gain plus dividends in excess of the Treasury bill rate on the transactions during the time interval.

Each portfolio acquired by a fund manager has a beta (β) which describes the relation between the return during the interval t to $t + 1$ on the portfolio of risky assets in excess of the risk free rate (Δp) and the return on the index in excess of the risk free rate (ΔI) during the same interval. Beta in equation (7.48) has no normative significance as it has in the CAPM, but is simply the manager's subjective view of the relation between the market excess return ΔI and the excess return Δp on this portfolio of securities. The first two terms $\beta \Delta I + \epsilon$ represent a return on the portfolio. It is the marginal efficiency of capital: the return on a 'stock' rather than on a 'flow'.

The third term in equation (7.48) reflects the effects of fund *transactions* upon the market price of the portfolio. It refers to costs involved in rapid acquisitions or sales of portfolios *per unit of time*. It is of fundamental importance in understanding how and why fund managers and principal sponsors use the futures markets in financial instruments and stock market indexes. This element is not captured at all by the portfolio models in the literature, due to their focus upon 'stocks', which have no time dimensions rather than flows per unit of time.

The *immediate* disposal by a manager of an 80 million dollar portfolio consisting of two million shares at 40 dollars per share will tend to depress the average price per share. Travelers Investment Management estimated this effect as being between an eighth and a quarter of a point, an estimate confirmed by other fund managers. This means that the sale (purchase) of an 80 million dollar portfolio of stocks sold (purchased) during a short time interval (for example, a day) will change its value by at least $250\,000$ (= 2 million shares $\times$ 1/8) and possibly by as much as $500\,000$ (= 2 million shares $\times$ 1/4). Term $\gamma s(t)/2$ describes the change in the market price that results from *transaction* s(t) *during the time interval*.

Coefficient γ has several determinants. It measures the adjustment costs and consists of the market power of a fund to affect price. First, a transaction during a given interval of time $s(t)$ by a fund involves a heterogeneous collection of securities. Some are actively traded in broad markets and others are traded in thin markets. The greater the fraction of the transaction consisting of the sales or purchases of securities with low daily volumes, the greater the effect upon the market price and the larger will be γ. Even if all securities had the same price elasticity of demand, the larger percentage change in volume of securities sold in thin markets would produce larger percentage price declines than in the case of actively traded securities. Secondly, in so far as the sale by a fund involves a nonrepresentative sample of securities, the number of other funds or large institutional investors who would be interested in acquiring the particular securities *during the time interval* may be small. The price elasticity of demand over the short time interval may be lower than that for a representative sample of corporations. Thirdly, there is a bias or negative signal that a fund transaction imparts to the market. The sale of a portfolio by a manager who is being replaced conveys a signal to the market that its ϵ is negative. There is a high probablity that this particular transaction consists of securities that are currently overhauled. As a result, the dealer or market may only absorb these securities at a substantial reduction in price.

The dynamic risk management problem facing institutional investors can be summarized in terms of Figure 7.3. The faster the manager or principal sponsor wants to change the portfolio (from A to M, or from M to B), the greater will be the costs of adjustment. The marginal efficiency of investment (Δp) is reduced below the marginal efficiency of capital ($\beta \Delta I + \epsilon$) by the costs of adjustment. The latter are positively related to the speed of adjustment.

Institutional investors use futures in two major ways. They engage in arbitrage, which permits them to earn at least the market rate of return on the index. They also use futures to reduce the adjustment costs of temporary changes in their portfolios. This raises the marginal efficiency of investment for any given marginal product of capital. These two factors improve the expected return–risk possibilities offered to savers, and thereby increases the savings available for risky investment.

7.4.2 *Arbitrage Between Futures and the Index*

There are several ways to invest in the S&P 500 index. Buy the index of stocks at time t at price $I(t)$ and receive dividends $VI(t)$ where V is the dividend rate. Alternatively, invest $I(t)$ in Treasury bills yielding rate r and purchase a futures contract on the index for $q_T(t)$. In each case at maturity the investment will be worth the same amount $I(T) = q_T(T)$. The gross return from the direct investment in the index R_I and the gross return from the indirect investment R_{FT} by buying Treasury bills and purchasing futures are defined below:

$$R_I \equiv I(T) - (1 - V)I(t) \tag{7.49a}$$

$$R_{FT} \equiv I(T) + rI(t) - q_T(t) \tag{7.49b}$$

$$\eta \equiv R_{FT} - R_I \equiv (1 + r - V)I(t) - q_T(t) \tag{7.49c}$$

Define η in equation (7.49c) as $(R_{FT} - R_I)$ the gross return from purchasing the futures contract on the index and investing in Treasury bills less the gross return from purchasing the stock index directly.

If the futures contract were to be held to maturity, the only stochastic element in η is the dividend–price ratio V on the index. 'Mispricing' and the possibility for quasi-arbitrage profits exist when the absolute value of η exceeds transactions costs (estimated by Merrill Lynch Capital Markets division at 0.5 percentage points). If η is positive then (gross of transactions costs) it is profitable to short the index of stocks, invest the proceeds in Treasury bills and purchase the futures. If η is negative then (gross of transactions costs) it is profitable to short the futures and invest in the index of stocks.

To take advantage of mispricing (when η is not zero), several institutional investors established performance index futures funds to do the quasi-arbitrage.

These funds cannot do worse than the S&P 500 Index. The returns are R_I plus the absolute value of η when there is mispricing. When there is no mispricing the fund earns $R_I = R_{FT}$. During the early period, these funds obtained a 5–6 per cent return above the S&P 500 index. As a result of these quasi-arbitrage activities by funds that hold approximations to the S&P 500 index, the absolute value of η has declined. Nevertheless, these funds still make arbitrage profits, but the quasi-arbitrage activities drive the absolute value of η towards the transactions costs.

7.4.3   Futures Facilitate Risk-Return Adjustment and Raise the Marginal Efficiency of Investment

Earlier it was claimed that the immediate purchase or sale of a portfolio of 80 million dollars (consisting of two million shares at 40 dollars per share) tends to affect the average price of a share by an eighth to a quarter of a point. This was described by the $\gamma s(t)$

term in equation (7.48). Funds do not have much power to affect futures prices in the index for several reasons.

First, no signals are conveyed to the market that the fund is disposing of overvalued stocks when it sells the future on the index. Such a sale cannot convey signals about relative prices of securities. Secondly, the price elasticity of demand for a representative sample of stocks in the S&P 500 should be greater than the elasticity of demand for a nonrepresentative subset of these stocks. Funds may invest in portfolios which are proxies to the market index as well as specializing in different portfolios of stock. If one fund is selling a block of a particular stock and another fund is purchasing another block of a particular stock, it is unlikely that what one is demanding is what the other is supplying. A price change would be required to induce a fund to change its proportions of securities. However, if one fund is decreasing its equity investment in the index by selling futures on the index it will be exactly the same future that another firm is purchasing to increase its equity investment in the index. The futures transaction on the index is equivalent to buying or selling the index of underlying securities. Consequently, both funds are trading the same homogeneous commodity: a representative sample of stocks. For this reason, no reduction in price must be offered to induce the buyer to purchase a different vector of securities than initially planned.

These reasons explain why there is a market power term $\gamma s(t)$ in equation (7.48) for the change in the price of portfolios and none for the change in the futures price. This is a formal way of stating that the *futures market in a broad-based index* is much more *liquid* than the market for underlying securities (or the market in narrow based sub-indexes). *The* raison d'être *of futures markets is the considerable liquidity relative to the markets in underlying securities.*

Transactions costs of purchases and sales in futures are approximately 15 per cent of those in the underlying securities. (The following example was provided by Travelers Investment Management Company and confirmed by other funds.) Suppose that a fund purchased or sold $80 million of equity. At an average price share of $40, the transaction involves two million shares. At a commission rate of five cents a share (a rate considerably lower than the average for all institutional trades), the one way commissions amount to $100 000 (= 2 million shares × 5 cents per share).

If $80 million of the S&P 500 future were sold, the commissions would be substantially lower. With the futures selling for 160, the value of a futures contract on the S&P 500 index is

\$80 000 (= 160 × \$500). To sell \$80 million, 1000 futures contracts must be sold. The one way commission rate is \$15 per contract. Total commissions involved in selling \$80 million in futures are \$15 000 (= \$15 × 1000). This is 15 per cent of the transactions costs in underlying securities.

The reason for this difference is the economy to scale. It may cost no more to process one futures contract for \$80 000 than for one block of 100 shares at \$40 per share, valued at \$4000. Bid-ask spreads are not standardized so that it is difficult to know how they compare in futures transactions and those in the underlying securities. The net result is that transactions costs for futures are less than for those in the underlying securities.

Futures markets in the stock market index and in Treasury securities reduce the adjustment costs of temporary changes in the portfolio of institutional investors and thereby raise the marginal efficiency of investment. This is the subject of the present section.

Equation (7.50) describes the return $\pi(t + h)$ to the fund or trust, when it can engage in futures transactions. The first three terms in equation (7.50), or the term in brackets in equation (7.50a), are $s\Delta p - T(s)$ the returns on the cash transactions $s(t)$ less transactions costs $T[s(t)]$.

Let $x_T(t)$ of futures which mature at time T be sold at time t. The current price is $q_T(t)$. These futures will be repurchased at subsequent date $t + h$ at price $q_T(t + h)$. Transactions costs on the futures are $\theta(x)$.

It was explained above that the futures market is so liquid that there is no term corresponding to $\gamma s(t)$ the monopoly power in the cash transactions market. In addition, transactions costs in futures $\theta(x)$ are much lower than $T(s)$ those in the cash instruments.

$$\pi(t + h) = \{\beta[I(t + h) - (1 + r - v)I(t)] + \epsilon\}s(t)$$
$$- \gamma s^2(t)/2 - T[s(t)] + x_T(t)[q_T(t) - q_T(t + h)]$$
$$- \theta[x(t)] \tag{7.50}$$

abbreviated as

$$\pi = [(\beta\Delta I + \epsilon)s - \gamma s^2/2 - T(s)] - x\Delta q - \theta(x) \tag{7.50a}$$

where π is the return on the transactions, $x(t)$ are the sales of futures $y(t) = -x(t) =$ purchases of futures, $q_T(t)$ is the price at time t of futures maturing at time T, $T(s)$, $\theta(x)$ are transactions costs and $I(t)$ is the price of the index. Using equation (7.7a) for the relation between the change in the futures price Δq and in the index ΔI, where η corresponds to ϵ_2, equation (7.51) is derived:

$$\pi = (\beta s - x)\Delta I + \epsilon s - \gamma s^2/2 - \eta x - T(s) - \theta(x) \qquad (7.51)$$

The first term $(\beta s - x)\Delta I$ is the gross return attributable to changes in the market (S&P 500) index. The second term ϵs is the gross return from changes in the relative price (ϵ) of the portfolio acquired or sold during the interval. The third term $\gamma s^2/2$ is the change in price induced by the fund's purchases or sales of the securities during the interval of time. The fourth term $-\eta x$ represents the basis risk. The last two terms are the transactions costs in dealing with the underlying securities $T(s)$ and the futures $\theta(x)$. Transactions costs on purchases are the same as on sales so $T(s) = T(-s)$ and $\theta(x) = \theta(-x) = \theta(y)$.

Expected return $E\pi$ is described by

$$E\pi = (\beta s - x)E(\Delta I) + sE(\epsilon) - (\gamma s^2/2) - T(s) - \theta(x) \qquad (7.52)$$

where the expectations are taken over stochastic variables: ΔI, ϵ and η. It is assumed that the expected value of η is zero, but it has a variance.

In deriving the variance of the return $\operatorname{var}\pi$, assume that the three stochastic elements are independent of each other:

$$\operatorname{var} \pi = (\beta s - x)^2 \operatorname{var} \Delta I + s^2 \operatorname{var} \epsilon + x^2 \operatorname{var} \eta \qquad (7.53)$$

There are three sources of risk: (a) $\operatorname{var} \Delta I$ is the variance of the return on the *market index* of securities; (b) $\operatorname{var} \epsilon$ is the risk of *relative price* changes between the portfolio in question and the market index; (c) $\operatorname{var} \eta$ which corresponds to $\operatorname{var} \epsilon_2$ is the *basis* risk.

Equations (7.50)–(7.53) just focus upon the returns and risk associated with transactions during the interval. The change in risk on the entire portfolio resulting from transactions $s(t)$ per unit of time also depends upon the particular subjective variance–covariance matrix, which differs among funds. The approach taken here can be generalized to take the latter into account, with no basic change in results. The present analysis brings out more clearly and simply the uses and advantages of futures markets to the institutional investors.

7.4.3.1 Transition to a New Portfolio

Two cases of risk management are considered. The first case concerns a principal sponsor who dismisses a fund manager whose performance put the trust at point A in Figure 7.3. A new manager is appointed who believes that he can select a portfolio M which will exceed the market performance at point I. I show how the use of futures markets raises the marginal efficiency of investment on the acquisition of a new portfolio.

If the new fund manager acts quickly to reinvest the allotted funds in the market during a short time interval, the fund will obtain a change in the expected returns $\partial E\pi/\partial s$ and a change in risk $\partial \text{ var } \pi/\partial s$ on the resulting transactions $s(t)$. Call the ratio MRT(s) in equation (7.54), the marginal rate of transformation between risk and expected return from investment in cash securities during the time interval. It is derived from equations (7.52) and (7.53):

$$\text{MRT}(s) = \frac{\partial E\pi/\partial s}{\frac{1}{2}\partial \text{ var } \pi/\partial s} = \frac{\beta E(\Delta I) + E(\epsilon) - \gamma s - T'(s)}{(\beta s - x)\beta \text{ var } \Delta I + s \text{ var } \epsilon} \qquad (7.54)$$

Evaluated at $x = 0$ when there is no futures position, this marginal rate of transformation is

$$\text{MRT}(s) = \frac{\beta E(\Delta I) + E(\epsilon) - \gamma s - T'(s)}{s(\beta^2 \text{ var } \Delta I + \text{ var } \epsilon)} \qquad (7.55)$$

This is graphed as curve OS in Figure 7.4. The numerator is the marginal efficiency of the investment. The marginal efficiency of capital exceeds the marginal efficiency of investment for two reasons. First, the faster the portfolio is acquired, the greater are the adjustment costs γs, where s represents the transactions during the given time interval. Secondly, the faster the portfolio is acquired, the lower will be $E(\epsilon)$, its performance relative to the index because an inadequate amount of time is devoted to the selection of a portfolio, i.e. to the formulation of an investment strategy. The fund cannot jump from point A to point M in Figure 7.3. The change in expected returns from a rapid purchase programme is the numerator in equation (7.55).

A different marginal rate of transformation results when the principal sponsor or fund manager uses the futures market. As the securities of the dismissed fund manager are sold, the principal sponsor can: (a) invest the proceeds in highly liquid assets such as Treasury bills; (b) purchase futures contracts on the S&P 500 index; and (c) the new fund manager carefully devises an investment strategy.

The marginal rate of transformation MRT(y) between the change in expected return per purchases of stock index futures per unit of time (the numerator) and the change in risk per purchases of stock index futures per unit of time (the denominator) is equation (7.56), based upon equation (7.52) and (7.53). Vari-

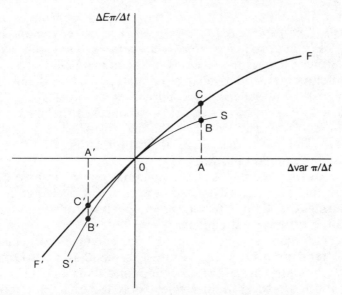

Figure 7.4   The curves describe the change in expected return over the time interval to the change in risk over the time interval. Curve SS' refers to the purchases or sales of securities and curve FF' refers to the purchase of sales of futures.

able $y = -x$ represents purchases of futures per unit of time:

$$\text{MRT}(y) = \frac{E(\Delta I) - \theta'}{(\beta s - x)\, \text{var}\, \Delta I - x\, \text{var}\, \eta} = \frac{\partial E(\pi)/\partial(y)}{\frac{1}{2}\partial\, \text{var}\, \pi/\partial(y)} \qquad (7.56)$$

When $\text{MRT}(y)$ is evaluated at $s = 0$ when there are no purchases of cash securities, the marginal rate of transformation is

$$\text{MRT}(y) = \frac{E(\Delta I) - \theta'}{y\,(\text{var}\, \Delta I + \text{var}\, \eta)} \qquad (7.57)$$

which is graphed as OF in Figure 7.4.

The numerator, derived from equation (7.52), is the change in the expected return from the purchases of futures on the index per unit of time. It is the expected return on the stock index in excess of the safe return $E(\Delta I)$ less the transactions costs θ'. It is assumed that there is no mispricing so that $E(\eta) = 0$. Due to the liquidity and depth of the futures market (discussed above), funds do not perceptibly affect the market price by their transactions.

With the purchase of futures, the fund can jump from point A to the market expected return. The trust is totally invested in the market without the physical purchases of stocks. *The essence of purchasing the futures is that the trust is in effect purchasing the entire S&P 500 index at low transactions costs and without market power.* This is the meaning of the numerator.

The denominator, derived from equation (7.53), is the change in total risk resulting from the purchases of futures per unit of time. The two components of risk are changes in the market index (var ΔI) and the risk involved if the futures are sold before maturity. The basis risk var η is small relative to the risk of changes in the market index.

Curve OF in Figure 7.4 is the marginal rate of transformation between the change in expected return and the change in total risk, during the time interval, when the investment of funds is done in the futures on the index.

In general, comparing equations (7.55) and (7.57), the marginal rate of transformation using futures exceeds that of using securities directly under any of the following conditions: (a) the expected appreciation of stocks hastily selected is less than the expected appreciation of the index, $\beta E(\Delta I) + E(\epsilon) \leqslant E(\Delta I)$; (b) there is considerable market power when purchases are made quickly, γs is large; (c) the basis risk var η is less than the relative price risk var ϵ.

A comparison of the two marginal rates of transformation is most vivid, if it is assumed that: (a) either the principal sponsor has a fund purchase s of securities or an equivalent value of futures, during an interval; and (b) the portfolio of securities that would be purchased has a β equal to unity. Then equations (7.55a) and (7.57a) are special cases of (7.55) and (7.57) respectively:

$$\text{MRT}(s) \qquad\qquad\qquad \text{MRT}(y)$$

$$(7.55a) \quad \frac{E(\Delta I) + E(\epsilon) - T' - \gamma s}{s\,(\text{var }\Delta I + \text{var }\epsilon)} < \frac{E(\Delta I) - \theta'}{s\,(\text{var }\Delta I + \text{var }\eta)} \quad (7.57a)$$

The numerator of the MRT when there are purchases of stocks is less than the value when futures are purchased, because hastily conceived stock purchases are expected to perform worse than the market $E(\epsilon) < 0$; and the concentration of these purchases during a short time interval will raise their prices $\gamma s > 0$. In addition, the transactions costs in futures θ' are considerably less than T' those involving the physical securities. The denominator of the MRT when there are purchases of futures is less than that involved in the direct purchases of securities, because the basis risk var η is substantially less than the relative price risk var ϵ.

Graphically, the change in expected return for a given change in risk exposure 0A is AB on curve 0S when the stocks are purchased rapidly during the transition period between fund managers and AC on curve 0F when futures are purchased and the stock acquisition programme has been spread out over a longer period of time.

7.4.3.2 Rapid Temporary Reduction of Risk

The second problem of risk management discussed above concerns the rapid but temporary reduction of total risk exposure. The principal sponsor (or fund manager) wants to reduce total risk from σ_1 to σ_2 in Figure 7.3 for a short period of time. He is anxious to keep the portfolio described by point M as a long-term investment. This portfolio is expected to outperform the market: $E(\epsilon) > 0$. It was explained earlier that the attempt to move quickly to point B by selling a fraction of the portfolio of risky assets, and then repurchasing them to return to point M, is very costly and disruptive. Costs of adjustment are reflected in term γs in equation (7.48) above.

A more efficient strategy is available to quickly reduce market risk temporarily without incurring adjustment costs γs. The principal sponsor sells futures contracts corresponding to the risks that he wants to avoid. If he wants to reduce the risks of declines in the stock index, he sells futures contracts on the S&P 500 index. If he wants to reduce the risks of a decline in the index of long-term bonds, he sells futures contracts on Treasury bonds. These sales correspond to $x(t)$ in equations (7.52) and (7.53) above.

Fund managers need not be informed of these actions and no fund portfolio is being disturbed. Managers continue to hold the desired stocks in what they believe are the optimal proportions and there are no costly sales during a short interval of time. By increasing sales of futures $x(t)$, the principal sponsor moves along segment $0F'$ of the transformation curve in Figure 7.4. Risk is reduced by $0A'$ at a cost of $A'C'$ in expected return, whereas the cost would have been $A'B'$ if the first strategy were followed.

Formally, consider the case where the following conditions are satisfied: (a) portfolio M is expected to appreciate by more than the index and has a $\beta = 1$ which means

$$E(\Delta p) = E(\Delta I) + E(\epsilon) > E(\Delta I);$$

(b) the choice is to sell securities $(-s)$ or sell an equivalent value $x = -s$ of futures on the index which means that $MRT(x)$ is evaluated at $s = 0$ and $x = -s$. The two marginal rates of transformation are as follows:

$$\text{MRT}(-s) = \frac{E(\Delta I) + E(\epsilon) + T' + \gamma s}{s\,(\text{var }\Delta I + \text{var }\epsilon)}$$

slope   OS'

$$> \frac{E(\Delta I) + \theta'}{s\,(\text{var }\Delta I + \text{var }\eta)} = \text{MRT}(x)$$

slope   OF'

in Figure 7.4. The intuitive explanation is as follows. By selling portfolio M the trust (or fund) loses the return on the portfolio net of the safe return $E(\Delta I) + E(\epsilon)$ and incurs transaction costs T' and adjustment costs of γs. This loss is the numerator of $\text{MRT}(-s)$.

By selling futures on the index, the trust loses the expected return on the index $E(\Delta I)$ and incurs transactions costs θ'. In so far as the portfolio M is expected to appreciate relative to the index $E(\epsilon) > 0$ and adjustment costs are significant $\gamma > 0$, the loss of expected return is much greater by selling the portfolio than by selling futures on the index. Moreover, transactions costs on futures are lower than on the securities $\theta' < T'$.

The reduction in risk by selling the portfolio is $s\,(\text{var }\Delta I + \text{var }\epsilon)$ and is $s\,(\text{var }\Delta I + \text{var }\eta)$ by selling an equal value of futures on the index. Since the basis risk var η is small relative to the risk var ΔI on the index, the risk that is diversified away by selling the futures is similar to that which would be eliminated by selling an equivalent value of the portfolio.

The net result is described by comparing several points in Figure 7.3.

1   If there were no adjustment costs ($\gamma = 0$), the trust or fund could move from point M to point B by selling part of the portfolio M, and investing the proceeds temporarily in safe assets.
2   With adjustment costs ($\gamma > 0$), the sale described above would move the trust or fund to point D. The faster the attempt to reduce risk, the greater the distance between points D and B.
3   By selling futures on the index, but keeping portfolio M, the trust or fund moves to point C. The difference between points C and B result from the lower transactions costs on futures.

Thus the advantages of using futures for temporary risk reduction are measured by distance DC:

$$DC = \qquad DB \qquad + \qquad BC$$

= save adjustment costs + lower transactions costs

Savings in risky assets (Table 7.1, item 3) depend upon the expected return–risk possibilities in the secondary market. By using futures in the ways described above, the institutional investors improve the risk–return trade-off in Figures 7.3 and 7.4. As a result, the use of futures raises savings invested in risky assets. It was shown in Section 7.3 how the use of futures by the FNMA raises the rate of investment in housing (Table 7.1, item 1).

This concluding chapter is an application of the theory developed in Chapters Two to Six to the specific institutions in the capital market. I have explained how the use of interest rate and stock index futures raises the rate of capital formation.

References

Agmon, T. and Amihud, Y. 1981: The forward exchange rate and the prediction of the future spot rate. *Journal of Banking and Finance*, 5, 425-37.

Anderson, R. W. and Danthine, J.-P. 1983: Hedger diversity in futures markets. *Economic Journal*, 93, 370-89.

Beckmann, M. J. 1965: On the determination of prices in futures markets. In M. J. Brennan (ed.), *Patterns of Market Behaviour*, Providence, R. I.: Brown University Press, 3-16.

Black, F., Jensen, M. C. & Scholes, M. 1972: The capital asset pricing model: some empirical tests. In M. C. Jensen (ed.), *Studies in the Theory of Capital Markets*, New York: Praeger Publishers.

Bodie, Z. and Rosansky, V. J. 1980: Risk and return in commodity futures. *Financial Analysts Journal*, 36, 3-14.

Bray, Margaret 1985: Rational expectations, information and asset markets: an introduction. *Oxford Economic Papers*, 37, 161-95.

Brennan, M. J. 1958: The supply of storage. *American Economic Review*, 48, 50-72.

Britto, Ronald 1984: The simultaneous determination of spot and futures prices in a simple model with production risk. *Quarterly Journal of Economics*, 99, 221-35.

Carter, Colin, Rausser, G. and Schmitz, A. 1983: Efficient asset portfolios and the theory of normal backwardation. *Journal of Political Economy*, 91, 319-31.

Chang, E. 1985: Returns to speculators and the theory of normal backwardation. *Journal of Finance*, 40, 193-207.

Cootner, Paul H. 1967: Speculation and hedging. *Food Research Institute Studies*, VII Supplement, 65-106.

Cox, C. 1976: Futures trading and market information. *Journal of Political Economy*, 84, 1215-37.

Danthine, Jean-Pierre, 1978: Information, futures prices, and stabilizing speculation. *Journal of Economic Theory*, 17, 79-98.

DeGroot, Morris 1970: *Optimal Statistical Decisions*. New York: McGraw-Hill.

Douglas, G. W. 1969: Risk in the equity markets: an empirical appraisal of market efficiency. *Yale Economic Essays*, 9, 3-45.

Draper, Dennis W. 1985: The small public trader in futures markets. In Anne E. Peck (ed.), *Futures Markets: Regulatory Issues*, Washington, D.C.: American Enterprise Institute.

Dusak, K. 1973: Futures trading and investor returns: an investigation of commodity market risk premiums. *Journal of Political Economy*, 81, 1387–406.

Ederington, Louis 1979: The hedging performance of the new futures markets. *Journal of Finance*, 34, 157–70.

Fama, Eugene 1970: Efficient capital markets: a review of theory and empirical work. *Journal of Finance*, 25, 383–417.

— 1981: *Investments*, New York: Prentice-Hall.

— 1984: Forward and spot exchange rates. *Journal of Monetary Economics*, 14, 319–38.

Feller, W. 1966: *An Introduction to Probability Theory and its Applications*, II, New York: John Wiley and Sons.

Figlewski, S. 1982: Information diversity and market behavior. *Journal of Finance*, XXXVII, 87–102.

Forsythe, R., Palfrey, T. R. and Plott, C. R. 1982: Asset valuation in an experimental market. *Econometrica*, 50(3), 537–67.

— 1984: Futures markets and informational efficiency: a laboratory examination. *Journal of Finance*, XXXIX(4), 955–81.

Goss, B. and Yamey, B. 1976: *The Economics of Futures Trading*, London: Macmillan.

Gray, R. W. 1972: The futures market for Maine potatoes: an appraisal. *Food Research Institute Studies*, 11, No. 3. Reprinted in A. E. Peck (ed.), 1977: *Selected Writings on Futures Markets*, II, Chicago: Board of Trade, 337–65.

Grossman, S. 1976: On the efficiency of competitive stock markets where traders have diverse information. *Journal of Finance*, 31, 573–85.

— 1977: The existence of futures markets, noisy rational expectations and informational externalities. *Review of Economic Studies*, 44, 431–49.

— and Stiglitz, J. 1976: Information and competitive price systems. *American Economic Review*, 66, 246–53.

Hartzmark, Michael 1984: The distribution of large trader returns in futures markets. Doctoral Dissertation, Department of Economics, University of Chicago.

Helmuth, John W. 1977: *Grain Pricing*, Commodity Futures Trading Commission, Washington, D.C.

Hobson, R. B. 1978: *Futures Trading in Financial Instruments*, Washington, D.C.: Commodity Futures Trading Commission.

Hodrick, R. J. and Srivastara, S. 1985: *Foreign Currency Futures*, Columbia University Business School, Center for the Study of Futures Markets, Working Paper Series CSFM-116.

Holthausen, Duncan 1979: Hedging and the competitive firm under price uncertainty. *American Economic Review*, 69, 989–95.

Houthakker, Hendrik 1957: Can speculators forecast prices? *Review of Economics and Statistics*, XXXIX(2), 143–51.

Jensen, Michael C. 1972: Capital markets: theory and evidence. *Bell Journal of Economics and Management Science*, 3, 357–398.

Kamara, Avraham 1982: Issues in futures markets: a survey. *Journal of Futures Markets*, 2, 261–94.

Kawai, M. 1983: Spot and futures prices of nonstorable commodities under rational expectations. *Quarterly Journal of Economics*, 98, 235–54.

Keynes, J. M. 1930: *A Treatise on Money*, II, London: Macmillan and Co.

Keynes, J. M. 1936: *The General Theory of Employment, Interest and Money*, Harcourt Brace.

Lerner, A. P. 1947: *The Economics of Control*, New York: Macmillan.

Levy, Haim 1978: Equilibrium in an imperfect market: a constraint on the number of securities in the portfolio. *American Economic Review*, 68, 643–58.

Lintner, J. 1965: The valuation of risk assets and the selection of risky investments in stock portfolio and capital budgets. *Review of Economics and Statistics*, 47, 13–37.

Longworth, D., Boothe, P. and Clinton, K. 1983: *A Study of the Efficiency of Foreign Exchange Markets*, Ottawa: Bank of Canada.

Maddala, G. S. 1977: *Econometrics*, New York: McGraw-Hill.

Mankiw, N. G. and Shapiro, M. D. 1985: Risk and return: consumption beta versus market beta. NBER Working Paper No. 1399, Revised, January 4.

Markowitz, H. 1959: *Portfolio Selection: Efficient Diversification of Investment*, New York: John Wiley & Sons.

Miller, M. H. and Scholes, M. 1972: Rate of return in relation to risk: a re-examination of some recent findings. In M. C. Jensen (ed.), *Studies in the Theory of Capital Markets*, New York: Praeger Publishers.

Muth, J. 1961: Rational expectations and the theory of price movements. *Econometrica*, 29, 215–35.

Newbery, D. M. G. and Stiglitz, J. E. 1982: The choice of techniques and the optimality of market equilibrium with rational expectations. *Journal of Political Economy*, 90, 223–46.

Paul, Allen B. 1985: The role of cash settlement in futures contract specification. In Anne E. Peck (ed.), *Futures Markets: Regulatory Issues*, Washington, D.C.: American Enterprise Institute.

—, Heifner, R. G. and Helmuth, J. W. 1976: Farmers' use of forward contracts and futures markets. US Department of Agriculture, Economic Research Service, Agriculture Economic Reports No. 320.

Peck, A. E. 1979–80: Reflections of hedging on futures market activity. *Food Research Institute Studies*, 17, No. 3. Reprinted in A. E. Peck (ed.), *Selected Writings on Futures Markets*, IV, 1984, Chicago: Board of Trade, 305–26.

— 1985: The economic role of traditional commodity futures markets. In Anne E. Peck (ed.), *Futures Markets: Their Economic Role*, Washington, D.C.: American Enterprise Institute.

Rockwell, Charles 1967: Normal backwardation, forecasting, and the returns to commodity futures traders. *Food Research Institute Studies*, Suppl. Vol. VII, 107–30.

Samuelson, Paul A. 1965: Proof that properly anticipated prices fluctuate randomly. *Industrial Management Review*, 6, 41-9.

— 1976: Is real world price a tale told by the idiot of chance? *Review of Economics and Statistics*, 58, 120-3.

Sandor, Richard 1973: Innovation by an exchange: a case study of the development of the plywood futures contract. *Journal of Law and Economics*, 16.

Sharpe, W. F. 1964: Capital asset prices: a theory of market equilibrium under conditions of risk. *Journal of Finance*, 19, 425-42.

Silber, William L. 1981: Innovation, competition, and new contract design in futures markets. *The Journal of Futures Markets*, I, 123-56.

— 1985: The economic role of financial futures. In Anne E. Peck (ed.), *Futures Markets: Their Economic Role*, Washington, D.C.: American Enterprise Institute.

Simmons, Will M. 1962: *An Economic Study of the U.S. Potato Industry*, U.S. Department of Agriculture, Economic Research Service, Agricultural Economic Report No. 6.

Stein, Jerome L. 1979: Spot, forward and futures. In Haim Levy (ed.), *Research in Finance* I, Greenwich, Connecticut: JAI Press.

— 1980: The dynamics of spot and forward prices in an efficient foreign exchange market with rational expectations. *American Economic Review*, 70, 565-83.

— 1982: *Monetarist, Keynesian and New Classical Economics*, Oxford: Blackwell.

— 1984: Rational, irrational and over-regulated speculative markets. In Robert Lanzillotti and Yoram Peles (eds), *Management under Government Intervention, Research in Finance*, Research in Finance, Supplement I, Greenwich, Connecticut: JAI Press.

— 1985: Futures markets and capital formation. In Anne E. Peck (ed.), *Futures Markets: Their Economic Role*, Washington, D.C.: American Enterprise Institute.

Stewart, Blair 1949: An analysis of speculative trading in grain futures. United States Department of Agriculture, Commodity Exchange Auhority, Washington, D.C., Technical Bulletin No. 1001.

Telser, Lester G. 1958: Futures trading and the storage of cotton and wheat. *Journal of Political Economy*, 46, 233-55.

Theil, H. 1971: *Principles of Econometrics*, New York: John Wiley & Sons.

Tobin, J. 1958: Liquidity preference as behaviour toward risk. *Review of Economic Studies*, 27, 65-85.

Tomek, William G. and Gray, Roger W. 1970: Temporal relationships among prices in commodity futures markets. *American Journal of Agricultural Economics*, 52, 372-80.

Turnovsky, S. 1983: The determination of spot and futures prices with storable commodities. *Econometrica*, 51, 1363-87.

— and Campbell, R. B. 1985. The stabilizing and welfare properties of futures markets: a simulation approach. *International Economic Review*, 26, 277-303.

Van Horne, James and Heaton, H. B. 1983: Government security dealers' positions, information and interest rate expectations. *Journal of Finance*, 38, 1643-49.

Working, H. 1949a: The investigation of economic expectations. *American Economic Review*, 39, 150-66.

— 1949b: The theory of price of storage. *American Economic Review*, 39, 1254-62.

— 1953a: Futures trading and hedging. Reprinted in Anne E. Peck (ed.), 1977: *Readings in Futures Markets I: Selected Writings of Holbrook Working*, Chicago Board of Trade.

— 1953b: Hedging reconsidered. In Anne E. Peck (ed.), 1977: *Readings in Futures Markets I: Selected Writings of Holbrook Working*, Chicago Board of Trade.

— 1960: Speculation on hedging markets. *Food Research Institute Studies*, I, 185-219.

Index